Data Science in Education Using R

Data Science in Education Using R is the go-to reference for learning data science in the education field. The book answers questions like: What does a data scientist in education do? How do I get started learning R, the popular open-source statistical programming language? And what does a data analysis project in education look like?

If you're just getting started with R in an education job, this is the book you'll want with you. This book gets you started with R by teaching the building blocks of programming that you'll use many times in your career. The book takes a "learn by doing" approach and offers eight analysis walkthroughs that show you a data analysis from start to finish, complete with code for you to practice with. The book finishes with how to get involved in the data science community and how to integrate data science in your education job.

This book will be an essential resource for education professionals and researchers looking to increase their data analysis skills as part of their professional and academic development.

Ryan A. Estrellado has served public schools for over seventeen years as a school psychologist and administrator. Ryan writes about working with data, education and other projects at https://ryanestrellado.com.

Emily A. Freer is the Director of Educational Development and Assessment at the Marquette University School of Dentistry. Learn more about Emily at https://emilyfreer.com.

Jesse Mostipak is a Community Advocate for Kaggle, and has worked both as a high school science teacher and lead data scientist within education non-profits. To follow Jesse's learning adventures in Python and deep learning, head over to https://jessemaegan.com.

Joshua M. Rosenberg is an Assistant Professor of STEM Education at the University of Tennessee, Knoxville. Follow Josh's work at http://joshuamrosenberg.com.

Isabella C. Velásquez is a data analyst committed to nonprofit work with the goal of reducing racial and socioeconomic inequities. To follow Isabella's personal projects, join her at https://ivelasq.rbind.io.

"The authors have provided the definitive guide to the topic. The combination of theory and hands-on practical tutorials make this an invaluable resource for the growing fields of learning analytics and educational data science".
—*Mark Warschauer, Professor of Education and Informatics at the University of California, Irvine*

"This book is a clear, compelling guide for real-world practitioners who are ready to use modern tools of data science in the education domain. The effective data analysis content would benefit almost anyone getting started with data today, but these authors' thoughtful, focused handling of the specific issues involved in working with education data sets it apart from most introductory data science books".
—*Julia Silge, Software Engineer at RStudio*

"There are many resources for learning how to analyze education data. But what has long been missing is an inclusive and pedagogically refined resource on how to leverage modern data science principles, workflows, and tools. *Data Science in Education Using R* fills this massive gap and more. It will be the go to resource for the next generation of data driven education professionals. And is a beautiful exposition of how to responsibly work with data from the real, messy, world".
—*Dustin Tingley, Deputy Vice Provost for Advances in Learning at Harvard University*

"*Data Science in Education Using R* provides a wide menu of resources for individuals in education who wish to both learn R and think more deeply about their relationship to data. The book provides both practical guidance through worked examples and discussions of relevant theory and past research. That the book is written by authors who have varied research and practice positions lends itself to its broad-ranging appeal".
—*Teomara (Teya) Rutherford, Assistant Professor of Learning Sciences, University of Delaware*

"Doing data science in education is an interdisciplinary endeavor. If you are a teacher, an administrator, or an educational researcher who's looking for a theory-informed, practice-oriented, and equity-minded introduction to educational data science, no need to look further than this book. It will help you unleash your data science 'superpower,' turbocharge your practice, and make real-world changes in your organization".
—*Bodong Chen, Associate Professor and Co-Director of Learning Informatics Lab at the University of Minnesota*

Data Science in Education Using R

Ryan A. Estrellado, Emily A. Freer,
Jesse Mostipak, Joshua M. Rosenberg
and Isabella C. Velásquez

Routledge
Taylor & Francis Group

LONDON AND NEW YORK

First published 2021
by Routledge
2 Park Square, Milton Park, Abingdon, Oxon OX14 4RN

and by Routledge
52 Vanderbilt Avenue, New York, NY 10017

Routledge is an imprint of the Taylor & Francis Group, an informa business

British Library Cataloguing-in-Publication Data
A catalogue record for this book is available from the British Library

Library of Congress Cataloging-in-Publication Data
Names: Estrellado, Ryan A., author.
Title: Data science in education using R / Ryan A. Estrellado, Emily A.
Freer, Jesse Mostipak, Joshua M. Rosenberg, Isabella C. Velásquez.
Description: Abingdon, Oxon; New York, NY: Routledge, 2021. |
Includes bibliographical references and index.
Identifiers: LCCN 2020019952 (print) | LCCN 2020019953 (ebook) |
ISBN 9780367422240 (hardback) | ISBN 9780367422257 (paperback) |
ISBN 9780367822842 (ebook)
Subjects: LCSH: Educational statistics—Data processing. | Educational
evaluation—Data processing. | R (Computer program language)
Classification: LCC LB2846 .E78 2021 (print) |
LCC LB2846 (ebook) | DDC 370.72/7—dc23
LC record available at https://lccn.loc.gov/2020019952
LC ebook record available at https://lccn.loc.gov/2020019953

ISBN: 978-0-367-42224-0 (hbk)
ISBN: 978-0-367-42225-7 (pbk)
ISBN: 978-0-367-82284-2 (ebk)

Typeset in Stone Serif
by codeMantra

Ryan:
To my wife, Lucy, and my sons, Dylan and Adam, for enduring so much typing during dinner. And to Dan Winters, for enduring so many plots over coffee.

Emily:
To my husband, Dan, who supports me every day and has believed in this book from day one. To my family and to Gus, who accompanied me on the journey.

Jesse:
To Leo, Miles, Abby, and Jinx.

Josh:
To Katie and Jonah and to Teri, Joel, Aaron, and Jess, for supporting and encouraging me (in different ways!) from the start to the finish of writing this book.

Isabella:
To my loving family: to my parents, for giving me everything. To my older brother Gustavo E., for never telling me to go read the manual. To my younger brother Gustavo A., for inspiring me to be the best programmer I can be. To Kitty, for her critical eye (and purrs).

Contents

Acknowledgments

This work was supported by many individuals from the DataEdu Slack channel (https://dataedu.slack.com/). Thank you to everyone who contributed code, suggested changes, asked questions, filed issues, and even designed a logo for us: Daniel Anderson, Abi Aryan, Jason Becker, William Bork, Jon Duan, Erin Grand, Ellis Hughes, Ludmila Janda, Jake Kaupp, Kasia Banas, Nathan Kenner, Zuhaib Mahmood, David Ranzolin, Kris Stevens, Bret Staudt Willet, and Gustavo Velásquez.

Thank you to the data scientists in education that took time to share their stories with us: Isabella Fante, LaCole Foots, Tobie Irvine, Arpi Karapetyan, John LaPlante, and Andrew Morozov.

Thank you to the editor of this book at Routledge, Hannah Shakespeare. We appreciated Hannah's incisive, constructive feedback, interest, and support for the book and our unique approach to writing it—one which involved writing the book "in the open" (through GitHub) and sharing it on a freely available website.

Preface

There's this story going around the internet about an eagle egg that hatches in a chicken farm. The eagle egg hatches near the chicken eggs. The local hens are so busy doing their thing that they don't notice the baby eagle egg is not their own. The eagle chick is born into the world and, having no knowledge of its own eagleness, joins its new family on a nervous and exciting first day of life. Over the next few years the baby eagle lives as chickens live. It eats chicken feed, learns to fly in short choppy hops a few feet at a time, and masters the rapid head jabs of the chicken strut.

One day, while strutting around the chicken farm, the young eagle sees something soaring through the sky. The flying creature has long wings, which it stretches wide before tucking them back in and angling itself downward for a dive towards the earth. The sight of this other-worldly bird stirs something in the young eagle.

Over the next few weeks the eagle finds it can't shake the vision of the soaring eagle from its mind. It tests the conversational waters during feeding time. It wonders out loud, "What if we tried to fly more than two feet off the ground?" The other chickens stare back. The young eagle, uncertain if these stares are ambivalence or the default chicken eye position, begins to ponder the only way forward. It must learn to fly high while living with the chicken family it loves.

This is a book about learning to program in R while working in education. It's for folks who feel at home in the education community but are looking out into the world and wondering how to use data better. It's about being a great educator and wondering if it's too late to learn to code. It's about being an educator who's learning to code and wondering if there are others you can learn with.

We were on Twitter a lot in November of 2017. We talked about things like debugging R code, interpreting model coefficients, and working on spreadsheets with three header rows. We kept coming back to these topics over and over again. It was like having an obscure hobby with online friends because it's hard to find local knitters who only knit Friends characters, or vinyl collectors who only collect Swedish disco albums. When you work as a data science consultant in education or as an educator learning data science, it's hard to find that professional community that just gets you. Going to education conferences is great, but the eyes glaze over when you start talking about regression models. The data science conferences are super, but the group at the cocktail table gets smaller when you vent about the state of aggregate test score data.

We started talking about data science in education online because we wanted to be around folks who do data science in education. We wrote this book for you, so you can learn data science with datasets you can find in education work. We don't claim to be experts at education or data science, but we're pretty good at talking about what it's like to do both in a time where doing both is just starting to take off.

So, give your chicken family a big hug, open up your laptop, and let's start learning together. Turns out, there are a lot more hatchlings wanting to be eagles and chickens at the same time.

Figure 0.1: The Tweet That Started It All

Chapter 1

Introduction

Data science in education—you're invited to the party!

Dear Data Scientists, Educators, and Data Scientists who are Educators:

This book is a warm welcome and an invitation. If you're a data scientist in education or an educator in data science, your role isn't exactly straightforward. This book is our contribution to a growing movement to merge the paths of data analysis and education. We wrote this book to make your first step on that path a little clearer and a little less scary.

Whether you're a data scientist using your skills in an education job or an educator who wants to learn data science skills, we invite you to read this book and put these techniques to work in the real world. We think that your work in the education community will help decide how education and data science come together going forward.

Inspired by {bookdown}, this book is open source. Its contents are reproducible and publicly accessible for people worldwide. The online version of the book is hosted at datascienceineducation.com.

Learning data science in education

Over the coming chapters we'll be learning together about what data science in education can look like. But to understand why we were compelled to write about the topic, we need to talk about why data science in education is not such a straightforward thing.

Learning data science in education is challenging because there isn't a universal vision for that role yet. Data science in education isn't straightforward because the role itself is not straightforward. If education were a building, it would be multi-storied with many rooms. There are privately and publicly funded schools. There are more than 18 possible grade levels. Students can learn alone or with others in a classroom.

This imaginary building we call education also has rooms most residents never see—rooms where business and finance staff plan the most efficient use of limited funds. The transportation department plans bus routes across vast spaces.

University administrators search for the best way to measure career readiness. Education consultants study how students perform on course work and even how they feel about class materials.

There are a lot of ways one *could* do data science in education, but building consensus on ways one *should* do data science in education is just getting started. The "data science in education" community is still working out how it all fits together.

And for someone just getting started, it can all seem very overwhelming.

Even if we did have perfect clarity on the topic, there's still the issue of helping education systems learn to leverage these new analytical tools. In many education settings, school administrators and their staff may have never had someone around who deeply understands education, knows how to write code, and uses statistical techniques all at once, as data science in education could be defined (Conway 2010).

Making the path a little clearer

As data science in education grows, the way we talk about and conceptualize it also needs to grow; doing so can help us advance data science in education as a discipline and speak to the unique opportunities and concerns that arise with analyzing data in our domain.

We begin this book by offering a primer for data science in education, including a discussion of unique challenges and foundational skills in the programming language R. This includes this chapter as well as suggestions for how to use this text (Chapter 2), our definition of the process of data science and what it "looks like" in terms of who does data science and how they do it (Chapter 3), and a discussion of data science in education in the context of the wider fields of both education and data science (Chapter 4).

Next, you'll take what you've learned and apply it in our data analysis in education walkthroughs. The walkthroughs in this book are our contribution towards a more example-driven approach to learning. They're meant to make the ambiguous path of learning data science in education a little clearer by way of recognizable and actionable demonstrations.

These examples fall into four different themes, with chapters applying to each theme:

Build a foundation to use R and RStudio

- Getting Started with R and RStudio

- Foundational Skills

Student perceptions of learning

- Walkthrough 1: The Education Dataset Science Pipeline

- Walkthrough 5: Text Analysis With Social Media Data

- Walkthrough 7: The Role (and Usefulness) of Multilevel Models

Analyze student performance data

- Walkthrough 2: Approaching Gradebook Data From a Data Science Perspective

- Walkthrough 8: Predicting Students' Final Grades Using Machine Learning Methods

Get value from publicly available data

- Walkthrough 3: Introduction to Aggregate Data

- Walkthrough 4: Longitudinal Analysis With Federal Students With Disabilities Data

We'll end the book by discussing how to bring data science skills into your education job, with strategic considerations for applying data science in your job (Chapter 15), an overview of teaching data science (Chapter 16), and chapters on learning more (Chapter 17), and additional resources (Chapter 18).

We hope after reading this book you'll feel like you're not alone in learning to do data science in education. We hope your experience with this book is the right balance of challenging and fun. Finally, we hope you'll take what you learned and share it with others who are looking to start this journey.

Conventions used in the book

The following typographical conventions are used in this book:

- Package names are surrounded by curly brackets: {caret}

- Function names are in `constant width` and then parentheses: `clean_names()`

- Variable names are in `constant width`: `var1`

Chapter 2

How to use this book

We've heard it from fellow data scientists and experienced it ourselves—learning a programming language is hard. Like learning a foreign language, it is not just about mastering vocabulary. It's also about learning the language's norms, its underlying structure, and the metaphors that hold the whole thing together.

The beginning of the learning journey is particularly challenging because it feels slow. If you have experience as an educator or consultant, you already have efficient solutions you use in your day-to-day work. Introducing code to your workflow slows you down at first because you won't be as fast as you are with your favorite spreadsheet software. However, you're probably reading this book because you realize that learning how to analyze data using R is like investing in your own personal infrastructure—it takes time while you're building the initial skills, but the investment pays off when you start solving complex problems faster and at scale. One person we spoke with shared this story about their learning journey:

> The first six months were hard. I knew how quickly I could do a pivot table in Excel. It took longer in R because I had to go through the syntax and take the book out. I forced myself to do it, though. In the long-term, I'd be a better data scientist. I'm so glad I thought that way, but it was hard the first few months.

Our message is this: learning R for your education job is doable, challenging, and rewarding all at once. We wrote this book for you because we do this work every day. We're not writing as education data science masters. We're writing as people who learned R and data science *after* we chose education. And like you, improving the lives of students is our daily practice. Learning to use R and data science helped us do that. Join us in enjoying all that comes with R and data science—both the challenge of learning and the joy of solving problems in creative and efficient ways.

Different strokes for different data scientists in education

As we learned in the introduction, it's tough to define data science in education because people are educated in all kinds of settings and in all kinds of age groups. Education organizations require different roles to make it work, which creates different kinds of data science uses. A teacher's approach to data analysis is different from an administrator's or an operations manager's.

We also know that learning data science and R is not in the typical job description. Most readers of this book are educators working with data and looking to expand their tools. You might even be an educator who *doesn't* work with data, but you've discovered a love for learning about the lives of students through data. Either way, learning data science and R is probably not in your job description.

Like most professionals in education, you've got a full work schedule and challenging demands in the name of improving the student experience. Your busy workday doesn't include regular professional development time or self-driven learning. You also have a life outside of work, including family, hobbies, and relaxation. We struggle with this ourselves, so we've designed this book to be used in lots of different ways. The important part in learning this material is to establish a routine that allows you to engage and practice the content every day, even if for just a few minutes at a time. That will make the content ever-present in your mind and will help you shift your mindset so you start seeing even more opportunities for practice.

We want all readers to have a rewarding experience, and so we believe there should be different ways to use this book. Here are some of those ways:

Read the book cover to cover (and how to keep going)

We wrote this book assuming you're at the start of your journey learning R and using data science in your education job. The book takes you from installing R to practicing more advanced data science skills like text analysis.

If you've never written a line of R code, we welcome you to the community! We wrote this book for you. Consider reading the book cover to cover and doing all the analysis walkthroughs. Remember that you'll get more from a few minutes of practice every day than you will from long hours of practice every once in awhile. Typing code every day, even if it doesn't always run, is a daily practice that invites learning and "aha" moments. We know how easy it is to avoid coding when it doesn't feel successful (we've been there), so we've designed this book to deliver frequent small wins to keep the momentum going. But even then, we all eventually hit a wall in our learning. When that happens, take a break and then come back and keep coding. When daily coding becomes a habit, so does the learning.

If you get stuck in an advanced chapter and you need a break, try reviewing an earlier chapter. You'll be surprised at how much you learn from reviewing old material with the benefit of new experience. Sometimes that kind of back-to-basics attitude is what we need to get a fresh perspective on new challenges.

Pick a chapter of interest and start there

We interviewed R users in education as research for this book. We chose people with different levels of experience in R, in the education field, and in statistics. We asked each interviewee to rate their level of experience on a scale from 1 to 5, with 1 being "no experience" and 5 being "very experienced". You can try this now—take a moment to rate your level of experience in:

- Using R

- Education as a field

- Statistics

If you rated yourself as a 1 in Using R, we recommend reading the book from beginning to end as part of a daily practice. If you rated yourself higher than a 1, consider reviewing the table of contents and skimming all the chapters first. If a particular chapter calls to you, feel free to start your daily practice there. Eventually, we do hope you choose to experience the whole book, even if you start somewhere in the middle.

For example, you might be working through a specific use case in your education job—perhaps you are analyzing student quiz scores, evaluating a school program, introducing a data science technique to your teammates, or designing data dashboards. If this describes your situation, feel free to find a section in the book that inspires you or shows you techniques that apply to your project.

This book is primarily about learning to use R as a tool for data science in education. Your experience level with R should be the main factor when you decide how to enjoy the book. But do consider how you rated your level of experience with education and statistics. If these are areas you want to focus on, take your time understanding the education scenarios and statistics techniques we describe. All three disciplines are important parts of being a data scientist in education.

Read through the walkthroughs and run the code

If you're experienced in data analysis using R, you may be interested in starting with the walkthroughs. Each walkthrough is designed to demonstrate basic analytic routines using datasets that look familiar to people working in the education field.

In this approach, we suggest readers be intentional about what they want to learn from the walkthroughs. For example, readers may seek out examples of aggregated datasets, exploratory data analysis, the {ggplot2} package, or the `pivot_longer()` function. Read the walkthrough and run the code in your R console as you go. After you successfully run the code, experiment with the functions and techniques you learned by changing the code and seeing new results (or new error messages!). After running the code in the walkthroughs, reflect on how what you learned can be applied to the datasets, problems, and analytic routines in your education work.

One last note on this approach to the book: we believe that doing data science in education using R is, at its heart, an endeavor aimed at improving the student experience. The skills taught in the walkthroughs are only one part of doing data science in education using R. As an experienced R user, you know that this endeavor involves complex problems and collaboration. Since part of your task may be to convince others around you of the merits of your analytic tools and approaches, we've written this book with that context in mind. Chapter 15 in particular explores ways to introduce these skills to your education job and invite others into analytic activities. We believe you'll glean useful perspectives from chapters on concepts you're already familiar with, too.

A note on statistics

Data science is the intersection between content expertise, programming, and statistics. You'll want to grow all three of these as you learn more about using data science in your education job. Your education knowledge will lead you to the right problems, your statistics skills will bring rigor to your analysis, and your programming skills will scale your analysis to reach more people.

What happens when we remove one of these pieces? Consider a data scientist working in education who is an expert programmer and statistician but has not learned about the real life conditions that generate education data. She might make analysis decisions that overlook the nuances in the data. As another example, consider a data scientist who is an expert statistician and an education veteran, but who has not learned to code. He will find it difficult to scale his analysis up, thereby foregoing the chance to make the largest possible improvement to the student experience. Finally, consider a data scientist who is an expert programmer and an education veteran. She can only scale surface level analysis and might miss chances to understand causal relationships or predict student outcomes.

In this book we will spend a lot of time learning R by way of recognizable education data examples. But doing a deep dive into statistics and how to use statistical techniques responsibly is better covered by books dedicated solely to the topic. It's hard to overstate how important this part of the learning is on the lives of students and educators. One education data scientist we spoke to said this about the difference between building a model for an online retailer and building a model in education:

> It's not a big deal if an online shopper gets mistakenly shown 1,000 brooms but if I got my model wrong and we close a school, that will change a child's entire life.

We want this book to be your go-to R reference as you start integrating data science tools into your education job. Our aim is to help you learn R by teaching data science techniques using education datasets. We'll demonstrate statistics techniques like hypothesis testing and model building and how to run these operations in R. However, the explanations in our chapters will not provide a complete background about the statistical techniques.

We wrote within these boundaries because we believe that the technical and ethical use of statistics techniques deserves its own space. If you already have a foundation in statistics, you will learn how to implement some familiar processes in R. If you have no foundation in statistics, you will be able to take a satisfying leap forward in your learning by successfully using R to run the models and experiencing the model interpretations in our walkthroughs. We provide enough background for you to understand the purpose of the analysis and its results. We encourage you to explore other excellent books like *Learning Statistics With R* (https://learningstatisticswithr.com/) (Navarro 2020), as you learn the required nuances of applying statistical techniques to scenarios outside our walkthroughs.

What this book is not about

While we wrote *Data Science in Education Using R* to be a wide-ranging introduction to the topic, there is a great deal that this book is not about. Some of these topics are those that we would have liked to have been able to include, but we did not because they did not fit our intention of providing a solid foundation in doing data science in education. We chose to not include other topics because, frankly, excellent resources for those topics already exist. We detail some of what we had to not include in the book here.

- Git/GitHub: Git and GitHub are version control software programs, which means that they help keep track of different versions of coding files and specific changes that were made for each version. Git and GitHub are parts of many data scientists' workflows for solo or collaborative work. However, there is a steep learning curve and these tools are not necessary to get started with coding in R. An outstanding introduction to Git and Github is Bryan (2020)'s freely available book *Happy Git with R* (https://happygitwithr.com/).

- Building R packages: If you are carrying out the same analyses many times, it may be helpful to create your own package. Packages are collections of code and sometimes data, such as the {roomba} (for tidying complex, nested lists) and {tidyLPA} (for carrying out Latent Profile Analysis) packages that authors of this book created. However, building an R package is not the focus of this book. Hadley Wickham wrote a very helpful—and freely available—book on the topic called *R Packages* (http://r-pkgs.had.co.nz/) (Wickham 2015).

- Advanced statistical methodologies: As noted above, there are other excellent books for learning statistics. While we do discuss basic and advanced statistical methods, this is not a statistical methods book. One advanced statistical book that we think is excellent from a machine learning perspective is James et al. (2013)'s *An Introduction to Statistical Learning with Applications in R*.

- Creating a website (or book): As you might already suspect, R is versatile and can be used for more than just performing data analyses. In fact, R can be used to write books (like this one, which we wrote using the {bookdown} package) and create websites (which some of the authors have done using the {blogdown} package). This book does not describe how to create books or websites; there are excellent, freely available books on these topics as well (see Xie, Thomas, and

Hill's (2019) *blogdown: Creating Websites with R Markdown* (https://bookdown.org/yihui/blogdown/) and Xie's (2019) *bookdown: Authoring Books and Technical Documents with R Markdown* (https://bookdown.org/yihui/bookdown/).

Supporting the book

If you find this book useful, please support it by:

- Communicating about the book on social media

- Citing or linking to it

- Starring the GitHub repository for the book (https://github.com/data-edu/data-science-in-education)

- Starring the GitHub repository for the {dataedu} package (https://github.com/data-edu/dataedu)

- Reviewing it (e.g., on Amazon or Goodreads)

- Buying a copy

- Letting others in education and data science know about it!

Contributing to the book

We designed this book to be useful and practical for our readers in education. We wrote it as a guide to getting up and running in R, but we know this book does not comprehensively cover every topic related to R. We did this to create a reference that is not intimidating to new users and that creates frequent, small wins while learning to use R.

One question we asked ourselves was: how do we expand this work as data science in education expands as a field? We want readers of this book to be equipped with an agile skill set, and we want this book to continue to provide that even as new R packages are developed and new methods arise. We wrote this book in the open on GitHub so that community members can help us evolve the work, even after it is formally published.

We want this to be the book new data scientists in education have with them as they grow their craft. To achieve that goal, it's important to us that the stories and examples in the book are based on **your** stories and examples. Therefore, we've built ways for you to share with us.

If you have some experience with Git and want to contribute that way, here's how you can contribute:

- Submit an "issue" to our GitHub repository (https://github.com/data-edu/data-science-in-education/issues) that describes a data science problem that is unique to the education setting

- Submit a pull request to share a solution for the problems discussed in the book to the education setting

- Share an anonymized dataset for use in the book (or a future version of it)

If you are new to data science in education, welcome! We would love to have your feedback by email (authors@datascienceineducation.com).

We hope that as the book evolves, it grows to reflect the changing needs of data scientists in education.

Chapter 3

What does data science in education look like?

You can think of a data scientist as someone who combines three skills to do data analysis: programming, statistics, and content knowledge (Conway 2010). However, if you Google "what is a data scientist", you won't find a simple answer. In reality, "data scientist" is not a clear description of a single job function: it is much like saying you are a "business person". Data science as a field describes a wide array of job functions: some data scientists work on database architecture, while others focus on data analysis and interpretation. Moreover, data science describes a wide variety of job skills.

Some of the time, for instance, data science in education refers to the application of data science methods, while other times it refers to data science as a context for teaching and learning (Rosenberg et al. 2020). In the former case, data science in education is seen more as a set of techniques for making sense from data about teaching, learning, and educational systems; in the latter, it is seen more as a content area, like science or mathematics education. Our emphasis in this book is *primarily* (although, not exclusively) on the former case—applying data science methods to ask and answer questions and identify and solve problems related to education.

This wide variety can make it difficult to know what data science in education really is, and how one could start to learn how to do it. Despite the heterogeneity in roles and capabilities involved, in this chapter, we'll provide a working definition of data science in education by sharing some of the roles that professionals occupy in this line of work. We'll also share some common day-to-day tasks for a data scientist in education. Last, we'll provide a definition of the process of doing data science, one that we use to help categorize the aspects emphasized in each of the walkthroughs included later in the book.

Data roles in education

We learned from talking with data scientists in the education field that their roles and specializations can be very different from each other. People working in education have specialized skills and passions that allow them to add value to their organizations' data culture. Here are some of the roles and specializations data scientists in education might take on.

Building systems that get data to the right people

School staff and leadership can't make data-informed decisions unless they have good data. Data scientists in education who specialize in data engineering and data warehousing build systems that organize data in one place. They also keep the data secure to protect the information of students and staff, and they distribute datasets to the people who need it. In this area of data science, you might also find people who specialize in data governance: the creation and maintenance of policies used to keep data collection, documentation, security, and communication to a high standard.

Measuring the impact of our work on the student experience

Scientific evaluation can help measure the impact of student-centered policies and instructional interventions. Such measurements are important because they inform the allocation of time, money, and attention to future improvements to education systems. Data scientists who specialize in measuring impact know how to use statistical techniques to isolate the effect of an intervention and estimate its value. For example, an education system may choose to work with their data analysts to quantify gains in student attendance that result from a new intervention aimed at chronic absenteeism.

Looking for patterns in student data

Now more than ever, students and school staff are generating data as they go about their day learning and teaching. Online quizzes generate quiz data. Student systems collect data about attendance, discipline, behavior, and native language. Online individualized education program (IEP) systems house information about students with disabilities. State-wide testing assessments are scored, stored in a database, and reported to families. Much of this data gets reported to the state education agency (SEA) for processing and publishing online as a part of an accountability system.

School systems that learn to use this data as it is generated get a lot of value from it. Data analysts are experts at systematically analyzing this data and finding useful ways to compare it across different categories. This technique, called "exploratory data analysis", is used to generate plausible hypotheses about relationships between variables in the data. These hypotheses can help generate material educational organizations use to create data-driven institutional changes for their students. For example, one way for school systems to support efforts towards equity in student outcomes is to frequently examine any differences in outcomes among student subgroups.

Improving how we use statistical models in education

There are many tried and true methods for data analysis in schools; even so, there is plenty of room for innovation. Data scientists in education take techniques that are commonly found in other industries, like business, and explore how they can improve the state of analytics in education. In particular, the data scientists we spoke to talked about going beyond exploratory data analysis by introducing more advanced techniques like inferential statistics and predictive modeling to the data culture of the schools where they work. This work is not only about improving how well schools implement their current practices, but is also about exploring how we might apply new techniques improve the learning experience of our students.

Defining the process of data science

While there is not wholesale agreement on the process of what doing data science entails, there are some aspects that most data scientists agree upon.

For example, Peng and Matsui (2015)'s representation of the process emphasizes its cyclical, iterative nature (and the critical importance of starting with a question), and includes data exploration and model building as steps of the process. Wickham and Grolemund (2018)'s depiction emphasizes the specific, technical steps involved with doing data science; in addition to including modeling, it highlights the importance of preparing and transforming data so that it can be used in the analyses that follow these steps. In this book, we use their depiction to define the process of doing data science.

These are:

1. **Importing data:** Accessing data from a number of sources (including Excel and Comma Separate Value [CSV] files, databases, and Application Programming Interfaces [or APIs]), which is then—typically—stored in a data frame in R.

2. **Tidying data:** Storing data in a "tidy" form (Wickham 2014), which may involve pivoting data from "wide" to "long" form and joining or combining two or more data frames in order to facilitate data visualization or modeling.

3. **Transforming data:** Selecting and naming columns and filtering, recoding incomplete cases of data, and calculating summary statistics based on other variables in a dataset.

4. **Visualizing data:** Creating visualizations to understand data and to present output from analyses.

5. **Modeling data:** Using statistical models, from simple to complex, to understand trends and patterns in the data.

6. **Communicating results:** Sharing the results of the analysis through visualizations, the output from models, or other products related to what you learned from the data.

In Wickham and Grolemund (2018)'s depiction, steps three, four, and five are grouped together as "understanding data": we can see how transforming, visualizing, and modeling data are each different ways to make sense of the trends and patterns among variables in a dataset.

Later, in the first walkthrough chapter (Chapter 7), we'll introduce these six steps in the context of describing the areas of emphasis for the walkthrough; we then use these in the remaining walkthroughs to do the same. While we use these aspects to categorize the topics emphasized in the walkthroughs, we do not think that these are necessarily the *only* important aspects of doing data science. Nevertheless, particularly given our use of many R packages and techniques that work well with tidy data (see "tidying data" above; Wickham et al. (2019)), we think these aspects satisfactorily describe the process of doing data science for us to use them for our purposes.

Common activities of data scientists

Now let's explore the tasks and techniques a data scientist in education uses on a daily basis.

We'll learn and practice these and other similar techniques later in the book; for now, we introduce the common activities.

Processing (preparing and tidying) data

Processing data, or cleaning data, is the act of taking data in its raw form and preparing it for analysis. It begins with *importing data*, which is often followed by *transforming* (e.g., selecting and renaming variables, or filtering or recoding incomplete cases) and *tidying* (e.g., joining or pivoting) data in order to facilitate data visualization or modeling.

When you start a data analysis, the data you have is in the same state as when it was generated and stored. Often, it isn't designed to support the specific analysis that that you're tasked with performing.

Here are some examples of common things you'll need to do to prepare your data:

The variable names have to be reworked so they're convenient to reference in your code. It's common for raw datasets to have generic variable names that don't describe the values in that dataset's column. For example, a dataset indicating students' grades at various points in the semester might have variable names that are just the date of the measurement. In this case, the variable name doesn't fully describe the data captured in the column: it just captures the date of the measurement of that data. These variable names should be changed into something that intuitively represents the values in that column. There are also format-related problems with variables. Things like spaces between words, lengthy variable names, or symbols in the variable names can be inconvenient or make it hard to keep track of the steps in a complicated analysis.

Datasets also have to be filtered to the subset that you're interested in analyzing. It's possible that the dataset you're given contains a larger group of students than you need for your project. For example, a principal at a school site may give you a dataset of every student and the number of days they've missed this school year. Now imagine she asks you to do an analysis of attendance patterns in first, second, and third graders. Before you start the analysis, you would need to filter the dataset so that it only contains data for first, second, and third graders.

Sometimes, your stakeholders will ask you to generate summary figures. Imagine that the director of curriculum and instruction asks you to report the percentage of students at each school that have scored in the "proficient" range on a state-wide assessment. The datasets you're given are (1) a list of students, (2) a list of the schools they attend, and (3) a list of their test scores. To produce the requested report, you'll need to merge these lists so that all the data for each student is in one place: student, school, and test score. Next, you'll need to identify the number of students who scored above the "proficient" threshold on the test at each school. Finally, you'll be able to calculate the percentage of students who met that threshold at each school.

Doing analysis (exploring, visualizing, and modeling data)

This is the part of our workflow that most people associate with data science. Analysis is the application of techniques to identify the nature and underlying structure of the dataset, or the relationships among the variables in it. This means that you are making educated guesses about the real life conditions that generated the dataset. This process involves a number of steps, including *visualizing data* and *modeling data* (with techniques that range from the relatively simple to the highly complex).

We realize this may be the first time you've heard data analysis described this way. We choose to describe it this way because, in the end, data analysis in education is about understanding what the data tells us about the student experience. If we can understand the underlying structure of a dataset, we can improve our understanding of the students whose academic behaviors generated the numbers.

Let's look at a concrete example. Imagine that you are an education consultant and your client is a school district superintendent. The superintendent has asked you to evaluate the impact of a teacher coaching initiative the school district has been using for a year. After processing a dataset that contains teachers, the number of hours they spent in coaching sessions, and the change in student quiz scores, you set out to analyze the data and fit a statistical model. Your initial visualization of the dataset—a line graph of the relationship between hours the teachers spent in coaching and the quiz scores of their students—suggests there might be a linear relationship: the more hours a teacher spent in coaching, the higher that teacher's students score on quizzes. While this relationship might seem intuitive, you can't draw a definitive conclusion just from the visualization, because it doesn't tell you whether the relationship between those two variables is meaningful.

Using a statistical model to analyze this dataset can help estimate how much of the change in test scores can be explained by the hours a teacher spent in coaching sessions, and how much can be explained by some other factor (even random chance!). In this example, an alternative explanation for the results is that more conscientious and passionate teachers seek out additional hours of coaching. The data visualization might accurately reflect a relationship between effective teaching style and quiz scores, but that's not enough to conclude that the coaching program is the cause; it's just that more effective teachers are more likely to attend more hours of coaching.

As you can see, when we try to describe human behavior, things tend to get complicated quickly. Data scientists in education are fundamentally interested in the people who generated the numbers, and understanding the circumstances in which data is being collected is critical to performing good analysis.

Sharing results

So far, we've discussed processing data and analyzing data. At these stages, the audiences for your output are usually you, other data scientists, or stakeholders who are in a position to give feedback about the process so far. But when you've sorted through your findings and have selected conclusions you want to share, your audience becomes much wider. Now you're tasked with *communicating* your findings with leadership, staff, parents, the community, or some combination of those audiences.

The strategy and techniques for sharing with a wider audience are different from the ones you use when processing and analyzing data. Sharing your results includes developing visualizations that clearly communicate a finding, writing narratives that give context and story to your analysis, and developing presentations that spark conversations about the student experience.

Who we are and what we do

In some fields, there is a clear path you must follow to do a specific job: if you want to be perform cardiac surgery, you have to go to medical school; if you want to hear trials in court, you have to go to law school first. That's not always true for data analysis. To prepare for this book, we talked to lots of folks who do data analysis in the education field. We found that there's quite a bit of variety in both how people work with data in education and how those people arrived at their education data science roles.

This is good news for people who want to start working with data in education in a more formalized way. You don't need a Ph.D. to do this kind of work, though some people we talked to had pursued graduate education. You don't need to be an expert in statistical modeling, though some people had a statistics background. We talked to consultants who moved to the education field. We also talked to teachers and administrators who became consultants. We talked to people who are the lone data scientist in their education organizations and we talked to people who are part of an analytics team.

You might not think of yourself as a data scientist because your job title doesn't include those words. However, we believe data science is more about the things that you do than the title on your business card. Our own paths toward doing data science in education are very different. Here's a little about us and how we practice data science:

Leading office culture toward a data-driven approach

Jesse, a director at an education nonprofit in Texas, is setting up a database to house student achievement data. This project requires a number of data science skills, which we'll discuss in Chapter 5, including processing data into a consistent format. Once the data is prepared, Jesse builds dashboards to help her teammates explore the data.

However, not all of Jesse's work can be found in a how-to manual for data scientists. She manages a team and serves as the de facto project manager for IT initiatives. Given her expertise and experience in data science, she's also leading the charge towards a more data-driven approach within the organization.

Helping school districts plan to meet their goals

Ryan, a special education administrator in California, uses data science to reproduce the state department of education's special education compliance metrics. Then, he uses the results to build an early warning system for compliance based on local datasets. In this case, Ryan uses foundational data science skills like data processing, visualization, and modeling to help school districts monitor and meet their compliance requirements.

Doing and empowering research on data scientists in education

Joshua, an Assistant Professor of STEM Education at University of Tennessee in Knoxville, researches how students do data science and helps teachers teach the next generation of data-informed citizens. He uses R and develops R packages—self-contained groups of related functions to solve a problem—that facilitate efficient data analysis for researchers.

Supporting student success with data

Emily, a dental education administrator in Wisconsin, guides faculty members on best practices in assessing student learning. Like Jesse, Emily works on merging multiple data sources to get a better understanding of the educational experience. For example, she merges practice national board exam scores with actual national board performance data. Later, Emily conducts statistical analyses to help identify the practice score threshold at which students are ready to sign up for the real exam. All this is possible because of R!

Placing schools and districts in context

Isabella, a data analyst at a large philanthropic organization, uses publicly available aggregated data to analyze the demographics of schools and districts, how they've changed over time, and other contextual information needed to better understand the field of education. These datasets are often in messy formats (even PDFs!), and sometimes, data from the same agency are organized in a slightly different way every year. Using R allows the downloading and cleaning process to be reproducible when new data comes in. The code clearly shows the decisions made to make aggregated data useful in models or visualizations. Packages and projects allow the entire process to be shared and reused across the analytics team.

Next steps for data science in education

As you saw above, there are a variety of ways to apply statistics and programming techniques to support educators and students, and to create new knowledge in the education field. We hope this book is part of a movement to develop the norms and expectations for the field as the relationship between data science and education grows.

Because data science in education is still a young field, it is important that the people growing the field understand the unique culture and challenges in their education job. After all, the feature that will differentiate data science in education from data science in general is the ability to meet the unique needs of students, staff, and administration.

As you progress through this book, we hope you begin to understand where your particular data interests and passions lie. There is more variety in educational backgrounds and in the daily work of education data analysis than one might think. We hope this book will help you combine your unique experiences and talents with new learning in order to create a practice that improves the experience of students, teachers, and the realm of education as a whole.

Chapter 4

Special considerations

Data science in education presents many opportunities, like those discussed in Chapter 3, but also many challenges. These are varied, and while some are common to *all* domains in which data science is carried out, others are very particular to the field of education. For example, data science in education includes not only accessing, processing, and modeling data, but also social and cultural factors, like the training and support that educational data scientists have available to them.

Because data science in education is relatively new, it's understandable that school staff may be wary of how data is collected and analyzed. It's common for them to question how data is used, particularly if it is used to describe and evaluate staff and student performance. One of the biggest challenges that can arise is when individuals feel concerned that they are being evaluated by unclear or unfair metrics. Usually, "data-driven" efforts mean different things to administrators and to educators. To an administrator, a data-driven effort might be an endeavor to better understand the strengths and weaknesses of pre-existing systems, with an eye to eventually proposing new systems that are more efficient. To an educator, a data-driven effort might feel like an approach that masks the individuality of students by reducing them to numbers. Neither perspective is exactly correct. While maximizing efficiency and preserving students' individual needs should certainly be goals of educators and educational administrators, data science is a versatile tool that can be leveraged to help answer a variety of meaningful questions. This chapter will present some thoughts to consider when adopting data science in educational contexts.

Things to consider when doing data science in any domain

Learning to code

Data scientists everywhere are combining content knowledge, programming, and statistics to solve problems. However, many people are not experts in all three areas when they begin their data science journeys, and you are not alone if your programming skills are lacking. Learning to code can seem like a daunting task, but we don't want you to feel paralyzed. We wrote this book for R learners without a computer science background or even any informal coding training. The great thing about entering a field as flexible as data science is that you are joining a vast crowd of individuals who are self-taught, and you will find that there is a very supportive online community to help you.

Addressing ambiguity: a reproducible approach

Educators often feel wary of data science processes because of their ambiguity. One way to address this concern is to build analytic processes that are transparent. Specifically, it is helpful if the data scientist in education is open about what data is collected, how it is collected, how it is analyzed, and how it is considered alongside other data when used in decision-making conversations. This transparency can be achieved through a number of activities, including having regular conversations about analytic methods, providing written reports describing data collection, and receiving input about analytic goals from staff members.

One such process for achieving openness in data collection and analysis is called "reproducible research". The concept of reproducible work (Wikipedia 2020) is the idea that a completed analysis should come with all the necessary materials, including a description of methodology and programming code, needed for someone else to run the analysis and achieve the same results.

A reproducible approach can be especially beneficial in transition periods. If a data-science-in-school advocate leaves their original position, they would leave behind not just descriptions of the analyses that they did, but also the specific files needed to run the analyses again. The new individual who takes their place will be able to seamlessly transition into the new role. If asked to run "the same report I always got from your predecessor", the new person will understand immediately what files were needed to create that original report and will be able to request all necessary data to generate a new version of the report.

To implement a reproducible approach in your organization, you can start by keeping all files related to each project you do in their own folders. As you create reports from the data, keeping notes in the files will help you easily generate similar reports in the future. Many educators find that even though changing administration might mean changing requests, having careful documentation of past processes allows for more efficiency in the way they use data to answer those requests.

Things to consider when doing data science in education

Addressing organizational resistance: a self-driven analytic approach

One consideration when adopting data science strategies in educational contexts is that, in some environments, there is no precedent for a data science approach. It is not common, for example, for a teacher to be conducting regression analyses on data. However, it's not necessary to wait for a district-wide or state-wide initiative to begin to implement the techniques you will learn in this book.

An organization should encourage their staff to do their own data analyses primarily for the purpose of testing their own hypotheses. In a school, for example, a teacher might wonder about student learning in their classroom and might want to utilize data to guide decisions about how they deliver instruction. There are at least two benefits to this approach. First, staff begin to realize the value of doing data analysis as an ongoing inquiry into their outcomes, instead of a special event once a year ahead of school board presentations. Second—and more importantly for the idea of reducing apprehension around data analysis in schools—school staff begin to demystify data analysis as a process. When school staff collect and analyze their own data, they know exactly how it is collected and exactly how it is analyzed. The long-term effect of this self-driven analytic approach might be more openness to analysis, whether it is self-driven or conducted by the school district.

Building and establishing a data governance system that advocates for an open and transparent analytic process is difficult and long-term work, but the likely result will be less apprehension about how data is used and more ways for school staff to participate in the analysis. Here are more practical steps a school district can take towards building a more open approach to analysis:

- Make technical write-ups of data analyses available so interested parties can learn more about how data was collected and analyzed

- Make datasets available to staff within the organization, to the extent that privacy laws and policies allow

- Establish an expectation that analysts present their work in a way that is accessible to people with many levels of data experience

- Hold regular forums to discuss how the organization collects and uses data

By adopting a self-driven analytic approach, individuals can help their education organization to embrace the potential of utilizing data to anticipate and possibly forestall problems in the future.

Lack of processes and guidelines

Educators have concerns about the ambiguity of data science processes because we do not yet have a good idea of the best practices in our field. While there is a body of past research on *students'* work with data (see Lee and Wilkerson (2018) for a review), there is limited information from case- or design-based research on how others in education—teachers, administrators, and data scientists—use data in their work. This challenge is reflected in part in the variability in the job titles of those who work with data: some are data analysts, some are research associates, and the list continues. However, as educational data science emerges as a field, some school districts are now hiring for data scientist positions. Even so, there is a lack of an organizing body that brings all these people together. There are a multitude of discipline-specific (e.g., science teaching) or department-specific (e.g., institutional research) conferences, but no overarching norms universal to those who work with data in education.

Education is a field that is rich with data: survey, assessment, written, and policy and evaluation data, and more. Nevertheless, there often is a lack of common consensus on processes and procedures for educators and data scientists to share data and the results of data analysis with each other. Academic and research settings sometimes can lead to silos of information. A group of researchers at one university could do a survey, and another group doing similar work may not see the results until the study is published, years later. Sometimes, the second group may never even become aware of the survey. The good news about this is that many education organizations are both curious and passionate about supporting student success. It is likely that even if many separate data collection efforts are being implemented (rather than one unified strategy), you will not be dealing with the problem of "I don't have enough data to analyze". As a pioneer for data science in your organization, you can help to clarify these redundant processes and can offer your skills to help make sense of the wealth of information already being gathered.

Limited training and educational opportunities

Right now, there are limited opportunities for those working in education to build their capabilities in educational data science (though this is changing; see Anderson and colleagues' work to create an educational data science certificate program at the University of Oregon and Baker's educational data mining Massive Open Online Course offered through Coursera). Many educational data scientists have been trained in fields other than statistics, business analytics, or research. Moreover, the training in terms of particular tools and approaches that educational data scientists use are highly varied. However, this diversity of training and background positions educators to tackle educational challenges creatively.

Advancing equity

Data science can be used to inform decisions that reduce inequities in the education system. However, it can also be used to exacerbate the marginalization of students we want to serve. An example is an algorithm that is not transparent, that is implemented poorly, and that prompts people to make decisions that have adverse effects.

For data scientists in education, it is crucial that before beginning an analysis, we fully understand how our organization defines equity. Additionally, we should formulate clear equity goals and consider the ways we will continuously check our biases. After defining equity and our equity goals, we can work to ensure that our data science life-cycle reflects what we are trying to learn.

Thoughtful decisions during the project design and data collection, analysis, and presentation can increase the data's ability to move an organization towards its equity goals. For example, if an organization hopes to decrease the opportunity gap between students affected by poverty and students not affected by poverty, then it is important that they (1) define what "affected by poverty" means, (2) identify the type of project design that will help them understand if they are moving towards their goals, and (3) determine whether their data collection allows them to disaggregate these demographics (see Chapter 9). The organization can then make sure the analyses take these disaggregations into account. The final report should be conscientious of any potential blind spots we may have about the results, as all data is biased and can only ever tell a partial story.

R and RStudio, both freely available and open, also serve to increase equity in data science. As opposed to proprietary tools, they are accessible to anybody with a computer and internet. The code behind the packages is available online, opening up the "black box" of research. If code is submitted alongside analyses and reports, we can see what decisions were made to produce the analysis and rerun it ourselves. Using R can enable more audiences to learn, understand, and reuse analyses.

Thoughtful and deliberate data science can help us understand what to do so our students reach their highest potential. Data science can make us more efficient in our tasks. It can increase transparency about what we are doing to help our students. It can also help monitor how we are progressing. However, we must continuously inspect our processes and work to make sure we do not do unintentional harm.

The complex nature of education data

Education data is difficult to collect and to analyze. It is often hierarchical in that data at multiple "levels" is collected. These levels include classrooms, schools, districts, states, and countries—quite the hierarchy! Additionally, an education dataset often requires linking with other datasets. For example, when data is collected on students at the school level, it might be important to also know about the preparation of the teachers in the school. Contextual data about the funding provided by the community in terms of per-pupil spending would be helpful to merge with data about the educational outcomes of students in that school district. The complexity does not end when the data is collected and merged with other relevant information: education data is not simple.

Often, the variables gathered in education are numeric, but just as often they are not. Education data involves characteristics of students, teachers, and other individuals that are categorical. A categorical variable is a descriptive type of variable with multiple levels for which the levels do not signify quantity but instead signify groups, such as sex or grade level. It is not quite right to interpret these data as numeric. Additionally, education data can involve open-ended responses that are stored as string variables (a type of variable used to store text), or even recordings that consist of audio and video data. All these types of data present challenges to the data scientist in education. As with the diversity of training for educational data scientists, though, the complexity of educational data also presents opportunities for educators to creatively approach their tasks. There are specific techniques to efficiently handle each type of data listed above, and we will explore some of those techniques in this book.

The complexity of education data need not discourage educators from pursuing their interests. If you are faced with a large and complicated dataset, you might begin by asking yourself what you are curious about and then carving out just a couple variables that you can use to answer your question. Your colleague might be interested in an entirely different question and might consider different variables from the same dataset in their analysis.

Ethical and legal concerns

There are a number of ethical and legal concerns in working responsibly with education data. At the K–12 level, most datasets require safeguards because youth are a protected population. There might be physical limitations to the places from which a data scientist in education could access confidential data, and there might be limitations on the ways that results of a data analysis can be shared with others within the organization. A closely related issue concerns the aims of education within predetermined constraints. Those working in education often seek to improve it and often work to do so with a scarcity of school and community resources. These ethical, legal, and even values-related concerns may become amplified as the role of data in education increases. They should be carefully considered and emphasized from the outset by those involved in educational data science. If you feel resistance in your organization as you begin to adopt the principles you learn in this book, you might begin by offering to analyze "de-identified" or "anonymous" data. In this way, you show your administration what is possible and foster additional buy-in further down the road.

Analytic considerations

Due to its nature, analyzing education data can be difficult, too. The data is often not ready to be used: it may be in a format that is difficult to open without specialized software, or it may need to be "cleaned" before it is usable. In data science, "cleaning" or "processing" data refers to reorganizing or restructuring the dataset to make it easier to analyze. This process would be analogous to the steps you would take if you received an Excel spreadsheet but found that the columns were in an order that didn't make sense to you and that there were some duplicate columns. The process you'd go through to reorganize the data to make it logical is data cleaning. Because of the different *types* of data, the data scientist in education must often use a variety of analytic approaches, such as multilevel models, models for longitudinal data, or even models and analytic approaches for text data. In later chapters of this book, you will learn more specifics about building models.

Conclusion

While there are many challenges to working with education data, there are many opportunities as well. Once they unlock the power of data science to reveal insights about their organizational context (their students, their teaching, etc.), many educators will become more interested in gathering data and continuing on this path. Data science becomes a useful tool to help connect with the purpose of your job. Once you begin to rely on data science, it can be hard to stop! As an educational professional, remember that you are more closely acquainted with your context than any outside analyst could ever be. This affords you the unique opportunity to become the data and analysis guru in your area.

In summary, educators that want to evolve their data analysis processes into something practical and meaningful to student progress will need to address some unique challenges in order to help all stakeholders understand the benefits of the questions being answered with data. That hard work will pay off.

Chapter 5

Getting started with R and RStudio

In this chapter, the following chapter (on Foundational Skills), and each of the walkthrough chapters, we include a broad overview of the topics emphasized and the functions introduced in the chapter.

Topic emphasized

For all of the topics emphasized sections (like this one), we indicate what topics, in general, are unique to each chapter. Especially for the walkthrough chapters, there is a great deal of overlap between chapters in what is emphasized because, for example, visualizing data is used so regularly as a part of carrying out a data science project in education. Therefore, consider these topics emphasized to be those that are the *particular* focus of the chapters they reference.

- Installing R, RStudio, and R packages

Functions introduced

For all of the functions introduced sections, you will notice that some look a little bit different than others. For example, `devtools::install_github()` is different than `install.packages()`.

The reason is that the `install_github()` function comes from a specific *package* (which we'll discuss in great depth in this and the following chapter). If you had a hunch that this function comes from the {devtools} package, then you'd be correct. The `::` symbols (described more in Chapter 6) simply mean that a specific function comes from a particular package, something that we wanted to point out so that you will know which package you will need to use if you want to use the function. Not sure what some of these terms mean quite yet? Read on in this chapter to learn more about installing and using packages!

- `install.packages()`
- `devtools::install_github()`
- `library()`
- `print()`
- `readr::read_csv()`
- `here::here()`
- `swirl::swirl()`
- `swirl::install_course()`

Chapter overview

This chapter is designed to help you to get started using R and RStudio, assuming no prior use of either.

We will be covering the following topics in this chapter:

- Downloading R and RStudio

- RStudio layout and customization

- Writing and running code in RStudio

- Installing the {dataedu} package

- Exploring R with the {swirl} package

If you already have experience using R and RStudio, you may find some of the contents of this chapter to be a refresher—or a chance to learn a few new things about setting up and using them. If you are looking to get started with the very basics of data loading and manipulation using the {tidyverse} (Wickham et al. 2019) right now, consider reading this chapter quickly and then starting Chapter 6, which covers foundational skills.

Downloading R and RStudio

First, you will need to download the latest versions of R (R Core Team 2019) and RStudio (RStudio Team 2015). R is a free environment for statistical computing and graphics using the programming language R. RStudio is a set of integrated tools that allows for a more user-friendly experience for using R.

Although you will likely use RStudio as your main console and editor, *you must first install R* as RStudio uses R behind the scenes. Both R and RStudio are freely available, cross-platform, and open-source.

To download R:

- Visit CRAN (https://cran.r-project.org/) to download R

- Find your operating system (Mac, Windows, or Linux)

- Select the "latest release" on the page for your operating system

- Download and install the application

Don't worry; you will not mess anything up if you download (or even install!) the wrong file. Once you've installed R, you can get started.

To download RStudio:

- Visit RStudio's website (https://www.rstudio.com/products/rstudio/download/) to download RStudio

- Under the column called "RStudio Desktop FREE", click "Download"

- Find your operating system (Mac, Windows, or Linux)

- Select the "latest release" on the page for your operating system

- Download and install the application

If you do have issues, consider the Data Carpentry page (https://datacarpentry.org/R-ecology-lesson/) and then reach out for help. Another excellent place to get help is the RStudio Community forums (https://community.rstudio.com/).

RStudio layout and customization: getting to know R through RStudio

Now that we've installed both R and RStudio, we will be accessing R *through* RStudio. One of the most reliable ways to tell if you're opening R or RStudio is to look at the icons:

Icon for R   Icon for RStudio

Figure 5.1: Icons

Whenever we want to work with R, we'll open RStudio. RStudio interfaces directly with R, and is an **I**ntegrated **D**evelopment **E**nvironment (IDE). This means that RStudio comes with built-in features that make using R a little easier. If you'd like more information on the difference between R and RStudio, we recommend the "Getting Started" section of the *Modern Dive* textbook (https://moderndive.com/1-getting-started.html#) (Ismay & Kim, 2019).

You do not *have* to use RStudio to access R, and many people don't!

Other IDEs that work with R include:

- Jupyter notebook (https://jupyter.org/)

- VisualStudio (https://visualstudio.microsoft.com/services/visual-studio-online/)

- VIM (https://github.com/jalvesaq/Nvim-R)

- IntelliJ IDEA (https://plugins.jetbrains.com/plugin/6632-r-language-for-intellij)

- EMACS Speaks Statistics (ESS) (https://ess.r-project.org/)

This is a non-exhaustive list, and most of these options require a good deal of familiarity with a given IDE. However we bring up alternative IDEs—particularly ESS—because RStudio, as of this writing, is not fully accessible for learners who utilize screen readers. We have chosen to use RStudio in this text in order to standardize the experience, but we encourage you to choose the IDE that best suits your needs!

RStudio layout

When we open RStudio for the first time, we should see something similar to this:

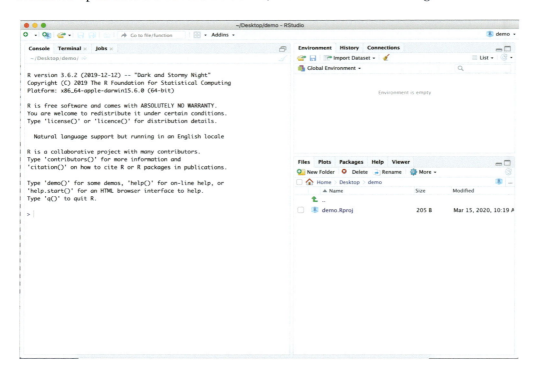

Figure 5.2: RStudio Layout

We'll refer to these three "panes" as the "Console pane", the "Environment pane", and the "Files pane". The large square on the left is the Console pane, the square in the top right is the Environment pane, and the square in the bottom right is the Files pane.

As you work with R more, you'll find yourself using the tabs within each of the panes.

When we create a new file, such as an R script, an R Markdown file, or a Shiny app, RStudio will open a fourth pane, known as the "Source pane". The Source pane should show up as a square in the top left. We can open up an .R script in the Source pane by going to "File", selecting "New File", and then selecting "R Script":

Figure 5.3: Creating a New R Script in RStudio

You do not need to do anything specific with this file, but we encourage you to experiment with it if you would like!

Customizing RStudio

One of the balances we've tried to strike in this text is a balance between best practices in your *workflow* (how you'll use R in your projects) and your *R code*. A best practice for your *workflow* is to ensure that you're starting with a blank slate every time you open R (through RStudio). To accomplish this, go to "Tools", and select "Global Options" from the dropdown menu.

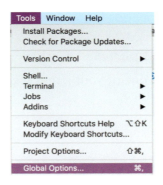

Figure 5.4: Selecting Global Options from the Tool Dropdown Menu

The "General" tab will open, with several checkboxes selected and unselected. The most important thing you can do is select "Never" next to the "Save workspace to .RData on exit:" prompt. After selecting "Never", go through and check and uncheck boxes so that your General tab looks like this:

Figure 5.5: General Tab from Global Options

Last, but certainly not least, click on the "Appearance" tab from within Global Options. From here you can select your RStudio Font, Font Size, and Theme. Go through the options and select an appearance that works best for you, and know that you can *always* come back and change it!

Minimized and missing panes

If, at any point, you find that one of your panes seems to have "disappeared", one of two things has likely happened:

- A pane has been minimized

- A pane has been closed

Let's look at the Environment pane as an example. If the Environment pane has been minimized, we'll see something like this:

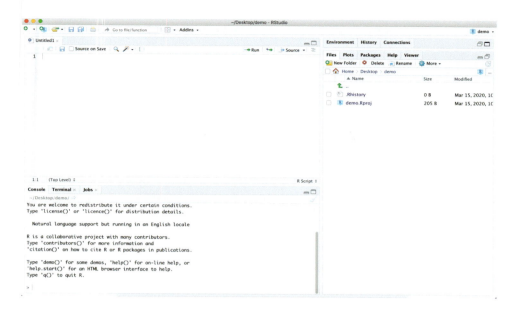

Figure 5.6: RStudio Layout with the Environment Pane Minimized

We know that the Environment pane has been minimized because although we can see the pane headers in the top right, we can't see the information *within* the Environment pane. To fix this, we can click on the icon of two squares in the top right of the Environment pane. If you click on the icon of the large square in the top right of the Environment pane, you'll maximize the Environment pane and minimize the Files pane. We do not want to do this, since we would prefer to see all the panes at once.

If the Environment pane has somehow been closed, you can recover it by going to the "View" menu, selecting "Panes", and then selecting "Pane Layout", like so:

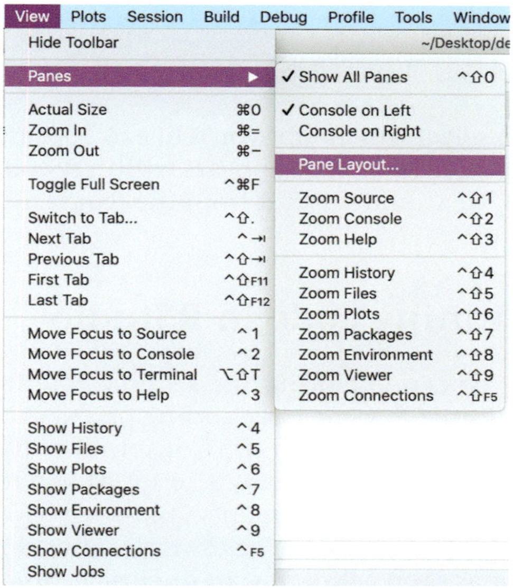

Figure 5.7: Accessing the Pane Layout from the View Dropdown Menu

When we select Pane Layout, we'll see this:

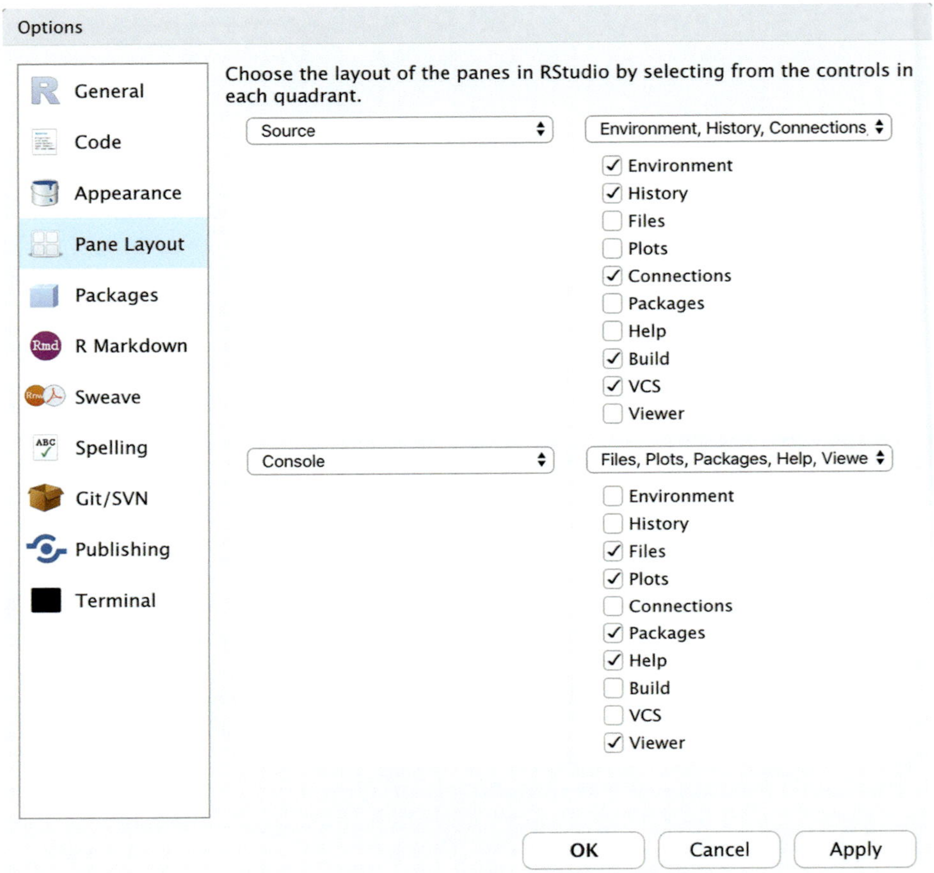

Figure 5.8: Pane Layout Options within RStudio

From here, you can select which tabs you'd like to appear within each pane, and you can even change where each pane appears within RStudio. If our Environment pane had been closed, we would select it from the Pane Layout in order to re-open it within RStudio.

Writing and running code in RStudio

Up to this point, we've been exploring the RStudio interface and setting up our preferences. Now, we'll shift to some basic coding practices. In order to run code in R, you need to type your code either in the Console or within an .R script.

We generally recommend creating an .R script as you're learning, as it allows you to type all of your code, add comments, and then save your .R script for reference. If instead you work entirely in the Console, anything that you type in the Console will disappear as soon as you restart or close R, and you will not be able to reference it in the future.

Writing code in the Console

To run code in the Console, you type your code next to the > and hit Enter .

We'll spend a little time practicing running code in the Console by exploring some basic properties of coding in R.

In the Console, type 3 + 4 and hit Enter. You should see the following:

```
> 3 + 4
[1] 7
>
```

Figure 5.9: Using the Console as a Calculator

We've just used R to add the numbers 3 and 4. R has returned the sum of 3 + 4 on a new line, next to [1]. The [1] tells us that there is one row of data.

We can also use R to print out text. Type the following in the Console and hit Enter:

```
print("I am learning R")
```

We should see this in the Console:

```
> print("I am learning R")
[1] "I am learning R"
>
```

Figure 5.10: Printing Text to the Console

There's one error that you're likely going to come across, both when running code in the Console as well as in an R script. Let's explore that error now by running the following code in the Console and hitting Enter:

```
print("This is going to cause a problem"
```

Make sure that you left off the closing parenthesis! What you'll see in the Console is:

```
> print("This is going to cause a problem"
+
```

Figure 5.11: Incomplete Parentheses Change What R Expects Next

When we're missing a closing parenthesis, R is expecting us to provide more code. We know this because instead of seeing a carat > in our Console, we see a +, and R has not returned the print statement that we were expecting! There are two ways to fix this problem:

- Type the closing) in the Console and hit Enter

- Hit the Esc key

Go ahead and run this intentional error, and try each of the options above. Compare the output of each, and think about how they're different. Can you think of when you might want to use one option instead of the other?

Writing code in an R script

There are three main ways to run code in an .R script:

- Highlight the line(s) of code you'd like to run and press `Ctrl + Enter`

- Highlight the line(s) of code you'd like to run and click the "Run" button in the `R script` pane

- To run *every* line of code in your file you can press `Ctrl + Shift + Enter`

Create a new .R script, or open the one you created earlier in this chapter. Next, type in the following code and run it using each of the options listed above.

```
print("We're going to use R as a calculator.")
print("First up, addition!")
12 + 8
632 + 41
print("Next, subtraction!")
48 - 6
0.65 - 1.42
```

Feel free to spend some more time writing and running code within your .R script, or move on to the next section, where we'll add comments to our code.

Commenting your code in R

It is considered good practice to comment your code when working in an .R script. Even if you are the only person to ever work on your code, it can be helpful to write yourself notes about what you were trying to do with a specific piece of code. Moreover, writing comments in your code as you work through the examples in this book is a great way to help reinforce what you're learning. Comments are ignored by R when running a script, so they will not affect your code or analysis.

To comment out a line of code, you can place a pound sign (also called an octothorpe!) # in front of the line of code that you want to exclude when you're running your script. Be careful when excluding certain lines of code, especially in longer files, as it can be easy to forget where you've commented out code. It is often better to simply start a new section of code to tinker with until you get it working as expected, rather than commenting out individual lines of code.

We can also write comments in-line with our code, like this:

```
#' this will be a short code example.
#' you are not expected to know what this does,
#' nor do you need to try running it on your computer.
library(readr)  # load the readr package
library(here)  # load the here package
data <- read_csv(here("file_path", "file_name.csv"))  # save file_
name.csv as data
```

If you think you'll be writing more than one line of comments, you can do a pound sign followed by a single quotation mark (#'). This will continue to comment out lines of text or code each time you hit Enter. You can delete the #' on a new line where you want to write code for R to run. This method is useful when you're writing a long description of what you're doing in R.

Note: when we refer to "commenting" we're referring to adding in actual text comments, whereas "commenting out" refers to using the pound sign (octothorpe) in front of a line of code so that R ignores it. We will also use the phrase "uncomment code", which means you should delete (or omit when typing out) the # or #' in an example.

Installing the {dataedu} package

This next section will briefly go over installing the {dataedu} package that's used throughout this book. We created this package to provide our readers with an opportunity to jump into R however they see fit.

The package serves four main functions:

1. Mass installation of all the packages used in the book

2. Reproducible code for the walkthroughs

3. Access to the data used in each of the walkthroughs

4. The "dataedu" theme and color palette for reuse

If you feel that you need more information before you're ready to install the package, you can skip this section, and rest assured that we'll cover packages, their installation, and how to load them into R in more depth in Chapter 6. However, if you're feeling a bit adventurous, go ahead and give it a shot by running the code below. *Please note that the {dataedu} package requires R version 3.6 or higher to run.*

```
# install devtools
install.packages("devtools", repos = "http://cran.us.r-project.org")
# install the dataedu package (requires R version 3.6 or higher)
devtools::install_github("data-edu/dataedu")
```

A special note on {tabulizer}: One of the walkthroughs uses {tabulizer}, created by ROpenSci to read PDFs. {tabulizer} requires the installation of {RJava}, which can be a tricky process. Neither {tabulizer} nor {RJava} are included in `install_dataedu()` and we recommend reading through the notes on the {tabulizer} GitHub repository if you choose to install them.

Exploring R with the {swirl} package

If you were able to install the {dataedu} package without any issues or concerns and you're eager to get started exploring everything that R can do, you can supplement your learning through {swirl} (https://swirlstats.com/students.html).

You can install {swirl} by running the following code:

```
install.packages("swirl")
```

{swirl} is set of packages (see more on packages in Chapter 6) that you can download, providing an interactive method for learning R by using R in the RStudio Console.

Since you've already installed R, RStudio, and the {swirl} package, you can follow the instructions on the {swirl} webpage or run the following code *in your Console pane* to get started with a beginner-level course in {swirl}:

```
library(swirl)
install_course("R_Programming_E")
swirl()
```

There are multiple courses available on {swirl}, and you can access them by installing them and then running the `swirl()` command in your console. We are not affiliated with {swirl} in any way, nor is {swirl} required in order to progress through this text, but it's a great resource that we want to make sure is on your radar!

Conclusion

Congratulations! At this point in the book you've installed R and RStudio, explored the RStudio IDE, and even written some basic code. At this point, you're set up to either move on to Chapter 6, where we'll do a deeper dive into projects, packages, and functions, and how those relate to your future data tasks. We will also introduce Help documentation and some skills for when you're working with new or unfamiliar information. If that all sounds familiar to you already, you can jump ahead to a walkthrough of your choosing!

Chapter 6

Foundational skills

Topics emphasized

- Preparing your programming environment
- Using the pipe operator
- Using the assignment operator

Functions introduced

- `function()`
- `janitor::clean_names()`
- `janitor::remove_empty()`
- `c()`
- `dplyr::mutate()`
- `janitor::excel_numeric_to_date()`
- `dplyr::coalesce()`
- `dplyr::select()`
- `stats::filter()`
- `dplyr::filter()`
- `names()`
- `dplyr::glimpse()`
- `summary()`
- `dplyr::group_by()`
- `dplyr::count()`
- `dplyr::arrange()`
- `dplyr::desc()`
- `dplyr::rename()`

Functions introduced in the appendix

- `read_csv()`
- `readxl::read_excel()`
- `haven::read_sav()`
- `googlesheets::gs_title()` and `googlesheets::gs_read()`

Chapter overview

This chapter is designed to give you the skills and knowledge necessary to *get started* in any of the walkthrough chapters. Our goal in this chapter is to give you insights into key areas of working with R, help you develop mental models for working with R, and ultimately to get you working with R using the RStudio Integrated Development Environment (IDE) through a series of introductory applied examples. If you have not yet installed R and/or RStudio, please go through the steps outlined in Chapter 5 before beginning this one. Please note that this chapter is not intended to be a full and complete introduction to programming with R nor to using R for data science. There are many excellent resources available which provide this kind of instruction, and we've listed them for you in Chapter 17.

We will be covering the following topics in this chapter:

- The foundational skills framework (understanding projects, functions, packages, and data)

- Using R's "Help" documentation

- Steps for working through new and unfamiliar content

- Getting started with a coding walkthrough

Foundational skills framework

No two data science projects are the same. Even so, we've created a general framework for you to use as a foundation and as a set of concepts to help you work through the walkthroughs in this book. The four core concepts we will use to build our framework are:

- Projects

- Functions

- Packages

- Data

Projects

One of the first steps of every workflow should be to set up a "Project" within RStudio. A Project is the home for all of the files, images, reports, and code that are used in any given project. Note that when we capitalize the word "Project", we're referring to a specific setup within RStudio, while we refer to general projects that you might work on with the lowercase "project".

We use Projects because they create a self-contained folder for a given analysis in R. This means that if you want to share your Project with a colleague, they will not have to reset file paths (or even know anything about file paths!) in order to re-run your analysis.

Furthermore, even if the only person you ever collaborate with is a future version of yourself, using a Project for each of your analyses will mean that you can move the Project folder around on your computer, or even move it to a new computer, and remain confident that the analysis will run in the future (at least in terms of file path structures).

Setting up your project

Creating a Project is one of the first steps in working on an R-based data science project in RStudio. To create a Project you will need to first open RStudio.

From within RStudio, follow these steps:

1. Click on "File"

2. Select "New Project"

3. Choose "New Directory"

4. Click on "New Project"

5. Enter your Project's name in the box that says, "Directory name". We recommend choosing a Project name that helps you remember that this is a project that involves data science in education. Avoid using spaces in your Project name, and instead, separate words with hyphens or underscore characters.

6. Choose where to save your Project by clicking on "Browse" next to the box labeled "Create project as a subdirectory of:". If you are just using this to learn and test out creating a Project, consider placing it in your downloads or another temporary directory so that you remember to remove it later.

7. Click "Create Project"

At this point, you should have a Project that will serve as a place to store any .R scripts that you create as you work through this text. If you'd like more practice, take a few moments to set up a couple of additional Projects by following the steps listed above. Within each Project, add and save .R scripts. Since this is just for practice, feel free to delete these Projects once you have the hang of the procedure.

We should point out that it is not *necessary* to create a Project for your work, although we *strongly* recommend it. When you utilize Projects in tandem with the {here} package, you will be set up with an easy-to-use workflow. For more on using Projects with the {here} package, read Bryan (2017)'s article (https://www. tidyverse.org/blog/2017/12/workflow-vs-script/). We will also explain more about the {here} package later in this text. If you choose not to create a Project, you will still be able to navigate the walkthroughs in this text—and even carry out future analyses—relatively easily. However, be aware that at some point you will run into issues with how the files are structured on your computer.

While we cannot emphasize enough how Projects and the {here} package streamline this process, you can always check where your computer is looking for your .R scripts by checking the working directory. To do that, you can run this code: `getwd()`. That code will let you know what file path R is currently pointing towards. If that is not what you wanted, you can then change your working directory manually by running `setwd()` and providing your file path name as an argument. The reason we do not advocate for this `getwd()` and `setwd()` workflow is that if you use it, it becomes impossible for someone on another computer (or you on a future computer) to run your code. The `getwd()` and `setwd()` commands point to a specific location on your own device.

Functions

A function is a reusable piece of code that allows us to consistently repeat a programming task. Functions in R can be identified by a word followed by a set of parentheses, like so: `word()`. More often than not, the word is a verb, such as `filter()`, suggesting that we're about to perform an action. Indeed, functions act like verbs: they tell R what to do with our data.

The word (or set of words) represents the name of the function, and the parentheses are where we can provide arguments to a function, if arguments are needed for the function to run. Many functions in R packages do not *require* arguments, and they will use a set of default arguments unless you provide something different from the default. There are not any hard and fast rules about when a function needs an argument (or series of arguments). However, if you are having trouble running your code, first check for typos, then check the Help documentation to see if you can provide arguments to more clearly direct R as to what to do. We'll cover how to access and navigate the Help documentation later in this chapter.

Writing your own functions

As you work in R more and more, you may find yourself copying and pasting the same lines of code and then making small modifications. This is perfectly fine while you're learning, but eventually, you're going to come across a large enough dataset where this approach is going to take a prohibitively large amount of time, not to mention increase the chance of accidentally introducing errors. This is when you *know* you need to write a function.

(We could argue that you need functions much sooner! For example, a general premise in programming is DRY, or Don't Repeat Yourself. What this translates to is the idea that once you find yourself copying and pasting code for the third time, it's time to write a function!)

We'll cover the very basics of writing a function, but we would strongly suggest you check out this Creating Functions (https://swcarpentry.github.io/r-novice -inflammation/02-func-R/) tutorial from (https://software-carpentry.org/) for more information and practice.

The template for writing a function is:

```
name_of_function <- function(argument_1, argument_2, argument_n)
{
code_that_does_something
code_that_does_something_else
}
```

Functions can be as simple or as complex as you like. For example, if we wanted to create a function that adds two numbers together, we would write:

```
#' writing our function
#' we've named the function "addition"
#' and asked for two arguments, "number_1" and "number_2"
addition <- function(number_1, number_2) {
number_1 + number_2
}

#' using our function
#' below are 3 separate examples of utilizing our new function
#' called "addition"
#' note that we provide each argument separated by commas
addition(number_1 = 3, number_2 = 1)

addition(0.921, 12.01)

addition(62, 34)
```

Challenge Questions

- For our newly written function "addition", what happens if we only provide one argument?

- What happens if we provide more than two arguments?

Packages

Packages are shareable collections of R code that can contain functions, data, and/or documentation. Packages increase the functionality of R by providing access to additional functions to suit a variety of needs. While it is entirely possible to do all of your work in R without ever using a package, we do not recommend that approach. There are a wealth of packages available, almost all of which help reduce both the learning curve associated with R and the amount of time spent on any given analytical project.

Installing and loading a package

Installing a package

In Chapter 5, you might have noticed at the very end that we installed two packages ({devtools} and {dataedu}), but we didn't talk too much about what we were doing. We'll get into more detail on installing and loading packages now.

In order to access the functions within a package, you must first install the package on your computer. There are a collection of R packages hosted on the internet on the CRAN website: *CRAN* (https://cran.r-project.org/), the Comprehensive **R** Archive Network. These packages must meet certain quality standards, and they are regularly tested.

If an R user feels that their package would benefit a broad audience, they may choose to submit their package to CRAN. The process of submitting a package and having it published through CRAN is beyond the scope of this book, but it's important to point out that you—yes, you!—can create a package that you use all for yourself, share with colleagues, or submit to CRAN. Most of the packages we'll be working with in this book are available on CRAN, which means that we can install them using the `install.packages()` function.

If the package is on CRAN, we can install it by running the following code in the RStudio Console:

```
# template for installing a package
install.packages("package_name")

# example of installing a package
install.packages("dplyr")
```

Note that the name of the package needs to be inside quotation marks when using the `install.packages()` function.

You can run the `install.packages()` functions within an .R script! However if you choose to do this, please make sure to comment out the line(s) of code that install packages after you have installed those packages. Commenting out the install packages commands will save you time in the future as you will not need to re-install packages each time you run a script.

If you do not want to write code for installing packages, you can also navigate to the "Packages" tab of the "Files" pane, click "Install", and then search for and install one or more packages.

Loading a package

Once a package is installed on your computer, you do not have to re-install it in order to use the functions in the package. However, every time you open RStudio and want to use the package, you will need to load the package into your RStudio environment. In this way, R will know where to look for the functions. We

Figure 6.1: Image of the Packages Pane, which is Found in the Bottom Right Corner of the RStudio IDE, along with the Files, Plots, Help, and Viewer Panes

can accomplish loading the package into our R environment using the `library()` function.

> A package is a like a book, a library is like a library; you use library() to check a package out of the library. –Hadley Wickham, Chief Scientist, RStudio

Loading a package into our R environment signals to R that we would like to have access to all the functions available to us in that package. We can load a package, such as the {dplyr} package (Wickham et al. 2020), using the following code:

```
# template for loading a package
library(package_name)

# example of loading a package
library(dplyr)
```

Note that unlike installing a package, we do not need to put the package name inside quotation marks when we load the package into RStudio using the `library()` function.

We only have to install a package once, but to use it, we have to load it each time we start a new R session.

Sometimes you'll see `require()` used instead of `library()`. We strongly advocate for the use of `library()`, as it forces R to load the package. If the package is not installed, or if there are issues with the package, RStudio will print out an error message. `require()`, on the other hand, will not give an error if the package is not available or if there are issues with it. Using `library()` will help to eliminate sources of confusion later.

How to find packages

As you begin your R learning journey, the bulk of the packages you will need to use are either already included when you install R or available on CRAN. *CRAN TaskViews* (https://cran.r-project.org/web/views/) is one of the best resources for seeing what packages are available and might be relevant to your work. Other great resources to learn about various R packages are through Twitter (following the "#rstats" hashtag) as well as through Google searches. As R has grown in popularity, Google has gotten significantly better at returning R-related results.

Learning more about a package

Sometimes when you look up a package, you will be able to identify the function that you need and continue on your way. Other times, you may need (or want!)

to learn more about a specific package. Packages on CRAN all come with something called a "vignette", which is a worked example using various functions from within the package. You can access a package's vignette(s) on CRAN TaskViews.

Packages do not need to be submitted to CRAN to be used by the public, and many are available directly from their respective developers via GitHub. Package authors may publish vignettes or blog posts about their package, and other R users may *also* publish tutorials about a specific package. If you find yourself on GitHub looking at information for a package, more often than not, the README file will have good information for getting started with a package. At the time of publication, the {dataedu} package we have created is available only through GitHub (but not yet through CRAN).

Installing the {dataedu} package

In Chapter 5, we provided the following code for installing the {dataedu} package. There are related packages that {dataedu} will install for you when you install the {dataedu} package. If you run into difficulties, a good place to start is re-installing the package to make sure you have the most updated version. If you installed the {dataedu} package already, you can skip to the next section. Otherwise, go ahead and run the following code. *Please note that the {dataedu} package requires R version 3.6 or higher to run.*

```
# install devtools
install.packages("devtools", repos = "http://cran.us.r-project.org")

# install the dataedu package
devtools::install_github("data-edu/dataedu")
```

Let's take this code apart a bit. The first function, `install.packages("devtools", repos = "http://cran.us.r-project.org")`, has two arguments, `"devtools"` and `repos = "http://cran.us.r-project.org"`. The first argument, `"devtools"`, is the name of the package we want to install. The second argument, `repos = "http://cran.us.r-project.org"`, tells R the URL of the repository to use. For now, all we need to know is that a repository is a place where code can be stored.

In order for us to load and use the {dataedu} package, we first needed to install the {devtools} package.

The second function, `devtools::install_github("data-edu/dataedu")`, has only one argument, `"data-edu/dataedu"`, but also looks a little different from the first function. What we're doing here is telling R to go to the {devtools} package to find the `install_github()` function. The `install_github()` function is telling R to go to a specific repository on GitHub to get the code for the {dataedu} package. You can also see the repository for the {dataedu} package on GitHub (https://github.com/data-edu/dataedu) yourself! We have to take this approach to loading the {dataedu} package because the package is not available on CRAN yet.

Loading the {dataedu} package

Now that we've installed the {dataedu} package, we can load it using `library()`. You can create an .R script in your Project to load and explore the {dataedu} package. We'll load the {dataedu} package by running the following code in an .R script:

```
# loading the dataedu package
library(dataedu)
```

When we work with packages, we *don't* include the install.packages() function in an .R script, but we *do* include any library() functions that we use. This ensures that we know what packages we need to load into our RStudio environment, and signals to anyone else using our code which packages they'll need to use to run our code.

Using the {dataedu} package

There are some basic functions in the {dataedu} package that are helpful to know.

Installing the packages used throughout this book

Type and run dataedu::install_dataedu() in your Console to install all the packages used in this book. If you run into issues, you can follow the prompts that are printed out in the RStudio Console.

If you find that you simply cannot get the packages to install, run the following code in the RStudio Console: dataedu::dataedu_packages.

This will print out a list of all the packages we used in the {dataedu} package. Although this is a monotonous task, you can then install each package individually using install.packages("package_name").

If you still encounter errors, please reach out to us! You can file an issue on GitHub, or email us at authors@datascienceineducation.com.

Accessing the datasets used in this book

All of the datasets are available within the {dataedu} package, as well as through downloadable .csv files stored in the data folder within our GitHub repository (https://github.com/data-edu/dataedu).

You can load any of the data files using the following code: dataedu::dataset_name. We'll practice doing this in a later section of this chapter, but if you want to try it out now, the names of the available datasets are:

- course_data
- course_minutes
- district_merged_df
- district_tidy_df
- child_counts
- ma_data_init
- pre_survey
- sci_mo_processed
- sci_mo_with_text
- tt_tweets

The relationship between packages and functions

Packages are a collection of functions, and most are designed for a specific dataset, field, and/or set of tasks. Functions are individual components within a package and are what we use to interact with our data.

To put it another way, an R user might write a series of functions that they find themselves needing to use repeatedly in a variety of projects. Instead of re-writing (or copying and pasting) the functions each time they need to use them, an R user can collect all of these individual functions inside a package. They can then load the package any time that they want to use the functions, using a single line of code instead of tens to tens of thousands of lines of code.

Data

We have *data* that we bring into a Project within RStudio, and you're likely using R because you have some data that you would like to explore. Throughout this book, you'll see data accessed in a multitude of ways. Sometimes, we've pulled the data directly from a website, while other times we ask you to load the data from a .csv or .xls file. We've also provided each of the datasets used in this book as .rda files that are accessible via the {dataedu} package (Estrellado et al. 2020). We've provided additional resources for loading data from Excel, SAV, and Google Sheets in Appendix A.

While it is possible to connect directly to a database from within R, we do not cover those skills in this text. For those curious about how to accomplish this, we recommend starting with the *Databases using R* (https://db.rstudio.com/) resource from RStudio.

Help documentation

Very few—if any—people in the world know everything there is to know about R. This means that we all need to look things up, sometimes every few minutes! Thankfully, there are some excellent built-in resources that we can leverage as we use R.

From within RStudio, we can access the "Help" documentation by using ? or ?? in the Console. For example, if I wanted to look up information on the data() function, I can type ?data or ?data() next to the carat (>) in the Console, and hit Enter. Try this now, and you should see the Help panel on the bottom right side of your RStudio environment populate with documentation on the data() function.

This works because the data() function is part of something called "base R"—that is, all of the functions included with R when you first install it. R comes with packages like this one pre-installed. However, as you saw in a previous section, we'll be asking you to install additional packages. These extend the functionality of base R and its pre-installed packages by providing us with access to new

```
> ?mutate
No documentation for 'mutate' in specified packages and libraries:
you could try '??mutate'
```

Figure 6.2: Error Message when Running ?mutate

functions. This means that instead of writing a function to do a common data analysis task, such as creating a new variable out of existing variables, you can use a function that someone has written and made available for you to use (almost always at no charge! Don't worry—all the packages we'll be using in this text are considered Open Source Software, and you will not have to purchase anything to complete any of the exercises or walkthroughs in this text). One of the functions that can accomplish the task of creating a new variable out of existing variables is called mutate(). What happens when you type ?mutate (or ?mutate()) into the Console and hit Enter? We've gotten one of our first error messages!

This is a fantastic error message because not only has it told us that something is wrong (there is no documentation for mutate), it tells us what we should try to do to solve the error. Let's see what happens when we follow the error message instructions by typing ??mutate (or ??mutate()) into the Console and hitting Enter.

What do you see?

The Help documentation is a great first stop when you've got a question about R. The next section will provide you with additional skills for working with new and unfamiliar content!

Steps for working through new and unfamiliar content

Great educators have the ability to ask great questions. Asking the learners in your classroom the right questions at the right time can facilitate understanding, uncover misconceptions, and indicate whether or not they have mastered the material. However, when you're learning on your own, you have to simultaneously fill the roles of both learner and educator. This means you must not only know how and when to ask yourself questions, but also answer your questions, evaluate your answers, and redirect your learning path as you progress. This section is intended to give you a series of steps you can use as you encounter new and unfamiliar content, both in reading this book and in your broader data science learning endeavors. For this section, we'll use the example of encountering a function for the first time, but you can use these steps with any new piece of information that you encounter!

Activate prior knowledge

You've been reading through a tutorial and have come across the coalesce() function in the vignette for the {janitor} package (https://github.com/sfirke/janitor):

```
library(tidyverse)
library(janitor)
roster <- roster_raw %>%
    clean_names() %>%
    remove_empty(c("rows", "cols")) %>%
    mutate(hire_date = excel_numeric_to_date(hire_date),
        cert = coalesce(certification, certification_1)) %>%
    select(-certification, -certification_1)
```

Note: you aren't expected to know what the chunk of code that you've just read does, nor are you expected to run it. By the time you've finished this book, you'll be able to run and understand everything in that code example!

Take a moment to think through the following questions:

- What does the word "coalesce" mean?

- Have you ever seen the `coalesce()` function before? If so, in what context?

Look for context clues

- Read a couple of lines of code both above and below where the `coalesce()` function appears—are there any clues as to what this function might do?

Check the Help documentation

- What information is available in the Help documentation?

- Are there any examples from the Help documentation that seem similar to what you're trying to accomplish? For example, this seems somewhat related to what we're trying to do:

```
# Or match together a complete vector from missing pieces
y <- c(1, 2, NA, NA, 5)
z <- c(NA, NA, 3, 4, 5)
coalesce(y, z)
```

Figure 6.3: Example from the `coalesce()` Help Documentation

Find the limits

Work through examples in the Help documentation (or examples that you've found online) and test the limits.

Testing the limits is a way of understanding the code by seeing how it handles different situations. Ultimately, what you're doing is recognizing a pattern, developing a hypothesis, and testing whether or not that hypothesis is true.

Some methods for testing the limits include:

- What happens if you substitute obviously larger (or smaller values)?

- What happens if you substitute different data types?

- What happens if you introduce NA values?

- Is the order of values important?

Test (and refine) your understanding

Take a moment to think through whether or not you could explain what you've just learned to someone else. Imagine the questions that they might ask of you, and try to answer them. If you can't, dig deeper into the documentation, online forums, or even in testing your own knowledge, until you feel like you can!

You won't necessarily have the time (or interest!) in doing this for each new or unfamiliar piece of content that you come across, but we hope that this provides you with a starting framework for furthering your understanding when you *do* come across content that you want to explore in a bit more depth.

Bringing it all together: getting started coding walkthrough

This section is going to take everything we've talked about so far and walk you through some introductory code. This code does not represent a comprehensive data analysis, but it does use some exploratory data analysis techniques.

At this point, we are assuming that you've installed the {dataedu} package and that you have also run `dataedu::install_dataedu()` to install the associated packages. If you have *not* installed the {dataedu} package and run `dataedu::install_dataedu()` yet, please do so before continuing.

Creating a project and an `.R` script and setting up our RStudio environment

If you haven't already, set up a Project in RStudio and create a new .R script. Save your .R script as "chapter_6_walkthrough" or another similar name. Run the following code in the RStudio Console:

```r
# Installing the skimr package, not included in {dataedu}
install.packages("skimr")
```

Now, take a few minutes to type out and run each of the following lines of code in your .R script, one by one, and notice what you see happening in the Console after you run each line.

```r
# Setting up your environment
library(tidyverse)
```

```
library(dataedu)
library(skimr)
```

- What do you think running the above lines of code accomplished?

- How do you know?

Function conflicts between packages

In your Console, you may have noticed the following message:

```
── Attaching packages ───────────────────────────────── tidyverse 1.3.0 ──
✓ ggplot2 3.2.1     ✓ purrr   0.3.3
✓ tibble  2.1.3     ✓ dplyr   0.8.4
✓ tidyr   1.0.2     ✓ stringr 1.4.0
✓ readr   1.3.1     ✓ forcats 0.4.0
── Conflicts ──────────────────────────────── tidyverse_conflicts() ──
x dplyr::filter() masks stats::filter()
x dplyr::lag()    masks stats::lag()
```

Figure 6.4: List of Attached Packages and Associated Conflicts
when Loading the tidyverse

This isn't an error, but it is some important information that we need to consider! When we first open R (via RStudio) we are working with base R—that is, everything that comes with R and a handful of pre-installed packages.

These are packages and functions that exist in R that we have access to without needing to first load the package using `library()`.

If you would like to see what functions are available to you in base R, you can run `library(help = "base")` in the Console. If you would like to see the packages that came pre-installed with R, you can run `installed.pack-ages()[ installed.packages()[,"Priority"] %in% "base", c("Package", "Priority")]` in the Console. Additionally, if you would like to see a list of *all* of the packages that have been installed (both pre-installed with base R as well as those that you have installed), you can run `rownames(installed.packages())` in the Console.

Due to the broad array of packages that have been created for use in R, it's not uncommon for two (or more!) packages to have functions with the same name.

What this message is telling us, then, is that if we use the `filter()` function, R will use the `filter()` function from the {dplyr} package (a package within the {tidyverse}) rather than the `filter()` function from within the {stats} package (one of the packages that accompanies base R).

Take a moment to use the Help documentation to explore how these two functions might differ.

It's important to note that R will give precedence to the most recently loaded package.

If R gives precedence to the most recently loaded package, you may be wondering what happens if we want to use the `filter()` function from the {stats} package *and* the `filter()` function from the {dplyr} package in the same R session.

One solution would be to reload the library you want to use each time you want to change the package you're using the `filter()` function from. However, this can be tricky for several reasons:

- It's best practice to keep your `library()` calls at the very top of your R script, so reloading a package using `library()` throughout your script can clutter things and cause you headaches down the road.

- If you scroll to the top of your script and reload the packages as you need them, it can be difficult to keep track of which one you recently loaded.

Instead, there's an easier way to handle this kind of problem. When we have conflicting function names from different packages, we can tell R which package we'd like to pull a function from by using `::`.

Using the example of the `filter()` function above, coupled with the examples in the Help documentation, we can specify which package to pull the `filter()` function using `::`, as outlined below.

Note: we haven't covered what any of this code does yet, but see what you can learn from running the code and using the Help documentation!

```r
# using the filter() function from the stats package
x <- 1:100

stats::filter(x, rep(1, 3))

# using the filter() function from the dplyr package
starwars %>%
    dplyr::filter(mass > 85)
```

Loading data from {dataedu} into our R Environment

In this section, we're going to explore not only how to load a dataset from the {dataedu} package into our R Environment but also how to assign that dataset to an object so that we can use it in downstream analyses.

In Appendix A, we show how to access directly data from a few other sources: Excel, SPSS (via `.SAV` files), and Google Sheets. For now, we will be loading datasets that are already stored in the {dataedu} package.

Take a few minutes to type out and run each of the following lines of code, one by one, and notice what you see happening in the Console after you run each line.

```r
dataedu::ma_data_init

dataedu::ma_data_init -> ma_data

ma_data_init <- dataedu::ma_data_init
```

Each of the three code examples above differs slightly, but two lines of code do almost exactly the same thing. The first example provided loads the data into our R environment, but not in a format that's immediately useful to us. The second

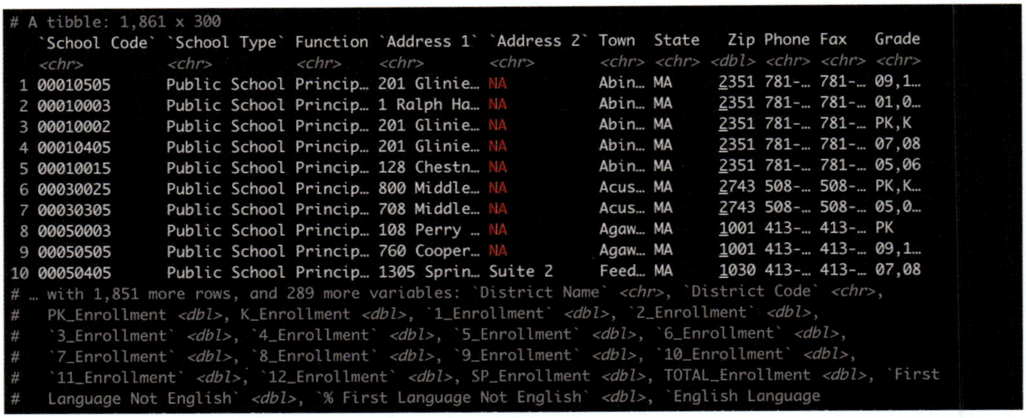

```
# A tibble: 1,861 x 300
   `School Code` `School Type` Function `Address 1` `Address 2` Town  State   Zip Phone Fax    Grade
   <chr>         <chr>         <chr>    <chr>       <chr>       <chr> <chr> <dbl> <chr> <chr>  <chr>
 1 00010505      Public School Princip… 201 Glinie… NA          Abin… MA     2351 781-… 781-… 09,1…
 2 00010003      Public School Princip… 1 Ralph Ha… NA          Abin… MA     2351 781-… 781-… 01,0…
 3 00010002      Public School Princip… 201 Glinie… NA          Abin… MA     2351 781-… 781-… PK,K
 4 00010405      Public School Princip… 201 Glinie… NA          Abin… MA     2351 781-… 781-… 07,08
 5 00010015      Public School Princip… 128 Chestn… NA          Abin… MA     2351 781-… 781-… 05,06
 6 00030025      Public School Princip… 800 Middle… NA          Acus… MA     2743 508-… 508-… PK,K…
 7 00030305      Public School Princip… 708 Middle… NA          Acus… MA     2743 508-… 508-… 05,0…
 8 00050003      Public School Princip… 108 Perry … NA          Agaw… MA     1001 413-… 413-… PK
 9 00050505      Public School Princip… 760 Cooper… NA          Agaw… MA     1001 413-… 413-… 09,1…
10 00050405      Public School Princip… 1305 Sprin… Suite 2     Feed… MA     1030 413-… 413-… 07,08
# … with 1,851 more rows, and 289 more variables: `District Name` <chr>, `District Code` <chr>,
#   PK_Enrollment <dbl>, K_Enrollment <dbl>, `1_Enrollment` <dbl>, `2_Enrollment` <dbl>,
#   `3_Enrollment` <dbl>, `4_Enrollment` <dbl>, `5_Enrollment` <dbl>, `6_Enrollment` <dbl>,
#   `7_Enrollment` <dbl>, `8_Enrollment` <dbl>, `9_Enrollment` <dbl>, `10_Enrollment` <dbl>,
#   `11_Enrollment` <dbl>, `12_Enrollment` <dbl>, SP_Enrollment <dbl>, TOTAL_Enrollment <dbl>, `First
#   Language Not English` <dbl>, `% First Language Not English` <dbl>, `English Language
```

Figure 6.5: Loading the `ma_data_init` Dataset

and third lines of code read in the data and assign it to a new object, `ma_data` and `ma_data_init`, respectively.

In our Environment pane, we can see the data that has been brought into R. We can even click on the table icon on the far right of the row that describes the data to get an interactive table (the dataset is rather large, so RStudio may lag slightly as you open the table and manipulate it).

The assignment operator

The second and third examples in the code chunk above are how you'll most commonly see things in R being saved to a variable. When we save something to a variable, we do so using what's called an "assignment operator", which in R is either a left- or a right-facing arrow (<- or ->).

Writing the name of your variable followed by a left-facing arrow is currently the most common convention used in R, but it is also perfectly acceptable to use the right-facing arrow. Intuitively, the right-facing arrow may make more sense for those of us who work predominantly in languages that read left to right as what we're essentially saying is "Take this entire chunk of code and save it to this variable name". Regardless of which option you choose, both are different means to the same end.

Exploring our data and common errors

This next chunk of code uses functions that help us explore our data, and also introduces us to some common errors in writing R code.

Take a few minutes to type out and run each of the following lines of code, one by one, and notice what you see happening in the Console after you run each line. If you'd like, practice commenting your code by noting what you see happening with each line of code that you run.

Note: we have intentionally included errors in this and subsequent code chunks to help highlight concepts as well as introduce you to error messages early on!

```r
# you probably wrote these 3 library() lines in your R script file
earlier
# if you have not yet run them, you will need to run these three
lines before running the rest of the chunk
library(tidyverse)
library(dataedu)
library(skimr)
library(janitor)

# Exploring and manipulating your data
names(ma_data_init)

glimpse(ma_dat_init)

glimpse(ma_data_init)

summary(ma_data_init)

glimpse(ma_data_init$Town)

summary(ma_data_init$Town)

glimpse(ma_data_init$AP_Test Takers)

glimpse(ma_data_init$`AP_Test Takers`)

summary(ma_data_init$`AP_Test Takers`)
```

What differences do you see between each line of code? What changes in the output to the Console with each line of code that you run?

Common errors: typos, spaces, and parentheses

There were two lines of code that resulted in errors and both were due to one of the most common sources of error in programming—typos!

The first was `glimpse(ma_dat_init)`.

This might be a tricky error to spot, because at first glance it might seem like nothing is wrong! However, we've left off the "a" in "data", which has caused problems with R.

Remember: R will do exactly as you tell it to do. This means if you want to run a function on a dataset, R will only run the function on the datasets that are available in its environment. Looking at our Environment pane, we can see that there is no dataset called `ma_dat_init`, which is what R is trying to tell us with its error message of `Error in glimpse(ma_dat_init) : object 'ma_dat_init' not found`.

The second error was with `glimpse(ma_data_init$AP_Test Takers)`. What do you think the error is here?

R is unhappy with the space in the file name, and it doesn't know how to read the code. To get around this, there are a couple of things we can do. First, we could make sure that data column names never have spaces in them. This is unlikely to be within our control, unless we are the ones creating every dataset we ever use. A second option would be to use R to manipulate the column names after we import the data, but before we start doing any exploration. Another method for dealing with the spaces in column names is to leave the column names as they are, but to use single backticks (`) to surround the column header with spaces in it.

Note: the single backtick key is usually in the top-left of your keyboard. It's common to try and use a set of single quotation marks ('   ') instead of the actual backticks, but they don't work the same way!

The $ operator

There are many ways to isolate and explore a single variable within your dataset. In this set of examples above, we used the $ symbol. The pattern for using the $ symbol is `name_of_dataset$variable_in_dataset`. We can see how this works in the last three lines of code in the code chunk above: it is a way of subsetting. It's important that the spelling, punctuation, and capitalization that you use in your code match what's in your dataset; otherwise, R will tell you that it can't find anything.

Exploring our data with the pipe operator

This next code chunk is going to introduce a funny little operator known as the pipe (`%>%`). The pipe operator allows us to link together functions so that we can run our data through multiple sequential functions. The keyboard shortcut for typing the pipe operator is `Ctrl + Shift + M`.

Note: You can find additional keyboard shortcuts for RStudio by going to "Help" in the top bar and then selecting "Keyboard Shortcuts Help".

Take a few minutes to type out and run each of the following lines of code, one by one, and notice what you see happening in the Console after you run each line. You will run into an error message in one of the code chunks, but just try to understand what it means and continue. We will explain this code below.

```
ma_data_init %>%
    group_by(District Name) %>%
    count()

ma_data_init %>%
    group_by(`District Name`) %>%
    count()

ma_data_init %>%
    group_by(`District Name`) %>%
    count() %>%
    filter(n > 10)
```

```
ma_data_init %>%
    group_by(`District Name`) %>%
    count() %>%
    filter(n > 10) %>%
    arrange(desc(n))
```

"Reading" code

When you encounter new-to-you code, it's helpful to pause and read through the code to see if you can come up with a hypothesis about what it is trying to accomplish. Doing this will help you not only understand code a bit better, but also spot errors more quickly when the code doesn't do what you thought it was going to do.

The way that we would read the last chunk of code we ran is:

> Take the `ma_data_init` dataset and then *group* it *by* District Name and then *count* (the number of schools in a district) and then *filter* for Districts with more than 10 schools and then *arrange* the list of Districts and the number of schools in each District in descending order, based on the number of schools.

That's a mouthful! But there are a couple of consistent points to make regarding this paragraph. Every time we see the pipe, we say "and then". This is because we're starting with our dataset, `ma_data_init`, *and then* doing one thing after another to it.

Because we're using the pipe operator between each function, R knows that all of our functions are being applied to the `ma_data_init` dataset. We do not need to call or refer to the `ma_data_init` data with each function on each line of code. When we link together functions using the pipe operator in this manner, we often refer to it as "chaining together functions".

Before we move on, let's go back to the first example in the code chunk we just ran. We got an error here due to an "unexpected symbol". Like the example we went over earlier in the chapter, this error is caused by the space in the variable name. In the second example in the code chunk we just ran, we enclose District Name in backticks to resolve this error.

The pipe operator

The pipe operator `%>%` can sometimes throw R learners for a loop, until all of a sudden something clicks for them and they decide that they either love it or hate it. We use the pipe operator throughout this text because we also heavily rely on use of the {tidyverse}, which is a package of packages designed for most data science workflows.

Note: as you progress in your R learning journey you will likely find that you need to move well beyond the tidyverse for accomplishing your analytical goals—and that's OK! We like the tidyverse for teaching and learning because it relies on the same syntax across packages, so as you learn how to use functions within one package, you're learning the syntax for functions in other tidyverse packages.

It's worth taking a few moments to talk about the context for the pipe operator and its package. The pipe operator first appeared in the {magrittr} package and is

a play on a famous painting by the artist Magritte, who painted The Treachery of
Images. In these images he would paint an object, such as a pipe, and accompany
it with the text "ceci n'est pas une pipe", which is French for "this is not a pipe".

At the risk of spoiling a joke by over-explaining it, it's common in the R programming world to name a package by choosing a word that represents what the
package does (or what the package is for) and either capitalizing the letter R if it
appears in the package name or adding an R to the end of the package ({dplyr},
{tidyr}, {stringr}, and even {purrr}).

In this case, the author of the {magrittr} package created a series of pipe operators and then collected them in a package named after the artist Magritte.

Exploring assignment vs. equality

We've introduced a couple operators already: namely the assignment operator (<-
or ->) and the pipe operator (%>%). We're now going to talk a bit more in-depth
about = and ==.

Take a few minutes to read through the code below before typing or running
anything in R. Try to guess what is happening in each code chunk by writing out
a sentence for each line of code so that you have a small paragraph for each chunk
of code. Once you've done that, type out and run each of the following lines of
code, one by one, and notice what you see happening in the Console after you run
each line.

```
ma_data_init %>%
    group_by(`District Name`) %>%
    count() %>%
    filter(n = 10)

ma_data_init %>%
    group_by(`District Name`) %>%
    count() %>%
    filter(n == 10)

ma_data_init %>%
    rename(district_name = `District Name`,
        grade = Grade) %>%
    select(district_name, grade)
```

The difference between = and ==

We talked earlier about using a left- or right-facing arrow to assign values or code to
a variable, but we could also use an equals sign (=) to accomplish the same thing.
When R encounters an equal sign (=) it is looking to create an object by assigning
a value to a variable. So when we saw filter(n = 10) in the first example in the
code chunk above, R didn't understand why we were trying to filter something we
were naming and told us so with an error message.

When we are looking to determine whether or not values are equal, we use a
double equals sign (==), as we did in filter(n == 10). When R sees a double equals

sign (==) it is evaluating whether or not the value on the left is equivalent to the value on the right.

Basics of object and variable names

Naming things is important!

The more you use R, the more you'll develop your own sense of how you prefer to name things, either as an organization or an individual programmer. However, there are some hard and fast rules that R has about naming things, and we'll cover them in this section. In the code chunk below, we will try saving our `ma_data_init` dataset into a few different object names. We will be using the `clean_names()` function from the {janitor} package, which you likely already loaded into your environment using the `library(janitor)` function earlier in this chapter. Take a few minutes to type out and run each of the following lines of code, one by one, and notice what you see happening in the Console after you run each line.

```r
ma data <-
    ma_data_init %>%
    clean_names()

01_ma_data <-
    ma_data_init %>%
    clean_names()

$_ma_data <-
    ma_data_init %>%
    clean_names()

ma_data_01 <-
    ma_data_init %>%
    clean_names()

MA_data_02 <-
    ma_data_init %>%
    clean_names()
```

As you saw in the above examples, R doesn't like it when you create a name that starts with a number or symbol. In addition, R is going to squawk when you give it a name with a space in it. As such, when we create variable names in R, they *must* start with a letter, although it doesn't matter if the letter is capitalized or in lower case.

Conclusion

It would be impossible for us to cover *everything* you can do with R in a single chapter of a book, but it is our hope that this chapter gives you a strong foundation from which to explore both subsequent chapters as well as additional R resources.

Appendix A[1] extends some of the techniques introduced in the foundational skills chapter—particularly, reading data from various sources (not only CSV files, but also SAV and XLSX files and spreadsheets from Google Sheets).

In this chapter, we've covered the concepts of Projects, functions, packages, and data. We have also walked through foundational ideas, concepts, and skills related to doing data science in R. It is our hope that you feel well prepared to tackle the subsequent walkthrough chapters, either in sequential order, or in the order that appeals to you!

---

1 We note that we will have a few other appendices like this one to expand on some of the content in the walkthrough chapters.

Chapter 7

Walkthrough 1

The education data science pipeline with online science class data

Topics emphasized

For this and the remaining walkthroughs, we refer to the topics emphasized in terms of distinct but related steps involved in the process of data science. In this book, we use the six steps—described in detail in Chapter 3—from Wickham and Grolemund (2018)'s depiction of the process.

As mentioned in Chapter 5, the topics emphasized are those that are the *particular* focus of each chapter. Most of the walkthroughs contain some element of all of the five aspects, but all have specific emphases.

For this chapter on the education data science pipeline, those emphases are:

- Tidying data

- Transforming data

Functions introduced

- `data.frame()`
- `dplyr::summarize()`
- `tidyr::pivot_longer()` and `tidyr::pivot_wider()`
- `tidyr::left_join()`, `tidyr::right_join()`, `tidyr::semi_join()`, and `tidyr::anti_join()`
- `lm()`
- `ggplot2::ggplot()`
- `apaTables::apa.cor.table()`
- `sjPlot::tab_model()`

Vocabulary

In this section, we include key terms that are introduced and used in the chapter.

- data frame
- item
- joins
- keys
- log-trace data
- passed arguments
- reverse scale
- regression
- survey
- tibble
- vectorize

Introduction to the walkthroughs

This chapter is the first of eight walkthroughs included in the book. In it, we present *one approach* to analyzing a specific dataset. In this chapter, the approach is what we refer to as the "education data science pipeline", or some of the steps taken in many data science projects, including cleaning and tidying data as well as exploring and visualizing or modeling it.

Here, we will be using data from a number of online science classes and will show the process of working with an education dataset from start to finish. While the walkthroughs are very different, the structure and section headings will be consistent throughout them. For example, each walkthrough will begin with a vocabulary section, followed by an introduction to the dataset and an introduction to the question or problem explored in the walkthrough.

We note that this chapter assumes familiarity with the four core concepts that comprise the foundational skills framework: projects, functions, packages, and data. If you would like a refresher about (or an introduction to) any of those, reading Chapter 6 and then writing and running some of the code in it may be helpful to you.

Chapter overview

In this walkthrough, we explore some of the key steps that are a part of many data science in education projects. In particular, we explore how to process and prepare data. These steps are sometimes referred to as "data wrangling". To do this, we rely heavily on a set of tools that we use throughout *all* the walkthroughs—those associated with the {tidyverse}.

The {tidyverse} is a set of packages for data manipulation, exploration, and visualization that uses the design philosophy of "tidy" data (Wickham 2014). Tidy data has a specific structure: each variable is a column, each observation is a row, and each type of observational unit is a table. We'll discuss both the {tidyverse} and tidy data much more throughout the book. For more information, see the "Foundational Skills" chapter or https://www.tidyverse.org/.

Background

The online science classes we explore in this chapter were designed and taught by instructors through a state-wide online course provider designed to supplement—but not replace—students' enrollment in their local school. For example, students may have chosen to enroll in an online physics class because one was not offered at their school. The data was originally collected for a research study, which utilized a number of different data sources to understand students' course-related motivation. These datasets included:

1. A self-report survey assessing three aspects of students' motivation

2. Log-trace data, such as data output from the learning management system (LMS)

3. Discussion board data

4. Academic achievement data

Our high-level *purpose* for this walkthrough is to conduct an analysis that helps explain students' performance in these online courses. The *problem* we are facing is a very common one when it comes to data science in education: the data is complex and in need of further processing before we can get to the step of running analyses. We will use this same dataset in the final walkthrough, Walkthrough 8, in Chapter 14, where we will provide more details about the dataset and context.

To understand students' performance, we will focus on an LMS variable that indicates the amount of time students spent within the course LMS. We will also explore the effects of the type of science course and the section in which students are enrolled on student performance.

First, these different data sources will be described in terms of how they were provided by the school.

Data sources

Data source #1: self-report survey about students' motivation

The first data source is a self-report survey. This was data collected before the start of the course. The survey included ten items, each corresponding to one of three motivation measures: interest, utility value, and perceived competence. A *measure* is a concept that we try to make concrete and assess using survey questions. The three motivation measures we explore here come from Expectancy-Value Theory, which states that students are motivated to learn when they both believe that they can achieve something (expectancy, also known as "perceived competence") and believe that the concept they are trying to learn is important (value) (Wigfield and Eccles 2000). There are multiple types of value, but we explore two of them here: interest and utility value. Utility value is the degree to which a person is able to connect the concept being learned with something they will utilize in their future. This survey included the following ten items:

1. I think this course is an interesting subject. (Interest)

2. What I am learning in this class is relevant to my life. (Utility value)

3. I consider this topic to be one of my best subjects. (Perceived competence)

4. I am not interested in this course. (Interest—reverse coded)

5. I think I will like learning about this topic. (Interest)

6. I think what we are studying in this course is useful for me to know. (Utility value)

7. I don't feel comfortable when it comes to answering questions in this area. (Perceived competence—reverse coded)

8. I think this subject is interesting. (Interest)

9. I find the content of this course to be personally meaningful. (Utility value)

10. I've always wanted to learn more about this subject. (Interest)

Data source #2: log-trace data

Log-trace data is data generated from our interactions with digital technologies, such as archived data from social media postings (see Chapters 11 and 12). In education, an increasingly common source of log-trace data is that generated from interactions with LMS and other digital tools (Baker and Siemens 2014). The data for this walkthrough is a summary type of log-trace data: the number of minutes students spent on the course. While this data type is fairly straightforward, there are even more complex sources of log-trace data out there (e.g., time stamps associated with when students started and stopped accessing the course).

Data source #3: academic achievement and gradebook data

This is a common source of data in the education realm: the graded assignments students completed. In this walkthrough, we examine only students' final grade for the course.

Data source #4: discussion board data

Discussion board data is both rich and unstructured because it is made up of large chunks of text that the students wrote. While discussion board data was collected for this research project, we do not examine it in this walkthrough. More information about analyzing text data can be found in Chapter 11.

Methods

In this walkthrough, we will concentrate on merging different datasets together by using the different "joins" available in the {dplyr} package. We will also start exploring how to run linear models in R.

Load packages

This analysis uses R packages, which are collections of R code that help users code more efficiently, as you will recall from Chapter 5. We load these packages with the function library(). The specific packages we'll use here will help us organize the structure of the data using the {tidyverse} (Wickham 2019b), create formatted tables using {apaTables} (Stanley 2018) and {sjPlot} (Lüdecke 2020), and export datasets using {readxl} (Wickham and Bryan 2019).

If you have not installed any of these packages before, you will need to do so before loading them (if you run the code below *prior* to installing the packages, you should see a message indicating that the package is not available). If you have installed these before, then you can skip this step.

You can install a single package, such as the {tidyverse} package, as follows:

```
install.packages("tidyverse")
```

If you must install two or more packages, you can do so in a single call to the install.packages() function; the names of the packages must be provided to the function as follows:

```
install.packages(c("tidyverse", "apaTables"))
```

When you're installing a package for the first time (which may be needed for the other walkthrough chapters, as well), you will need to take these same steps, first. The good news is that you only need to install a package *once*, after which you can simply load it using library() (as below).

More on the installation of packages is included in the "Packages" section of Chapter 6.

```
library(tidyverse)
library(apaTables)
library(sjPlot)
library(readxl)
library(dataedu)
```

Import data

This code chunk loads the log-trace data and self-report survey data from the {dataedu} package. Note that we assign a dataset to an object three different times, once for the three different datasets. We assign each of the datasets a name using <-.

```
# Pre-survey for the F15 and S16 semesters

pre_survey <- dataedu::pre_survey

# Gradebook and log-trace data for F15 and S16 semesters

course_data <- dataedu::course_data

# Log-trace data for F15 and S16 semesters - this is for time spent

course_minutes <- dataedu::course_minutes
```

View data

Now that we've successfully loaded all three log-trace datasets, we can visually inspect the data by typing the names that we assigned to each dataset. Running each line, one at a time, will show the first several rows of each dataset.

```
pre_survey
## # A tibble: 1,102 x 12
##    opdata_username opdata_CourseID Q1Maincellgroup… Q1Maincell
group…
##    <chr>           <chr>                       <dbl>      <dbl>
##  1 _80624_1        FrScA-S116-01                   4          4
##  2 _80623_1        BioA-S116-01                    4          4
##  3 _82588_1        OcnA-S116-03                   NA         NA
##  4 _80623_1        AnPhA-S116-01                   4          3
##  5 _80624_1        AnPhA-S116-01                  NA         NA
##  6 _80624_1        AnPhA-S116-02                   4          2
##  7 _80624_1        AnPhA-T116-01                  NA         NA
##  8 _80624_1        BioA-S116-01                    5          3
##  9 _80624_1        BioA-T116-01                   NA         NA
## 10 _80624_1        PhysA-S116-01                   4          4
## # … with 1,092 more rows, and 8 more variables: Q1Maincellgroup
Row3 <dbl>,
## #   Q1MaincellgroupRow4 <dbl>, Q1MaincellgroupRow5 <dbl>,
## #   Q1MaincellgroupRow6 <dbl>, Q1MaincellgroupRow7 <dbl>,
## #   Q1MaincellgroupRow8 <dbl>, Q1MaincellgroupRow9 <dbl>,
## #   Q1MaincellgroupRow10 <dbl>
course_data
## # A tibble: 29,711 x 8
## CourseSectionOr… Bb_UserPK Gradebook_Item Grade_Category Final
GradeCEMS
```

```
##     <chr>          <dbl>     <chr>          <chr>   <dbl>
##  1  AnPhA-S116-01   60186     POINTS EARNED…  <NA>    86.3
##  2  AnPhA-S116-01   60186     WORK ATTEMPTED  <NA>    86.3
##  3  AnPhA-S116-01   60186     0.1: Message …  <NA>    86.3
##  4  AnPhA-S116-01   60186     0.2: Intro As…  Hw      86.3
##  5  AnPhA-S116-01   60186     0.3: Intro As…  Hw      86.3
##  6  AnPhA-S116-01   60186     1.1: Quiz       Qz      86.3
##  7  AnPhA-S116-01   60186     1.2: Quiz       Qz      86.3
##  8  AnPhA-S116-01   60186     1.3: Create a…  Hw      86.3
##  9  AnPhA-S116-01   60186     1.3: Create a…  Hw      86.3
## 10  AnPhA-S116-01   60186     1.4: Negative…  Hw      86.3
## # … with 29,701 more rows, and 3 more variables: Points_Possible
<dbl>,
## #   Points_Earned <dbl>, Gender <chr>
course_minutes
## #   A tibble: 598 x 3
## Bb_UserPK CourseSectionOrigID TimeSpent
##     <dbl> <chr>              <dbl>
##  1  44638  OcnA-S116-01       1383.
##  2  54346  OcnA-S116-01       1191.
##  3  57981  OcnA-S116-01       3343.
##  4  66740  OcnA-S116-01        965.
##  5  67920  OcnA-S116-01       4095.
##  6  85355  OcnA-S116-01        595.
##  7  85644  OcnA-S116-01       1632.
##  8  86349  OcnA-S116-01       1601.
##  9  86460  OcnA-S116-01       1891.
## 10  87970  OcnA-S116-01       3123.
## # … with 588 more rows
```

Process data

Often, survey data needs to be processed in order to be most useful. We are going to start with one of the three datasets we just saved as objects into our environment: the dataset with the pre-survey items. Here, we process the self-report items into three scales for (1) interest, (2) perceived competence, and (3) utility value. We do this by:

- Renaming the question variables to something more manageable

- Reversing the response scales on questions 4 and 7

- Categorizing each question into a measure

- Computing the mean of each measure

Let's take these steps in order:

1. Take the pre-survey data, and save it as a new object with the same name pre-survey. Rename the question columns to something much simpler. To do this, we will use the `rename()` function and will input first the new variable name, then the "=" sign, and then the old variable name. You'll notice another function at the bottom called `mutate_at()`. We'll explain that below this code chunk.

```
pre_survey <-
  pre_survey %>%
  # Rename the questions something easier to work with because R
is case sensitive
  # and working with variable names in mix case is prone to error
  rename(
    q1 = Q1MaincellgroupRow1,
    q2 = Q1MaincellgroupRow2,
    q3 = Q1MaincellgroupRow3,
    q4 = Q1MaincellgroupRow4,
    q5 = Q1MaincellgroupRow5,
    q6 = Q1MaincellgroupRow6,
    q7 = Q1MaincellgroupRow7,
    q8 = Q1MaincellgroupRow8,
    q9 = Q1MaincellgroupRow9,
    q10 = Q1MaincellgroupRow10
  ) %>%
  # Convert all question responses to numeric
  mutate_at(vars(q1:q10), list( ~ as.numeric(.)))
```

Let's take a moment to discuss the {dplyr} function `mutate_at()`. `mutate_at()` is a version of `mutate()`, which changes the values in an existing column or creates new columns. It's useful in education datasets because you'll often need to transform your data before analyzing it. In the code chunk we just ran, we used `mutate_at()` to convert the data in all ten variables into a numeric format.

To learn a little more about `mutate()`, try the example below, where we create a new data frame called `df`. A data frame is a two-dimensional structure that stores tables. The table has a header and data rows and each cell stores values.

We fill this data frame with two columns: `male` and `female`. Each column has only one value, and that value is 5. In the second part of the code, we add a `total_students` column by adding the number of `male` students and `female` students.

Note that we create the dataset with `tibble()`, which is from the {tibble} package included in the tidyverse. A tibble is a special type of data frame that makes working with the tidy data a little easier. More information is available in R for Data Science (Wickham and Grolemund 2018).

```
# Dataset of students
df <- tibble(
  male = 5,
  female = 5
)
```

```
# Use mutate to create a new column called "total_students"
  # populate that column with the sum of the "male" and "female"
variables
df %>% mutate(total_students = male + female)
## # A tibble: 1 x 3
##      male female total_students
##     <dbl> <dbl>          <dbl>
## 1       5      5             10
```

To return to our original data, we used `mutate_at()`, a special version of `mutate()` which conveniently changes the values of multiple columns. In our dataset `pre_survey`, we let `mutate_at()` know we want to change the variables q1 through q10. We do this with the argument `vars(q1:q10)`.

2. Next we'll reverse the scale of the survey responses on questions 4 and 7 so the responses for all questions can be interpreted in the same way. As you can see from the survey questions we listed earlier in the chapter, the phrasing of questions 4 and 7 is opposite the phrasing of the other questions. Rather than write a lot of code once to reverse the scales for question 4 then writing it again to reverse the scales on question 7, we'll build a function that does that job for us. Then we'll use the same function that we wrote to recode both question 4 and question 7. This will result in much less code, and it will make it easier for us to change in the future.

We'll use the function `case_when()` within our function to reverse the scale of the item responses. `case_when()` is useful when you need to replace the values in a column with other values based on some criteria. Education datasets use a lot of codes to describe demographics, like numerical codes for disability categories, race groups, or proficiency in a test. When you work with codes like this, you'll often want to change the codes to values that are easier to understand. For example, a consultant analyzing how students did on state testing might use `case_when()` to replace proficiency codes like 1, 2, or 3 with more descriptive words, like "below proficiency", "proficient", or "advanced".

`case_when()` lets you vectorize the rules you want to use to change values in a column. When a sequence of criteria is vectorized, R will evaluate a value in a column against each criteria in your `case_when()` sequence. `case_when()` is helpful because it does this without requiring you to write complicated code loops. Instead, you can systematically evaluate your criteria using code that is compact and readable (once you understand how all the arguments work).

The left hand side of each `case_when()`argument will be a formula that returns either a `TRUE` or a `FALSE`. In the function below, we'll use logical operators in the left hand side of the formula like this: `question == 1 ~ 5`. Here are some logical operators you can use in the future:

- `==`: equal to

- `>`: greater than

- `<`: lesser than

- >=: greater than or equal to

- <=: lesser than or equal to

- !=: not equal to

- !: not

- &: and

- |: or

Let's make this all concrete and use it here in our function that reverses the scale of the survey responses. In the first part of the code chunk below, we will write our function. Note that by running the first bit of code here, we won't be changing anything in our data. Instead, we are creating a reusable, general-purpose code chunk that we will then apply to the specific survey questions we want to recode.

```r
# This part of the code is where we write the function:
# Function for reversing scales
reverse_scale <- function(question) {
  # Reverses the response scales for consistency
  #    Arguments:
  #       question - survey question
  #    Returns:
  #     a numeric converted response
  # Note: even though 3 is not transformed, case_when expects a
  match for all
  # possible conditions, so it's best practice to label each possible
  input
  # and use TRUE ~ as the final statement returning NA for unexpected
  inputs
  x <- case_when(
      question == 1 ~ 5,
      question == 2 ~ 4,
      question == 3 ~ 3,
      question == 4 ~ 2,
      question == 5 ~ 1,
      TRUE ~ NA_real_
  )
  x
}
# And here's where we use that function to reverse the scales
# We use the pipe operator %>% here
# Reverse scale for questions 4 and 7
pre_survey <-
  pre_survey %>%
  mutate(q4 = reverse_scale(q4),
         q7 = reverse_scale(q7))
```

You'll notice that we call the `reverse_scale()` function we wrote, but we call it within the `mutate()` function. By doing things this way, we are overwriting the previous data in the columns for questions 4 and 7 with our newly recoded values.

3. Next, we'll use a function called `pivot_longer()` in order to transform our `pre_survey` dataset from wide format to long format. That means instead of having 1,102 observations of 12 variables, we will now have 11,020 observations of 4 variables. By using `pivot_longer()`, we make it so that each question & response pair has its own line in the data. Therefore, since we have ten question variables (columns) in the `pre_survey` dataset, after we use `pivot_longer()` we will end up with ten times as many observations (rows) as before. Additionally, we no longer need a separate column for each individual question since each question-response pair is now on its own line. What was previously one row of data now takes up ten rows of data. `pivot_longer()` automatically deletes those empty columns after condensing all the data. We'll save this new dataset as an object called `measure_mean` in order to represent new variables we will create in future data processing steps.

```
# Pivot the dataset from wide to long format
measure_mean <-
  pre_survey %>%
  # Gather questions and responses
  pivot_longer(cols = q1:q10,
               names_to = "question",
               values_to = "response")
```

4. Next, we'll take our new `measure_mean` dataset and create a column called `measure`. We'll fill that column with one of three question categories:

- `int`: interest
- `uv`: utility value
- `pc`: perceived competence

We will use the `case_when()` function we learned earlier in order to do this. When we pivoted from wide format to long format in the prior step, we ended up with one variable containing all possible question numbers (q1, q2, etc.). Now, we want to tell R which question numbers correspond to which categories. To do this, we will supply `case_when()` with a list of all the question numbers that correspond to each category: interest, utility value, and perceived competence. We'll introduce a new operator in order to do this: `%in%`. Practically, this operator means that R should look within a list for something. In the code below, we tell R to use questions 1, 4, 5, 8, and 10 to create the category `int`. We then tell R to use questions 2, 6, and 9 to calculate `uv` and to use questions 3 and 7 to calculate `pc`. We indicate the start of each list with the letter "c" and an open parenthesis, and we indicate the end of each list with a close parenthesis.

```
# Add measure variable
measure_mean <- measure_mean %>%
  # Here's where we make the column of question categories called
  "measure"
```

```
  mutate(
    measure = case_when(
      question %in% c("q1", "q4", "q5", "q8", "q10") ~ "int",
      question %in% c("q2", "q6", "q9") ~ "uv",
      question %in% c("q3", "q7") ~ "pc",
      TRUE ~ NA_character_)
  )
```

5. Last, we'll take that same `measure_mean` dataset and create a new variable called `mean_response`. Since we are calculating the mean by category, we will need to first group the responses together using a function called `group_by()`. This function helps us get set up to calculate new columns with grouped data. Next, we'll use the function `summarize()` to create two new variables: `mean_response` and `percent_NA`. We'll find the mean response of each category using the `mean()` function.

```
# Add measure variable
measure_mean <- measure_mean %>%
  # First, we group by the new variable "measure"
  group_by(measure) %>%
  # Here's where we compute the mean of the responses
  summarize(
    # Creating a new variable to indicate the mean response for
    each measure
    mean_response = mean(response, na.rm = TRUE),
    # Creating a new variable to indicate the percent of each
    measure that
    # had NAs in the response field
    percent_NA = mean(is.na(response))
    )
```

```
measure_mean
## # A tibble: 3 x 3
##    measure mean_response percent_NA
##    <chr>        <dbl>        <dbl>
## 1 int          4.25         0.178
## 2 pc           3.65         0.178
## 3 uv           3.74         0.178
```

With that last step, we have finished processing the `pre_survey` dataset. We have renamed the relevant variables and computed some means that we can use later.

Processing the course data

When we loaded the data earlier in the chapter, we loaded three datasets: `pre_survey`, `course_data`, and `course_minutes`. Next, we can process the course data that we already loaded into the environment in order to create new variables which we can use in analyses.

Information about the course subject, semester, and section are stored in a single column, `CourseSectionOrigID`. This format of data storage is not ideal. If we instead give each piece of information its own column, we'll have more opportunities for later analysis. We'll use a function called `separate()` to do this. Below, we will load `course_data` and run the `separate()` function to split up the subject, semester, and section so we can use them later on.

```
# split course section into components
course_data <-
  course_data %>%
  # Give course subject, semester, and section their own columns
  separate(
      col = CourseSectionOrigID,
      into = c("subject", "semester", "section"),
      sep = "-",
      remove = FALSE
  )
```

After running the code chunk above, take a look at the dataset `course_data` to make sure it looks the way you'd expect it to look. In this case, we are expecting that we will add three new variables, taking the total number of variables in this dataset from eight to 11. We will still see the original variable `CourseSectionOrigID` in the data as well.

Joining the data

In this chapter, we are looking at two datasets that are derived from the same courses. In order for these datasets to be most useful to us, we'd like all that data to be in one place.

To join the course data and pre-survey data, we need to create similar keys. Our goal here is to have one variable that matches across both datasets. Once we have that common variable in both datasets, we can merge the datasets on the basis of that variable.

When we look at the `course_data` and `pre_survey` datasets in our environment, we see that both have variables for the course and the student. However, this information is captured in different variable names in each dataset. Our first goal will be to rename two variables in each dataset so that they will match. One variable will correspond to the course, and the other will correspond to the student. We are not changing anything in the data itself at this step—instead, we are just cleaning up the column headers so we can look at the data all in one place.

Let's start with the pre-survey data. We will rename `opdata_username` and `opdata_CourseID` to be `student_id` and `course_id`, respectively. Here, we are going to use the same `rename()` function we learned earlier in this chapter.

```
pre_survey <-
  pre_survey %>%
  rename(student_id = opdata_username,
         course_id = opdata_CourseID)
```

```
pre_survey
## # A tibble: 1,102 x 12
##    student_id course_id q1 q2 q3 q4 q5      q6     q7     q8     q9
## <chr> <chr> <dbl> <dbl> <dbl> <dbl> <dbl> <dbl> <dbl> <dbl> <dbl>
##  1 _80624_1 FrScA-S1… 4 4 4      5     5     4     5     5     5
##  2 _80623_1 BioA-S11… 4 4 3      4     4     4     4     3     4
##  3 _82588_1 OcnA-S11… NA NANA NA    NA    NA    NA    NA    NA
##  4 _80623_1 AnPhA-S1… 4 3 3      4     3     3     3     4     2
##  5 _80624_1 AnPhA-S1… NA NANA NA    NA    NA    NA    NA    NA
##  6 _80624_1 AnPhA-S1… 4 2 2      4     4     4     5     4     4
##  7 _80624_1 AnPhA-T1… NA NANA NA    NA    NA    NA    NA    NA
##  8 _80624_1 BioA-S11… 5 3 3      5     5     4     5     5     3
##  9 _80624_1 BioA-T11… NA NANA NA    NA    NA    NA    NA    NA
## 10 _80624_1 PhysA-S1… 4 4 3      4     4     4     4     4     3
## # … with 1,092 more rows, and 1 more variable: q10 <dbl>
```

Those variable names look better now!

When we look at the data more closely, though, we notice that the `student_id` variable has another issue—the variable has some additional characters before and after *the actual ID* that we will need to be able to join this data with the other data sources we have. Why does this variable have these additional characters? Why is there a "1" at the end of every five-digit ID number? We are not sure! Sometimes, educational data from different systems (used for different purposes) may have additional "meta"-data added on. In any event, here is what the variables look like before processing:

```
head(pre_survey$student_id)
## [1] "_80624_1" "_80623_1" "_82588_1" "_80623_1" "_80624_1" "_80624_1"
```

What we need is the five characters in between the underscore (_) symbols.

One way to do this is to use the `str_sub()` function from the {stringr} package. This function lets us subset "string" variables—variables that store text data. You can specify the indices of the variables you want the string to start and end with.

Here, for example, is how we can select only the content starting with the second character, skipping the first underscore in the process. This next chunk of code will not change our data, but will show you how the `str_sub()` function works by supplying a number-and-underscore combination to the function that is in the same format as our data.

```
str_sub("_99888_1", start = 2)
## [1] "99888_1"
```

We can apply the same thinking to delete characters from the end of a string. We will use a – to indicate that we want to start from the right side of the string of characters. Interestingly, when we specify the argument `end` below, we will tell it the placement of the first character we want to *include*. When we type `end = -3`, we end up deleting only the last two characters. Our new rightmost character will be the final eight.

```
str_sub("_99888_1", end = -3)
## [1] "_99888"
```

Putting the pieces together, the following should return what we want. Try running the code below to see if it yields the five-digit ID number we are shooting to extract.

```
str_sub("_99888_1", start = 2, end = -3)
## [1] "99888"
```

Note: you may receive a warning telling you that NA values were introduced by coercion. This happens when we change data types, and we will overlook this warning message for the purposes of this walkthrough.

We can apply this process to our data using `mutate()`. We convert the string into a number using `as.numeric()` in the next portion of the code. This step is important so the data can be joined to the other numeric `student_id` variables (in the other datasets):

```
# Re-create the variable "student_id" so that it excludes the ex-
traneous characters
pre_survey <- pre_survey %>%
  mutate(student_id = str_sub(student_id, start = 2, end = -3))
# Save the new variable as numeric so that R no longer thinks it
is text
pre_survey <- pre_survey %>%
  mutate(student_id = as.numeric(student_id))
## Warning: NAs introduced by coercion
```

Now that the `student_id` and `course_id` variables are ready to go in the `pre_survey` dataset, let's proceed to the course data. Our goal is to rename the two variables that correspond to the course and the student so we can match them with the other variables we created for the pre-survey data. In the code chunk below, we will rename both those variables.

```
course_data <-
  course_data %>%
  rename(student_id = Bb_UserPK,
         course_id = CourseSectionOrigID)
```

Now that we have two variables that are consistent across both datasets—we have called them `course_id` and `student_id`. We can now join the two datasets using the {dplyr} function `left_join()`, which is named based on the "direction" that the data is being joined. Note the order of the data frames passed to our "left" join. Left joins retain all of the rows in the data frame on the "left" and joins every matching row in the right data frame to it. We will use two variables as keys for joining the datasets, and we will specify those after the word `by`.

Let's save our joined data as a new object called `dat`.

```
dat <-
  left_join(course_data, pre_survey,
            by = c("student_id", "course_id"))
dat
## # A tibble: 40,348 x 21
##      course_id subject semester section student_id Gradebook_
Item Grade_Category
##      <chr>     <chr>   <chr>    <chr>   <dbl>      <chr>            <chr>
## 1  AnPhA-S1… AnPhA   S116     01      60186      POINTS EARNED… <NA>
## 2  AnPhA-S1… AnPhA   S116     01      60186      WORK ATTEMPTED <NA>
## 3  AnPhA-S1… AnPhA   S116     01      60186      0.1: Message … <NA>
## 4  AnPhA-S1… AnPhA   S116     01      60186      0.2: Intro As… Hw
## 5  AnPhA-S1… AnPhA   S116     01      60186      0.3: Intro As… Hw
## 6  AnPhA-S1… AnPhA   S116     01      60186      1.1: Quiz       Qz
## 7  AnPhA-S1… AnPhA   S116     01      60186      1.2: Quiz       Qz
## 8  AnPhA-S1… AnPhA   S116     01      60186      1.3: Create a… Hw
## 9  AnPhA-S1… AnPhA   S116     01      60186      1.3: Create a… Hw
## 10 AnPhA-S1… AnPhA   S116     01      60186      1.4: Negative… Hw
## # … with 40,338 more rows, and 14 more variables: FinalGrade-
CEMS <dbl>,
## # Points_Possible <dbl>, Points_Earned <dbl>, Gender <chr>, q1 <dbl>,
## # q2 <dbl>, q3 <dbl>, q4 <dbl>, q5 <dbl>, q6 <dbl>, q7 <dbl>,
q8 <dbl>,
## # q9 <dbl>, q10 <dbl>
```

Let's hone in on how this code is structured. After `left_join()`, we see `course_data` and then `pre_survey`. In this case, `course_data` is the "left" data frame (passed as the *first* argument), while `pre_survey` is the "right" data frame (passed as the *second* argument). So, in the above code, what happens? You can run the code yourself to check.

Our aim with that code is that all of the rows in `course_data` are retained in our new data frame, `dat`, with matching rows of `pre_survey` joined to it. An important note is that there are not multiple matching rows of `pre_survey`; otherwise, you would end up with more rows in `dat` than expected. There is a lot packed into this one function. Joins are extremely powerful—and common—in many data analysis processing pipelines, both in education and in other fields. Think of all the times you have data in more than one data frame, but you want everything to be in a single data frame! As a result, we think that joins are well worth investing the time to be able to use.

With most types of data, `left_join()` is helpful for carrying out most tasks related to joining datasets. However, there are functions for other types of joins that we want to make sure you know how to use. They may be less frequently used than `left_join()`, but they are still worth mentioning. Note that, for all of these, the "left" data frame is always the first argument, and the "right" data frame is always the second. When running the code chunks below, it can be helpful to pay attention to the number of observations and variables in the datasets before and after the joining. Eventually, the obscure names of these types of joins will start to become more intuitive as you use them more often.

semi_join()

`semi_join()`joins and retains all of the *matching* rows in the "left" and "right" data frame. This is useful when you are only interested in keeping the rows (or cases/observations) that are able to be joined. `semi_join()` will not create duplicate rows of the left data frame, even when it finds multiple matches on the right data frame. It will also keep only the columns from the left data frame.

For example, the following returns only the rows that are present in both `course_data` and `pre_survey`:

```
dat_semi <-
  semi_join(course_data,
            pre_survey,
            by = c("student_id", "course_id"))
```

```
dat_semi
## # A tibble: 28,655 x 11
##      course_id subject semester section student_id Gradebook_
Item Grade_Category
##      <chr>     <chr>   <chr>   <chr>   <dbl>  <chr>           <chr>
##   1  AnPhA-S1… AnPhA   S116    01      60186  POINTS EARNED…  <NA>
##   2  AnPhA-S1… AnPhA   S116    01      60186  WORK ATTEMPTED  <NA>
##   3  AnPhA-S1… AnPhA   S116    01      60186  0.1: Message …  <NA>
##   4  AnPhA-S1… AnPhA   S116    01      60186  0.2: Intro As…  Hw
##   5  AnPhA-S1… AnPhA   S116    01      60186  0.3: Intro As…  Hw
##   6  AnPhA-S1… AnPhA   S116    01      60186  1.1: Quiz       Qz
##   7  AnPhA-S1… AnPhA   S116    01      60186  1.2: Quiz       Qz
##   8  AnPhA-S1… AnPhA   S116    01      60186  1.3: Create a…  Hw
##   9  AnPhA-S1… AnPhA   S116    01      60186  1.3: Create a…  Hw
## 10  AnPhA-S1… AnPhA   S116    01      60186  1.4: Negative…  Hw
## # … with 28,645 more rows, and 4 more variables: FinalGradeCEMS
<dbl>,
## # Points_Possible <dbl>, Points_Earned <dbl>, Gender <chr>
```

anti_join()

`anti_join()`*removes* all of the rows in the "left" data frame that can be joined with those in the "right" data frame.

```
dat_anti <-
  anti_join(course_data,
            pre_survey,
            by = c("student_id", "course_id"))
```

```
dat_anti
## # A tibble: 1,056 x 11
## course_id subject semester section student_id Gradebook_Item
Grade_Category
```

```
##      <chr>       <chr>    <chr>  <chr>  <dbl>  <chr>                <chr>
##  1  AnPhA-S1... AnPhA    S116   01     85865  POINTS EARNED...     <NA>
##  2  AnPhA-S1... AnPhA    S116   01     85865  WORK ATTEMPTED       <NA>
##  3  AnPhA-S1... AnPhA    S116   01     85865  0.1: Message ...     <NA>
##  4  AnPhA-S1... AnPhA    S116   01     85865  0.2: Intro As...     Hw
##  5  AnPhA-S1... AnPhA    S116   01     85865  0.3: Intro As...     Hw
##  6  AnPhA-S1... AnPhA    S116   01     85865  1.1: Quiz            Qz
##  7  AnPhA-S1... AnPhA    S116   01     85865  1.2: Quiz            Qz
##  8  AnPhA-S1... AnPhA    S116   01     85865  1.3: Create a...     Hw
##  9  AnPhA-S1... AnPhA    S116   01     85865  1.3: Create a...     Hw
## 10  AnPhA-S1... AnPhA    S116   01     85865  1.4: Negative...     Hw
## # ... with 1,046 more rows, and 4 more variables: FinalGradeCEMS
<dbl>,
## # Points_Possible <dbl>, Points_Earned <dbl>, Gender <chr>
```

right_join()

Perhaps the least helpful of the three, right_join(), works the same as left_join() but by retaining all of the rows in the "right" data frame and joining matching rows in the "left" data frame (so, the opposite of left_join()).

```
dat_right <-
  right_join(course_data,
             pre_survey,
             by = c("student_id", "course_id"))

dat_right
## # A tibble: 39,593 x 21
##      course_id subject  semester  section  student_id  Gradebook_
Item Grade_Category
##      <chr>       <chr>    <chr>    <chr>    <dbl>    <chr>    <chr>
##  1  FrScA-S1... <NA>     <NA>     <NA>     80624    <NA>     <NA>
##  2  BioA-S11... <NA>     <NA>     <NA>     80623    <NA>     <NA>
##  3  OcnA-S11... <NA>     <NA>     <NA>     82588    <NA>     <NA>
##  4  AnPhA-S1... <NA>     <NA>     <NA>     80623    <NA>     <NA>
##  5  AnPhA-S1... <NA>     <NA>     <NA>     80624    <NA>     <NA>
##  6  AnPhA-S1... <NA>     <NA>     <NA>     80624    <NA>     <NA>
##  7  AnPhA-T1... <NA>     <NA>     <NA>     80624    <NA>     <NA>
##  8  BioA-S11... <NA>     <NA>     <NA>     80624    <NA>     <NA>
##  9  BioA-T11... <NA>     <NA>     <NA>     80624    <NA>     <NA>
## 10  PhysA-S1... <NA>     <NA>     <NA>     80624    <NA>     <NA>
## # ... with 39,583 more rows, and 14 more variables: FinalGradeCEMS
<dbl>,
## # Points_Possible <dbl>, Points_Earned <dbl>, Gender <chr>, q1 <dbl>,
## # q2 <dbl>, q3 <dbl>, q4 <dbl>, q5 <dbl>, q6 <dbl>, q7 <dbl>, q8 <dbl>,
## # q9 <dbl>, q10 <dbl>
```

If we wanted this to return exactly the same output as left_join() (and, in doing so, create a data frame that is identical to the dat data frame we created above), we could simply switch the order of the two data frames to be the opposite of those used for the `left_join()` above:

```
dat_right <-
  right_join(pre_survey,
             course_data,
             by = c("student_id", "course_id"))

dat_right
# A tibble: 40,348 x 21
   student_id course_id   q1    q2    q3    q4    q5    q6    q7    q8    q9
        <dbl> <chr>     <dbl> <dbl> <dbl> <dbl> <dbl> <dbl> <dbl> <dbl> <dbl>
 1      85791 FrScA-S1...   3     3     3     3     4     3     3     3     2
 2      85791 FrScA-S1...   3     3     3     3     4     3     3     3     2
 3      85791 FrScA-S1...   3     3     3     3     4     3     3     3     2
 4      85791 FrScA-S1...   3     3     3     3     4     3     3     3     2
 5      85791 FrScA-S1...   3     3     3     3     4     3     3     3     2
 6      85791 FrScA-S1...   3     3     3     3     4     3     3     3     2
 7      85791 FrScA-S1...   3     3     3     3     4     3     3     3     2
 8      85791 FrScA-S1...   3     3     3     3     4     3     3     3     2
 9      85791 FrScA-S1...   3     3     3     3     4     3     3     3     2
10      85791 FrScA-S1...   3     3     3     3     4     3     3     3     2
# ... with 40,338 more rows, and 10 more variables: q10 <dbl>, subject <chr>,
#   semester <chr>, section <chr>, Gradebook_Item <chr>, Grade_Category <chr>,
#   FinalGradeCEMS <dbl>, Points_Possible <dbl>, Points_Earned <dbl>,
#   Gender <chr>
```

Now that we've gone through the different types of joins available, we will return to our main focus: joining our course datasets together. While we didn't do any data processing steps on it, we still have the `course_minutes` dataset in our environment from when we loaded it there earlier in the chapter. In the code chunk below, we will rename the necessary variables in that dataset so that it is ready to merge. Then, we will merge the `course_minutes` dataset and its newly renamed variables `student_id` and `course_id` with our `dat` dataset.

```
course_minutes <-
  course_minutes %>%
  rename(student_id = Bb_UserPK,
         course_id = CourseSectionOrigID)


course_minutes <-
  course_minutes %>%
  # Change the data type for student_id in course_minutes so we
can match to
```

```
# student_id in dat
mutate(student_id = as.integer(student_id))

dat <-
  dat %>%
  left_join(course_minutes,
            by = c("student_id", "course_id"))
```

Note that they're now combined, even though the course data had many more rows. The pre-survey data has been joined for each student-course combination. We have a pretty large data frame! Let's take a quick look.

```
dat
## # A tibble: 40,348 x 22
##      course_id subject semester section student_id Gradebook_
Item Grade_Category
##      <chr>      <chr>  <chr>    <chr>   <dbl>  <chr>          <chr>
##  1   AnPhA-S1... AnPhA  S116     01      60186  POINTS EARNED... <NA>
##  2   AnPhA-S1... AnPhA  S116     01      60186  WORK ATTEMPTED   <NA>
##  3   AnPhA-S1... AnPhA  S116     01      60186  0.1: Message ... <NA>
##  4   AnPhA-S1... AnPhA  S116     01      60186  0.2: Intro As... Hw
##  5   AnPhA-S1... AnPhA  S116     01      60186  0.3: Intro As... Hw
##  6   AnPhA-S1... AnPhA  S116     01      60186  1.1: Quiz        Qz
##  7   AnPhA-S1... AnPhA  S116     01      60186  1.2: Quiz        Qz
##  8   AnPhA-S1... AnPhA  S116     01      60186  1.3: Create a... Hw
##  9   AnPhA-S1... AnPhA  S116     01      60186  1.3: Create a... Hw
## 10   AnPhA-S1... AnPhA  S116     01      60186  1.4: Negative... Hw
## # ... with 40,338 more rows, and 15 more variables: FinalGradeCEMS
<dbl>,
## # Points_Possible <dbl>, Points_Earned <dbl>, Gender <chr>, q1 <dbl>,
## # q2 <dbl>, q3 <dbl>, q4 <dbl>, q5 <dbl>, q6 <dbl>, q7 <dbl>, q8 <dbl>,
## # q9 <dbl>, q10 <dbl>, TimeSpent <dbl>
```

It looks like we have 40,348 observations from 22 variables.

Finding distinct cases at the student-level

If a student was enrolled in two courses, she will have a different final grade for each of those two courses. However, our data in its current form has many rows representing each course. An easy way we can visually inspect to make sure every row is the same for the same student by course is to use the `glimpse()` function. Try it below.

```
glimpse(dat)
## Rows: 40,348
## Columns: 22.
## $ course_id <chr> "AnPhA-S116-01", "AnPhA-S116-01", "AnPhA-S116-01", "A...
## $ subject   <chr> "AnPhA", "AnPhA", "AnPhA", "AnPhA", "AnPhA", "AnPhA",...
## $ semester  <chr> "S116", "S116", "S116", "S116", "S116", "S116", "S116...
## $ section   <chr> "01", "01", "01", "01", "01", "01", "01", "01", "01",...
```

```
## $ student_id <dbl> 60186, 60186, 60186, 60186, 60186, 60186, 60186, 6018...
## $ Gradebook_Item <chr> "POINTS EARNED & TOTAL COURSE POINTS",
"WORK ATTEMPTE...
## $ Grade_Category <chr> NA, NA, NA, "Hw", "Hw", "Qz", "Qz", "Hw",
"Hw", "Hw",...
## $ FinalGradeCEMS <dbl> 86.272, 86.272, 86.272, 86.272, 86.272,
86.272, 86.27...
## $ Points_Possible <dbl> 5, 30, 105, 140, 5, 5, 20, 50, 10, 50,
5, 5, 24, 10, ...
## $ Points_Earned <dbl> 4.050, 24.000, 71.675, 140.970, 5.000, 4.000, NA, 50....
## $ Gender <chr> "F", "F", "F", "F", "M", "F", "F", "F", "F", "F", "M"...
## $ q1 <dbl> 5, 5, 5, 5, 5, 5, 5, 5, 5, 5, 5, 5, 5, 5, 5, 5, 5,...
## $ q2 <dbl> 4, 4, 4, 4, 4, 4, 4, 4, 4, 4, 4, 4, 4, 4, 4, 4, 4,...
## $ q3 <dbl> 5, 5, 5, 5, 5, 5, 5, 5, 5, 5, 5, 5, 5, 5, 5, 5, 5,...
## $ q4 <dbl> 5, 5, 5, 5, 5, 5, 5, 5, 5, 5, 5, 5, 5, 5, 5, 5, 5,...
## $ q5 <dbl> 5, 5, 5, 5, 5, 5, 5, 5, 5, 5, 5, 5, 5, 5, 5, 5, 5,...
## $ q6 <dbl> 5, 5, 5, 5, 5, 5, 5, 5, 5, 5, 5, 5, 5, 5, 5, 5, 5,...
## $ q7 <dbl> 5, 5, 5, 5, 5, 5, 5, 5, 5, 5, 5, 5, 5, 5, 5, 5, 5,...
## $ q8 <dbl> 5, 5, 5, 5, 5, 5, 5, 5, 5, 5, 5, 5, 5, 5, 5, 5, 5,...
## $ q9 <dbl> 5, 5, 5, 5, 5, 5, 5, 5, 5, 5, 5, 5, 5, 5, 5, 5, 5,...
## $ q10 <dbl> 5, 5, 5, 5, 5, 5, 5, 5, 5, 5, 5, 5, 5, 5, 5, 5, 5,...
## $ TimeSpent <dbl> 2087.05, 2087.05, 2087.05, 2087.05, 2087.05, 2087.05,...
```

You can also use `View(dat)` in order to view the data in RStudio's viewer.

Visually inspecting the first several rows of data, we see that they all correspond to the same student for the same course. As we expected, the `FinalGradeCEMs` variable (representing students' final grade) is also consistent across these rows.

Since we are not carrying out a finer-grained analysis using the `Gradebook_Item`, these duplicate rows are not necessary. We only want variables at the student level and *not* at the level of different gradebook items. We can extract only the unique student-level data using the `distinct()` function. This function takes as arguments the name of the data frame and the name of the variables used to determine what counts as a unique case.

Imagine having a bucket of Halloween candy that has 100 pieces of candy. You know that these 100 pieces are really just a bunch of duplicate pieces from a relatively short list of candy brands. `distinct()` takes that bucket and returns one containing a single piece from each distinct "brand".

Another thing to note about `distinct()` is that it will only return the variable(s)—it is possible to pass more than one variable to `distinct()`—you used to determine uniqueness, *unless* you include the argument `.keep_all = TRUE`. For the sake of making it simple to view the output, we will omit this argument for now.

Were we to run `distinct(dat, Gradebook_Item)`, what do you think would be returned? Running the following code returns a one-column data frame that lists the names of every distinct gradebook item.

```
distinct(dat, Gradebook_Item)
## # A tibble: 222 x 1
##    Gradebook_Item
##    <chr>
```

```
##  1 POINTS EARNED & TOTAL COURSE POINTS
##  2 WORK ATTEMPTED
##  3 0.1: Message Your Instructor
##  4 0.2: Intro Assignment - Discussion Board
##  5 0.3: Intro Assignment - Submitting Files
##  6 1.1: Quiz
##  7 1.2: Quiz
##  8 1.3: Create a Living Creature
##  9 1.3: Create a Living Creature - Discussion Board
## 10 1.4: Negative Feedback Loop Flowchart
## # … with 212 more rows
```

You might be wondering whether some gradebook items have the same names across courses. We can return the unique *combination* of courses and gradebook items by adding another variable to `distinct()`:

```
distinct(dat, course_id, Gradebook_Item)
## # A tibble: 1,269 x 2
##      course_id       Gradebook_Item
##      <chr>           <chr>
##  1 AnPhA-S116-01 POINTS EARNED & TOTAL COURSE POINTS
##  2 AnPhA-S116-01 WORK ATTEMPTED
##  3 AnPhA-S116-01 0.1: Message Your Instructor
##  4 AnPhA-S116-01 0.2: Intro Assignment - Discussion Board
##  5 AnPhA-S116-01 0.3: Intro Assignment - Submitting Files
##  6 AnPhA-S116-01 1.1: Quiz
##  7 AnPhA-S116-01 1.2: Quiz
##  8 AnPhA-S116-01 1.3: Create a Living Creature
##  9 AnPhA-S116-01 1.3: Create a Living Creature - Discussion Board
## 10 AnPhA-S116-01 1.4: Negative Feedback Loop Flowchart
## # … with 1,259 more rows
```

The data frame we get when we run the code chunk above yields a much longer (more observations) dataset. It looks like *a lot* of gradebook items were repeated across courses—likely across the different sections of the same course. If you'd like, you can continue to investigate this: we would be curious to hear what you find if you do!

Next, let's use a similar process to find the unique values at the student level. Instead of exploring unique gradebook items, we will explore unique students (still accounting for the course, as students could enroll in more than one course). This time, we will add the `.keep_all = TRUE` argument.

```
dat <-
  distinct(dat, course_id, student_id, .keep_all = TRUE)
```

This is a much smaller data frame—with one row for each student in the course. Whereas our prior version of the `dat` dataset had over 40,000 rows, that prior version is only helpful if we wanted to do an analysis at the level of specific students' grades for specific gradebook items. Our new dataset keeps only the unique combinations of student and course, leaving us with a more manageable number of observations: 603. Now that our data is ready to go, we can start to ask some questions of it.

Let's take one last step. Since we will be using the final grade variable in many of the figures and analyses that follow, let's rename it using the {dplyr} `rename()` function to something that is a bit easier to type and remember than `FinalGradeCEMS`:

```
dat <- rename(dat, final_grade = FinalGradeCEMS)
```

Analysis

In this section, we focus on some initial analyses in the form of visualizations and some models. We expand on these in Chapter 13. Before we start visualizing relationships between variables in our survey dataset, let's introduce {ggplot2}, a visualization package we'll be using in our walkthroughs.

About {ggplot2}

{ggplot2} is a package we'll be using a lot for graphing and visualizing our education datasets. It is designed to build graphs layer by layer, where each layer is a building block for your graph. Making graphs in layers is useful because we can think of building up our graphs in separate parts: the data comes first, then the x-axis and y-axis, and finally other components like text labels and graph shapes. When something goes wrong and your {ggplot2} code returns an error, you can learn about what's happening by removing one layer at a time and running it again until the code works properly. Once you know which line is causing the problem, you can focus on fixing it.

The first two lines of {ggplot2} code look similar for most graphs. The first line tells R which dataset to graph and which columns the x-axis and y-axis will represent. The second line tells R which shape to use when drawing the graph. You can tell R which shape to use in your graphs with a family of {ggplot2} functions that start with `geom_`. {ggplot2} has many graph shapes you can use, including points, bars, lines, and boxplots. Here's a {ggplot2} example using a dataset of school mean test scores to graph a bar chart:

```
# make dataset
students <-
  tibble(
    school_id = c("a", "b", "c"),
    mean_score = c(10, 20, 30)
  )

# tell R which dataset to plot and which columns the x-axis and
y-axis will represent
students %>%
  ggplot(aes(x = school_id, y = mean_score)) +
```

```
# draw the plot
geom_bar(stat = "identity",
         fill = dataedu_colors("darkblue")) +
theme_dataedu()
```

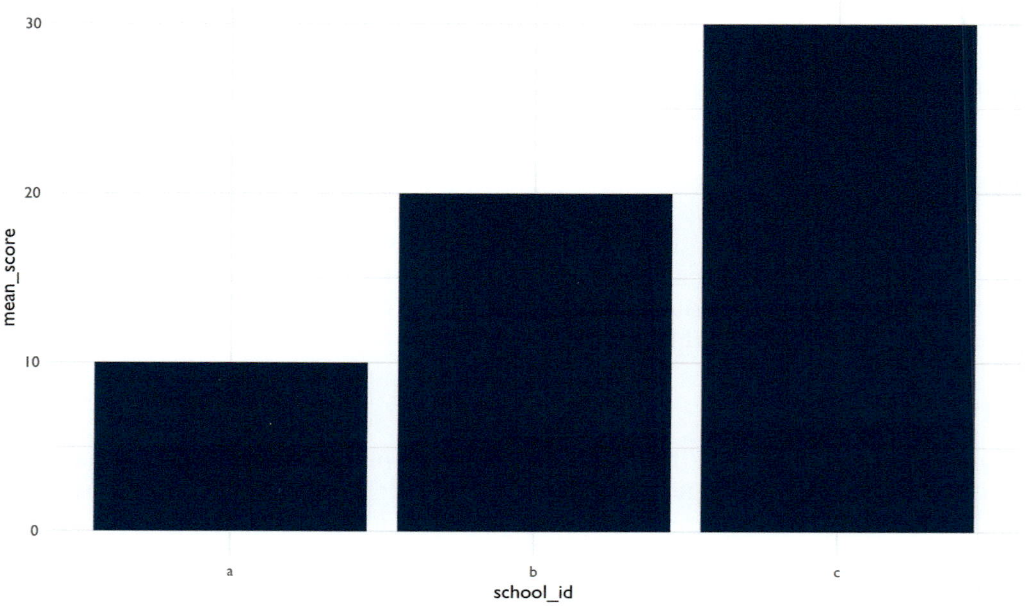

Figure 7.1 Example Plot

The `data` argument in the first line tells R we'll be using the dataset called `students`. The `aes` argument tells R we'll be using values from the `school_id` column for the x-axis and values from the `mean_score` column for the y-axis. In the second line, the `geom_bar` function tells R we'll drawing the graph using the bar chart format. Each line of {ggplot2} code is connected by a + at the end to tell R the next line of code is an additional {ggplot2} layer to add.

Writing code is like writing essays. There's a range of acceptable styles and certainly you can practice unusual ways of writing, but other people will find it harder to understand what you want to say. In this book, you'll see variations in {ggplot2} style, but all within what we believe is the range of acceptable conventions. Here are some examples:

- Piping data to `ggplot()` using `%>%` vs including it as an argument in `ggplot()`

- Using `ggtitle()` for labels vs using `labs()`

- Order of `ggplot()` levels

It's okay if those terms are new to you. The main point is there are multiple ways to make the plot you want. You'll see that in this book and in other peoples' code. As you learn, we encourage you to practice empathy and think about how well your code conveys your ideas to others, including yourself when you look at it many weeks from when you wrote it.

The relationship between time spent on course and final grade

One thing we might be wondering is how time spent on course is related to students' final grades. Let's make a plot to depict that relationship. Below, we'll use `geom_point` instead of `geom_bar`.

```r
dat %>%
    # aes() tells ggplot2 what variables to map to what feature of a plot
    # Here we map variables to the x- and y-axis
    ggplot(aes(x = TimeSpent, y = final_grade)) +
    # Creates a point with x- and y-axis coordinates specified above
    geom_point(color = dataedu_colors("green")) +
    theme_dataedu() +
    labs(x = "Time Spent",
         y = "Final Grade")
```

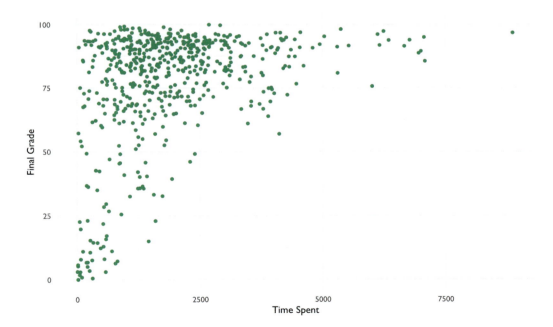

Figure 7.2 Percentage Earned vs. Time Spent

Note: you may receive a warning that reads `Warning message: Removed 5 rows containing missing values (geom_point).` *This is due to the* `NA` *values that were introduced through coercion earlier in this walkthrough and are not a cause for alarm!*

There appears to be *some* relationship. What if we added a line of best fit—a linear model? The code below is the same plot we just made, but it includes the addition of another layer called `geom_smooth`.

```
dat %>%
  ggplot(aes(x = TimeSpent, y = final_grade)) +
    geom_point(color = dataedu_colors("green")) + # same as above
    # this adds a line of best fit
    # method = "lm" tells ggplot2 to fit the line using linear regression
    geom_smooth(method = "lm") +
    theme_dataedu() +
    labs(x = "Time Spent",
        y = "Final Grade")
```

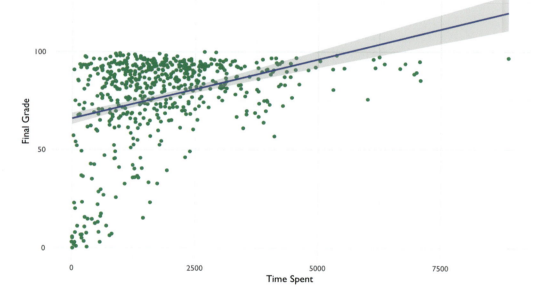

Figure 7.3 Adding a Line of Best Fit

Looking at this plot, it appears that the more time students spent on the course, the higher their final grade.

What is the line doing in the upper right part of the graph? Based upon the trend observable in the data, the line of best fit predicts that students who spend a particular amount of time on the course *earn greater than 100* for their final grade! Of course, this is not possible and highlights the importance of understanding your data and carefully interpreting lines of best fit (and other, more sophisticated analyses) carefully, keeping that understanding and knowledge in mind as you present and make sense of the results.

Linear model (regression)

We can find out exactly what the relationship between these two variables is using a linear model. We discuss linear models in more detail in Chapter 10.

Let's use this technique to model the relationship between the time spent on the course and students' final grades. Here, we predict `final_grade`. The student's final reported grade is the dependent, or y-variable, and so we enter it first, after the `lm()` command and before the tilde (~) symbol. To the right of the tilde is one independent variable, `TimeSpent`, or the time that students spent on the course. We also pass, or provide, the data frame, `dat`. At this point, we're ready to run the model. Let's run this line of code and save the results to an object—we chose `m_linear`, but any name will work. We will then run the `summary()` function on the output.

```
m_linear <-
lm(final_grade ~ TimeSpent, data = dat)

summary(m_linear)
##
## Call:
## lm(formula = final_grade ~ TimeSpent, data = dat)
##
## Residuals:
##     Min      1Q  Median      3Q     Max
## -67.136  -7.805   4.723  14.471  30.317
##
## Coefficients:
##               Estimate Std. Error t value Pr(>|t|)
## (Intercept) 6.581e+01  1.491e+00   44.13   <2e-16 ***
## TimeSpent   6.081e-03  6.482e-04    9.38   <2e-16 ***
## ---
## Signif. codes:  0 '***' 0.001 '**' 0.01 '*' 0.05 '.' 0.1 ' ' 1
##
## Residual standard error: 20.71 on 571 degrees of freedom
##   (30 observations deleted due to missingness)
## Multiple R-squared: 0.1335, Adjusted R-squared: 0.132
## F-statistic: 87.99 on 1 and 571 DF, p-value: < 2.2e-16
```

Another way that we can generate table output is with a function from the {sjPlot} package, `tab_model()`. When you run this code, you should see the results pop up in the "Viewer" pane of RStudio. If you haven't changed the default settings, this will be in the lower right quadrant of your screen.

```
tab_model(m_linear,
          title = "Table 7.1")
```

	Final Grade		
Predictors	Estimates	CI	p
(Intercept)	65.81	62.88–68.74	<0.001
TimeSpent	0.01	0.00–0.01	<0.001
Observations	573		
R^2 / R^2 adjusted	0.134 / 0.132		

Table 7.1 Time Spent (Minutes) Regressed on Final Grade

This will work well for R Markdown documents (or simply to interpret the model in R). If you want to save the model for use in a Word document, the {apaTables} (https://cran.r-project.org/web/packages/apaTables/vignettes/apaTables.html) package may be helpful. To save a table in Word format, just pass the name of the regression model to a function from the {apaTables} package, like we did with the `tab_model()` function. Then, you can save the output to a Word document, by adding a `filename` argument:

```
apa.reg.table(m_linear, filename = "regression-table-output.doc")
```

You might be wondering what else the {apaTables} package does. We encourage you to read more about the package here: https://cran.r-project.org/web/packages/apaTables/index.html. The vignette is especially helpful. One function that may be useful for writing manuscripts is the following function for creating correlation tables. This function takes, as an input, a data frame with the variables for which you wish to calculate correlations.

Before we proceed to the next code chunk, let's talk about some functions we'll be using a lot in this book. `filter()`, `group_by()`, and `summarize()` are functions in the {dplyr} package that you will see a lot in upcoming chapters. You got a preview of these functions earlier in this chapter, and now that you've seen how they are used, we want to provide clear definitions for each of these functions.

- `filter()` removes rows from the dataset that don't match a criteria. Use it for tasks like only keeping records for students in the fifth grade.

- `group_by()` groups records together so you can perform operations on those groups instead of on the entire dataset. Use it for tasks like getting the mean test score of each school instead of a whole school district.

- `summarize()` and `summarise()` reduce your dataset down to a summary statistic. Use it for tasks like turning a dataset of student test scores into a dataset of grade levels and their mean test score.

Now let's use these {dplyr} functions in our survey analysis. We will create the same measures (based on the survey items) that we used earlier to understand how they relate to one another.

```
survey_responses <-
  pre_survey %>%
  # Gather questions and responses
```

```r
pivot_longer(cols = q1:q10,
             names_to = "question",
             values_to = "response") %>%
mutate(
    # Here's where we make the column of question categories
    measure = case_when(
        question %in% c("q1", "q4", "q5", "q8", "q10") ~ "int",
        question %in% c("q2", "q6", "q9") ~ "uv",
        question %in% c("q3", "q7") ~ "pc",
        TRUE ~ NA_character_
    )
) %>%
group_by(student_id, measure) %>%
# Here's where we compute the mean of the responses
summarize(
    # Mean response for each measure
    mean_response = mean(response, na.rm = TRUE)
    ) %>%
    # Filter NA (missing) responses
filter(!is.na(mean_response)) %>%
pivot_wider(names_from = measure,
            values_from = mean_response)

survey_responses
## # A tibble: 515 x 4
## # Groups:    student_id [515]
##    student_id   int    pc     uv
##         <dbl> <dbl> <dbl>  <dbl>
## 1      43146   5     4.5    4.33
## 2      44638   4.2   3.5    4
## 3      47448   5 4   3.67
## 4      47979   5     3.5    5
## 5      48797   3.8   3.5    3.5
## 6      49147   4.25  3.73   3.71
## 7      51943   4.6   4      4
## 8      52326   5     3.5    5
## 9      52446   3     3      3.33
## 10     53248   4     3      3.33
## # … with 505 more rows
```

Now that we've prepared the survey responses, we can use the `apa.cor.table()` function:

```r
survey_responses %>%
  apa.cor.table()
##
##
## Means, standard deviations, and correlations with confidence
intervals
```

```
##
##
##    Variable        M           SD          1                 2                 3
##    1. student_id 85966.07  10809.12
##
##    2. int          4.22        0.59        .00
##                                            [-.08,  .09]
##
##    3. pc           3.60        0.64        .04    .59**
##                                            [-.05,  .13] [.53,  .64]
##
##    4. uv           3.71        0.71        .02    .57**     .50**
##                                            [-.06, .11] [.51, .62] [.43, .56]
##
##
## Note. M and SD are used to represent mean and standard devi-
ation, respectively.
## Values in square brackets indicate the 95% confidence interval.
##  The confidence interval is a plausible range of population
correlations
## that could have caused the sample correlation (Cumming, 2014).
## * indicates p < .05. ** indicates p < .01.
##
```

The time spent variable is on a very large scale (minutes); what if we transformed it to represent the number of *hours* that students spent on the course? Let's use the `mutate()` function we used earlier. We'll end the variable name with _hours to represent what this variable means.

```
# creating a new variable for the amount of time spent in hours
dat <-
  dat %>%
  mutate(TimeSpent_hours = TimeSpent / 60)

# the same linear model as above, but with the TimeSpent variable
in hours
m_linear_1 <-
  lm(final_grade ~ TimeSpent_hours, data = dat)

# viewing the output of the linear model
tab_model(m_linear_1,
          title = "Table 7.2")
```

	Final Grade		
Predictors	Estimates	CI	p
(Intercept)	65.81	62.88–68.74	<0.001
TimeSpent_hours	0.36	0.29–0.44	<0.001
Observations	573		
R^2 / R^2 adjusted	0.134 / 0.132		

Table 7.2 Time Spent (Hours) Regressed on Final Grade

The scale still does not seem quite right. What if we standardized the variable to have a mean of zero and a standard deviation of one?

```
# this is to standardize the TimeSpent variable to have a mean of
0 and a standard deviation of 1
dat <-
  dat %>%
  mutate(TimeSpent_std = scale(TimeSpent))

# the same linear model as above, but with the TimeSpent variable
standardized
m_linear_2 <-
  lm(final_grade ~ TimeSpent_std, data = dat)

# viewing the output of the linear model
tab_model(m_linear_2,
          title = "Table 7.3")
```

	Final Grade		
Predictors	Estimates	CI	p
(Intercept)	76.75	75.05–78.45	<0.001
TimeSpent_std	8.24	6.51–9.96	<0.001
Observations	573		
R^2 / R^2 adjusted	0.134 / 0.132		

Table 7.3 Time Spent (Standardized) Regressed on Final Grade

When we look at this output, it seems to make more sense. However, there is a different interpretation now for the time spent variable: for every one standard deviation increase in the amount of time spent on the course, students' final grades increased by 8.24, or around eight percentage points.

Results

Let's extend our regression model and consider the following to be the final model in this sequence: What other variables may matter? Perhaps there are

differences based on the subject of the course. We can add subject as a variable
as follows:

```
# a linear model with the subject added

# independent variables, such as TimeSpent_std and subject, can
simply be separated with a plus symbol:
m_linear_3 <-
  lm(final_grade ~ TimeSpent_std + subject, data = dat)
```
We can use tab_model() once again to view the results:
```
tab_model(m_linear_3,
          title = "Table 7.4")
```

Predictors	Estimates	CI	p
		Final Grade	
(Intercept)	70.19	66.76–73.61	<0.001
TimeSpent_std	9.63	7.90–11.37	<0.001
Subject [BioA]	−1.56	−8.64–5.52	0.665
Subject [FrScA]	11.73	7.38–16.08	<0.001
Subject [OcnA]	1.10	−3.96–6.16	0.670
Subject [PhysA]	16.04	10.00–22.07	<0.001
Observations	573		
R^2 / R^2 adjusted	0.213 / 0.206		

Table 7.4 Time Spent (Standardized) and Course Subject Regressed on Final Grade

It looks like subjects FrSc—forensic science—and PhysA—Physics—are associated
with a higher final grade. This indicates that students in those two classes earned
higher grades than students in other science classes in this dataset.

Conclusion

In this walkthrough, we focused on taking unprocessed or raw data and loading,
viewing, and then processing it through a series of steps. The result was a dataset which we could use to create visualizations and a simple (but powerful!) linear
model, also known as a regression model. We found that the time that students
spent on the course was positively (and statistically significantly) related to students'
final grades, and that there appeared to be differences by subject. While we focus on
using this model in a traditional, explanatory sense, it could also potentially be used
for predictive analytics in that knowing how long a student spent on the course and
what subject their course is could be used to estimate what that student's final grade
might be. We focus on uses of predictive models further in Chapter 14.

In the follow-up to this walkthrough (see Chapter 13), we will focus on visualizing and then modeling the data using an advanced methodological technique,
multilevel models, using the data we prepared as a part of the data processing pipeline used in this chapter.

Chapter 8

Walkthrough 2

Approaching gradebook data from a data science perspective

Topics emphasized

- Tidying data
- Transforming data
- Visualizing data
- Modeling data

Functions introduced

- `janitor::remove_empty()`
- `stringr::contains()`
- `cor()`

Vocabulary

- correlation
- directory
- environment
- linear model
- linearity
- missing values/NA

- outliers

- string

Chapter overview

Whereas Walkthrough 1 in Chapter 7 focused on the education data science pipeline in the context of an online science class, this walkthrough further explores the ubiquitous but not-often-analyzed classroom gradebook dataset. We will use data science tools and techniques, and focus more on analyses, including correlations and linear models.

There are a variety of data sources to explore in the education field. Student assessment scores can be examined for progress towards goals. The text from a teacher's written classroom observation notes about a particular learner's in-class behavior or emotional status can be analyzed for trends. We can tap into the exportable data available from common learning software or platforms popular in the K–12 education space.

Background

This walkthrough goes through a series of analyses using the data science framework. The first analysis centers around a common K–12 classroom tool: the gradebook. While gradebook data is common in education, it is sometimes ignored in favor of data collected by evaluators and researchers or data from state-wide tests. Nevertheless, it represents an important untapped data source. A data science approach can reveal the value of analyzing a range of education data sources.

Data sources

We use an Excel gradebook template, *Assessment Types Points* (https://web.mit.edu/jabbott/www/excelgradetracker.html), coupled with simulated student data. On your first pass through this section, try using our simulated dataset found in this book's data folder.

You can access the "data" folder by navigating to the book's GitHub repository (https://github.com/data-edu/data-science-in-education) and clicking on the "data" folder. From inside the "data" folder, click on "gradebooks". The file with simulated gradebook data is named ExcelGradeBook.xlsx. When you click on the file name, you will see two buttons: one that says "Download" and another that says "History". Click on the "Download" button to download the Excel-GradeBook.xlsx file to your computer.

Methods

This analysis uses a linear model, which relates one or more X (or independent variables) to a Y (or dependent variable) and a correlation analysis.

Load packages

As mentioned in the "Foundational Skills" chapter, begin by loading the libraries that will be used. We will load the {tidyverse} package used in Walkthrough 1 in Chapter 7. This chapter has an example of using the {readxl} package to read and import Excel spreadsheets—these file types are very common in the education field. We will also use the {janitor} package (Firke 2020). {janitor} provides a number of functions related to cleaning and preparing data.

Make sure you have installed the packages in R on your computer before starting (for an overview and some instructions, see the "Packages" section of the "Foundational Skills" chapter). Load the libraries, as they must be loaded each time we start a new project.

```
# Load libraries
library(tidyverse)
library(here)
library(readxl)
library(janitor)
library(dataedu)
```

Import data

In Appendix A, we recommended the use of .csv files, or comma-separated values files, when working with datasets in R. This is because .csv files, with the .csv file extension, are common in the digital world. They are "plain text"—they tend to be faster when imported, do not have formatting, and are generally easier to deal with than Excel files.

However, data won't always come in your preferred file format. Fortunately, R can import a variety of data file types. This walkthrough imports an Excel file because Excel file types, with the .xlsx or .xls extensions, are very likely to be encountered in the K–12 education world. We'll show you two ways to import the gradebook dataset. The first uses a file path, and the second uses the here() function from the {here} package. We recommend using here(), but it's worthwhile to review both methods.

Import using a file path

First, let's look at importing the dataset using a file path. This code uses the read_excel() function of the {readxl} package to find and read the data of the desired file. Note the file path that read_excel() takes to find the simulated dataset file named ExcelGradeBook.xlsx, which sits in a folder on your computer if you have downloaded it. The function getwd() will help locate your current working directory. This tells where on the computer R is currently working with files.

```
# See the current working directory
getwd()
```

For example, an R user on Linux or Mac might see their working directory as: /
home/username/Desktop. A Windows user might see their working directory as:
C:\Users\Username\Desktop.

From this location, go deeper into files to find the desired file. For example,
if you downloaded the book repository (https://github.com/data-edu/data-science-
in-education) from Github to your Desktop, the path to the Excel file might look
like one of these below:

- /home/username/Desktop/data-science-in-education/data/grade-
  books/ExcelGradeBook.xlsx (on Linux & Mac)

- C:\Users\Username\Desktop\data-science-in-education\data\
  gradebooks\ExcelGradeBook.xlsx (on Windows)

After locating the sample Excel file, use the code below to run the function read_
excel(), which reads and saves the data from ExcelGradeBook.xlsx to an object also called ExcelGradeBook. Note the two arguments specified in this code:
sheet = 1 and skip = 10. This Excel file is similar to one you might encounter
in real life with superfluous features that we are not interested in. This file has
three different sheets, and the first ten rows contain things we won't need. Thus,
sheet = 1 tells read_excel() to just read the first sheet in the file and disregard
the rest. Then, skip = 10 tells read_excel() to skip reading the first 10 rows of
the sheet and start reading from row 11, which is where the column headers and
data actually start inside the Excel file. Remember to replace path/to/file.xlsx
with your own path to the file you want to import.

```
ExcelGradeBook <- read_excel("path/to/file.xlsx", sheet = 1, skip = 10)
```

Import using here()

Whenever possible, we prefer to use here() from the {here} package because it
conveniently guesses the correct file path based on the working directory. In your
working directory, place the ExcelGradeBook.xlsx file in a folder called "gradebooks". Then place the "gradebooks" folder in a folder called "data". The last
step is to make sure your new "data" folder and all its contents are in your working directory. Following those steps, use this code to read the data in:

```
# Use readxl package to read and import file and assign it a name
ExcelGradeBook <-
  read_excel(
    here("data", "gradebooks", "ExcelGradeBook.xlsx"),
    sheet = 1,
    skip = 10
  )
```

The ExcelGradeBook file has been imported into RStudio. Next, assign the data
frame to a new name using the code below. Renaming cumbersome filenames can

improve the readability of the code and make it easier for the user to call on the dataset later on.

```
# Rename data frame
gradebook <- ExcelGradeBook
```

Your environment will now have two versions of the dataset. There is Excel-GradeBook, which is the original dataset we've imported. There is also gradebook, which is a copy of ExcelGradeBook. As you progress through this section, we will work primarily with the gradebook version. While working through this walkthrough, if you make a mistake and mess up the gradebook data frame and are not able to fix it, you can reset the data frame to return to the same state as the original ExcelGradeBook data frame by running gradebook <- ExcelGrade-Book again. This will overwrite any errors in the gradebook data frame with the originally imported ExcelGradeBook data frame.

Process data

Tidy data

This walkthrough uses an Excel data file because it is one that we are likely to encounter. Moreover, the messy state of this file mirrors what might be encountered in real life. The Excel file contains more than one sheet, has rows we don't need, and uses column names that have spaces between words. The data is *not* tidy. All these things make the data tough to work with. We can begin to overcome these challenges before importing the file into RStudio by deleting the unnecessary parts of the Excel file then saving it as a .csv file. However, if you clean the file outside of R, this means if you ever have to clean it up again (say, if the dataset is accidentally deleted and you need to re-download it from the original source), you would have to do everything from the beginning and may not recall exactly what you did in Excel prior to importing the data to R. We recommend cleaning the original data in R so that you can recreate all the steps necessary for your analysis. Also, the untidy Excel file provides realistic practice for tidying up the data programmatically (using a computer program) with R itself, instead of doing these steps manually.

First, we want to modify the column names of the gradebook data frame to remove any spaces and replace them with an underscore. Using spaces in column names in R can present difficulties later on when working with the data.

Second, we want the column names of our data to be easy to use and understand. The original dataset has column names with uppercase letters and spaces. We can use the {janitor} package to quickly change them to a more usable format.

About {janitor}

The {janitor} package is a great resource for anybody who works with data, and particularly fantastic for data scientists in education. Created by Sam Firke, the

Analytics Director of The New Teacher Project, it is a package created by a practitioner in education with education data in mind.

{janitor} has many handy functions to clean and tabulate data. Some examples include:

- `clean_names()`, which takes messy column names that have periods, capitalized letters, spaces, etc., and changes the column names into an R-friendly format

- `get_dupes()`, which identifies and examines duplicate records

- `tabyl()`, which tabulates data in a `data.frame` format, and can be "adorned" with the `adorn_` functions to add total rows, percentages, and other dressings

Let's use {janitor} with this data!

First, let's have a look at the original column names. The output will be long, so let's just look at the first ten by using `head()`.

```
# look at original column names
head(colnames(gradebook))
## [1] "Class"              "Name"              "Race"              "Gender"
## [5] "Age"                "Repeated Grades"
```

You can look at the full output by removing the call to `head()`.

```
# look at original column names
colnames(gradebook)
```

Now let's look at the cleaned names:

```
gradebook <-
  gradebook %>%
  clean_names()
```

```
# look at cleaned column names
head(colnames(gradebook))
## [1] "class"              "name"              "race"              "gender"
## [5] "age"                "repeated_grades"
```

Review what the `gradebook` data frame looks like now. It shows 25 students and their individual values in various columns like `projects` or `formative_assessments`.

```
View(gradebook)
```

The data frame looks cleaner but there still are some things we can remove. For example, there are rows without any names in them. Also, there are entire columns that are unused and contain no data (such as gender). These are called missing values and are denoted by NA. Since our simulated classroom only has 25 learners and doesn't use all the columns for demographic information, we can safely remove these to tidy up our dataset even more.

We can remove the extra columns rows that have no data using the {janitor} package. The handy `remove_empty()` removes columns, rows, or both that have no information in them.

```
# Removing rows with nothing but missing data
gradebook <-
  gradebook %>%
  remove_empty(c("rows", "cols"))
```

Now that the empty rows and columns have been removed, notice that there are two columns, `absent` and `late`, where it seems someone started to input data but then decided to stop. These two columns didn't get removed by the last chunk of code because they technically contained some data. Since the simulated enterer of this simulated class data decided to abandon using the `absent` and `late` columns in this gradebook, we can remove it from our data frame as well.

In the "Foundational Skills" chapter, we introduced the `select()` function, which tells R what columns we want to keep. Let's do that again here. This time we'll use negative signs to say we want the dataset without `absent` and `late`.

```
# Remove a targeted column because we don't use absent and late
at this school.
gradebook <-
  gradebook %>%
  select(-absent, -late)
```

At last, the formerly untidy Excel sheet has been turned into a useful data frame. Inspect it once more to see the difference.

```
View(gradebook)
```

Create new variables and further process the data

R users transform data to facilitate working with it during later phases of visualization and analysis. A few examples of data transformation include creating new variables and grouping data. This code chunk first creates a new data frame named `classwork_df`, then selects particular variables from our gradebook dataset using `select()`, and finally "gathers" all the homework data into new columns.

As mentioned previously, `select()` is very powerful. In addition to explicitly writing out the columns you want to keep, you can also use functions from the package {stringr} within `select()`. The {stringr} package is contained within the {tidyverse} meta-package. Here, we'll use the function `contains()` from {stringr} to tell R to select columns that contain a certain string (that is, text). The function searches for any column with the string `classwork_`. The underscore makes sure the variables from `classwork_1` all the way to `classwork_17` are included in `classwork_df`.

pivot_longer() transforms the dataset into tidy data, where each variable forms a column, each observation forms a row, and each type of observational unit forms a table.

Note that scores are in character format. We use mutate() to transform them to numeric.

```
# Creates new data frame, selects desired variables from grade-
book, and gathers all classwork scores into key/value pairs
classwork_df <-
  gradebook %>%
  select(
    name,
    running_average,
    letter_grade,
    homeworks,
    classworks,
    formative_assessments,
    projects,
    summative_assessments,
    contains("classwork_")) %>%
  mutate_at(vars(contains("classwork_")), list(~ as.numeric(.))) %>%
  pivot_longer(
    cols = contains("classwork_"),
    names_to = "classwork_number",
    values_to = "score"
  )
```

View the new data frame and notice which columns were selected for this new data frame. Also, note how all the classwork scores were gathered under new columns classwork_number and score. We will use this classwork_df data frame later.

```
view(classwork_df)
```

Analysis

Visualize data

Visual representations of data are more human friendly than just looking at numbers alone. This next line of code shows a summary of the data by each column, similar to what we did in Walkthrough 1 in Chapter 7.

```
# Summary of the data by columns
summary(gradebook)
```

But R can do more than just print numbers to a screen. We'll use the {ggplot2} package from within {tidyverse} to graph some of the data to help get a better grasp of what the data looks like. This code uses {ggplot2} to graph categorical variables into a bar graph. Here we can see the variable `letter_grade` is plotted on the x-axis showing the counts of each letter grade on the y-axis.

```
# Bar graph for categorical variable
gradebook %>%
  ggplot(aes(x = letter_grade,
             fill = running_average > 90)) +
  geom_bar() +
  labs(title = "Bar Graph of Student Grades",
       x = "Letter Grades",
       y = "Count",
       fill = "A or Better") +
  scale_fill_dataedu() +
  theme_dataedu()
```

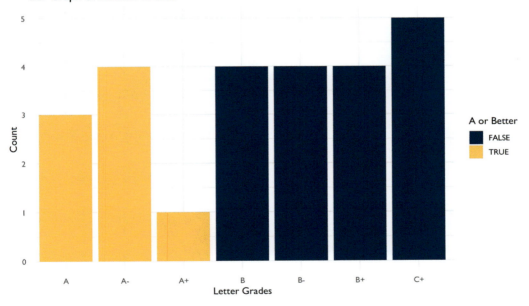

Figure 8.1: Bar Graph of Student Grades

Using {ggplot2}, we can create many types of graphs. Using our `classwork_df` from earlier, we can see the distribution of scores and how they differ from classwork to classwork using boxplots. We are able to do this because we have made the `classworks` and `scores` columns tidy.

```
# Boxplot of continuous variable
classwork_df %>%
  ggplot(aes(x = classwork_number,
```

```
              y = score,
              fill = classwork_number)) +
geom_boxplot() +
labs(title = "Distribution of Classwork Scores",
     x = "Classwork",
     y = "Scores") +
scale_fill_dataedu() +
theme_dataedu() +
theme(
  # removes legend
  legend.position = "none",
  # angles the x axis labels
  axis.text.x = element_text(angle = 45, hjust = 1)
  )
```

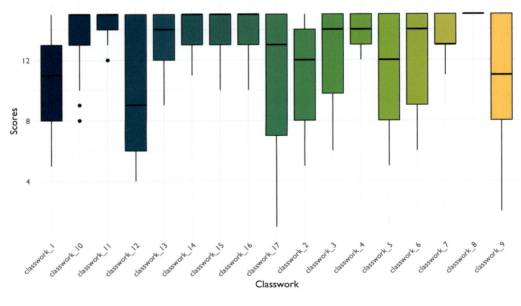

Figure 8.2: Distribution of Classwork Scores

Model data

Deciding on an analysis

Using this spreadsheet, we can start to form hypotheses about the data. For example, we can ask ourselves, "Can we predict overall grade using formative assessment scores?" For this, we will try to predict a response variable Y (overall grade) as a function of a predictor variable X (formative assessment scores). The goal is to create a mathematical equation for overall grade as a function of formative assessment scores when only formative assessment scores are known.

Visualize data to check assumptions

It's important to visualize data to see any distributions, trends, or patterns before building a model. We use {ggplot2} to understand these variables graphically.

Linearity

First, we plot X and Y to determine if we can see a linear relationship between the predictor and response. The x-axis shows the formative assessment scores while the y-axis shows the overall grades. The graph suggests a correlation between overall class grade and formative assessment scores. As the formative scores goes up, so does the overall grade.

```r
# Scatterplot between formative assessment and grades by percent
# To determine linear relationship
gradebook %>%
  ggplot(aes(x = formative_assessments,
             y = running_average)) +
  geom_point(color = dataedu_colors("green")) +
  labs(title = "Relationship Between Overall Grade and Formative
  Assessments",
       x = "Formative Assessment Score",
       y = "Overall Grade in Percentage") +
  theme_dataedu()
```

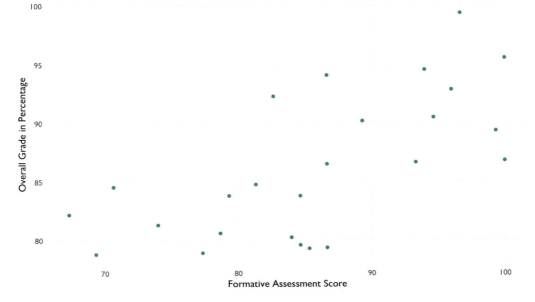

Figure 8.3: Relationship between Overall Grade and Formative Assessments

We can layer different types of plots on top of each other in {ggplot2}. Here the scatterplot is layered with a line of best fit, suggesting a positive linear relationship.

```
# Scatterplot between formative assessment and grades by percent
# To determine linear relationship
# With line of best fit
gradebook %>%
  ggplot(aes(x = formative_assessments,
             y = running_average)) +
  geom_point(color = dataedu_colors("green")) +
  geom_smooth(method = "lm",
              se = TRUE) +
  labs(title = "Relationship Between Overall Grade and Formative
Assessments",
       x = "Formative Assessment Score",
       y = "Overall Grade in Percentage") +
  theme_dataedu()
```

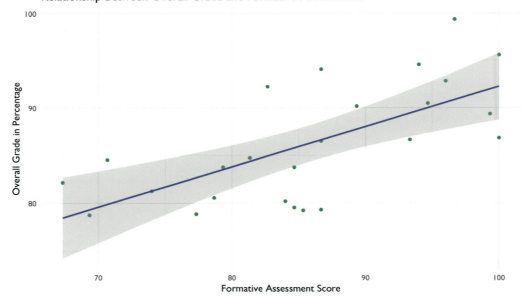

Figure 8.4: Relationship between Overall Grade and Formative Assessments (with Line of Best Fit)

Outliers

Now we use boxplots to determine if there are any outliers in the formative assessment scores or overall grades. As we would like to conduct a linear regression, we're hoping to see no outliers in the data. We don't see any for these two variables, so we can proceed with the model.

```
# Boxplot of formative assessment scores
# To determine if there are any outliers
gradebook %>%
  ggplot(aes(x = "",
             y = formative_assessments)) +
  geom_boxplot(fill = dataedu_colors("yellow")) +
  labs(title = "Distribution of Formative Assessment Scores",
       x = "Formative Assessment",
       y = "Score") +
  theme_dataedu()
```

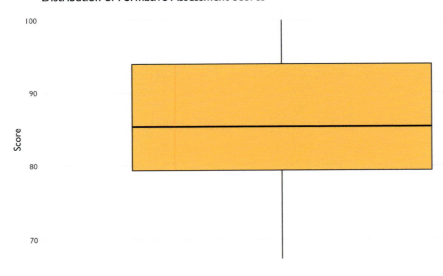

Distribution of Formative Assessment Scores

Figure 8.5: Distribution of Formative Assessment Scores

```
# Boxplot of overall grade scores in percentage
# To determine if there are any outliers
gradebook %>%
  ggplot(aes(x = "",
             y = running_average)) +
  geom_boxplot(fill = dataedu_colors("yellow")) +
  labs(title = "Distribution of Overall Grade Scores",
       x = "Overall Grade",
       y = "Score in Percentage") +
  theme_dataedu()
```

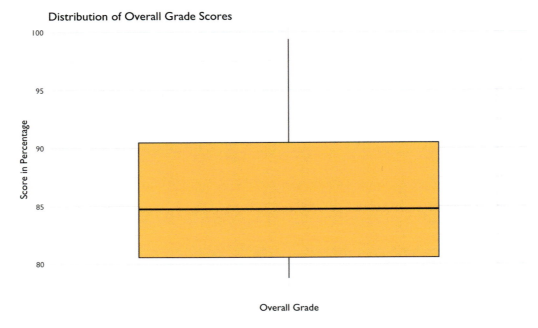

Figure 8.6: Distribution of Overall Grade Scores

Correlation analysis

We want to know the strength of the relationship between the two variables, formative assessment scores and overall grade percentage. The strength is denoted by the "correlation coefficient". The correlation coefficient goes from -1 to 1. If one variable consistently increases with the increasing value of the other, then they have a positive correlation (towards 1). If one variable consistently decreases with the increasing value of the other, then they have a negative correlation (towards -1). If the correlation coefficient is 0, then there is no relationship between the two variables.

Correlation is good for finding relationships but it does *not* imply that one variable causes the other (*correlation* does not mean *causation*).

```
cor(gradebook$formative_assessments, gradebook$running_average)
## [1] 0.6632553
```

Results

In Chapter 7, we introduced the concept of linear models. Let's use that same technique here. Now that you've checked your assumptions and seen a linear relationship, we can build a linear model—a mathematical formula that calculates your running average as a function of your formative assessment score. This is done using the lm() function, where the arguments are:

- Your predictor (formative_assessments)

- Your response (`running_average`)

- The data (`gradebook`)

`lm()` is available in "base R"—that is, no additional packages beyond what is loaded with R automatically are necessary.

```
linear_mod <-
  lm(running_average ~ formative_assessments, data = gradebook)
summary(linear_mod)
##
## Call:
## lm(formula = running_average ~ formative_assessments, data =
##     gradebook)
##
## Residuals:
##     Min       1Q  Median      3Q     Max
## -7.2814 -2.7925 -0.0129  3.3179  8.5353
##
## Coefficients:
##                        Estimate Std. Error t value Pr(>|t|)
## (Intercept)             50.11511    8.54774   5.863 5.64e-06 ***
## formative_assessments    0.42136    0.09914   4.250 0.000302 ***
## ---
## Signif. codes:  0 '***' 0.001 '**' 0.01 '*' 0.05 '.' 0.1 ' ' 1
##
## Residual standard error: 4.657 on 23 degrees of freedom
## Multiple R-squared:  0.4399, Adjusted R-squared:  0.4156
## F-statistic: 18.06 on 1 and 23 DF,  p-value: 0.0003018
```

When you fit a model to two variables, you create an equation that describes the relationship between them based on their averages. This equation uses the (`Intercept`), which is 50.11511, and the coefficient for `formative_assessments`, which is 0.42136. The equation reads like this:

```
running_average = 50.11511 + 0.42136*formative_assessments
```

We interpret these results by saying, "For every one unit increase in formative assessment scores, we can expect a 0.421 unit increase in running average scores". This equation estimates the relationship between formative assessment scores and running average scores in the student population. Think of it as an educated guess about any one particular student's running average, if all you had was their formative assessment scores.

More on interpreting models

Challenge yourself to apply your education knowledge to the way you communicate a model's output to your audience. Consider the difference between describing the relationship between formative assessment scores and running averages for a large group of students and for an individual student.

If you were describing the formative assessment system to stakeholders, you might say something like, "We can generally expect our students to show a 0.421 increase in their running average score for every one point increase in their formative assessment scores". That makes sense because your goal is to explain what happens *in general*.

But we can rarely expect every prediction about individual students to be correct, even with a reliable model. So when using this equation to inform how you support an individual student, it's important to consider all the real-life factors, visible and invisible, that influence an individual student outcome.

To illustrate this concept, consider predicting how long it takes for you to run around the block right outside your office. Imagine you ran around the block five times and after each lap you jotted your time down on a sheet of paper. After the fifth lap, you do a calculation on your cell phone and see that your average lap time is five minutes. If you were to guess how long your sixth lap would take, you'd be smart to guess five minutes. But intuitively you know there's no guarantee the sixth lap time will land right on your average. Maybe you'll trip on a crack in the sidewalk and lose a few seconds, or maybe your favorite song pops into your head and gives you a 30-second advantage. Statisticians would call the difference between your predicted lap time and your actual lap time a "residual" value. Residuals are the differences between predicted values and actual values that aren't explained by your linear model equation.

It takes practice to interpret and communicate these concepts well. A good start is exploring model outputs in two contexts: first, as a general description of a population and, second, as a practical tool for helping individual student performance.

Conclusion

This walkthrough chapter followed the basic steps of a data analysis project. We first *imported* our data, then *cleaned* and *transformed* it. Once we had the data in a tidy format, we were able to *explore* it using data visualization before *modeling* it using linear regression. Imagine that you ran this analysis for someone else: a teacher or an administrator in a school. In such cases, you might be interested in sharing the results in the form of a report or document. Thus, the only remaining step in this analysis would be to communicate our findings using a tool such as R Markdown (https://rmarkdown.rstudio.com/). While we do not discuss R Markdown in this book, we note that it provides the functionality to easily generate reports that include both text (like the words you just read) and code, and the output from code, which are displayed together in a single document (PDF, Word, HTML, and other formats).

While we began to explore models in this walkthrough, we will continue to discuss analyses and statistical modeling in more detail in later chapters (i.e., Chapter 9 on aggregate data, Chapter 10 on longitudinal analyses, Chapter 13 on multi-level models, and Chapter 14 on random forest machine learning models).

Chapter 9

Walkthrough 3

Using school-level aggregate data to illuminate educational inequities

Topics emphasized

- Importing data
- Tidying data
- Transforming data
- Visualizing data

Functions introduced

- `dplyr::mutate_at()`
- `readRDS()`
- `purrr::map` and `purrr::map_df()`
- `purrr::set_names()`
- `dplyr::slice()`

Vocabulary

- aggregate data
- disaggregated data
- data frame
- Free/Reduced Price Lunch (FRPL)
- histogram

- lists

- subgroup

- trim

- weighted average

Chapter overview

Data scientists working in education don't always have access to student-level data, so knowing how to model aggregate datasets is very valuable. This chapter explores what aggregate data is and how to access, clean, and explore it. It is a "companion" to Chapter 10, which also explores aggregate data but does so with an emphasis on "longitudinal analyses"—analyses that involve data at more than one time point.

Background

A common situation encountered when searching for education data, particularly by analysts who are not directly working with schools or districts, is the prevalence of publicly available *aggregate* data. Aggregate data refers to numerical information (or non-numerical information, such as the names of districts or schools) that has the following characteristics:

1. collected from multiple sources and/or on multiple measures, variables, or individuals and

2. compiled into data summaries or summary reports, typically for the purposes of public reporting or statistical analysis (Great Schools, n.d.)

Examples of publicly available aggregate data include school-level graduation rates, state test proficiency scores by grade and subject, or mean survey responses. In this walkthrough, we explore the role of aggregate data, with a focus on educational equity.

Aggregate data is essential both for accountability purposes and for providing useful information about schools and districts to those who are monitoring them. For example, district administrators might aggregate row-level (also known as individual-level or student-level) enrollment reports over time. This allows them to see how many students enroll in each school, in the district overall, and at any grade-level variation. Depending on their state, the district administrator might submit these aggregate data to their state education agency (SEA) for reporting purposes. These datasets might be posted on the state's Department of Education website for anyone to download and use.

Federal and international education datasets provide additional information. In the US, some federal datasets aim to consolidate important metrics from all states. This can be useful because each state has its own repository of data and to go through each state website to download a particular metric is a significant effort. The federal government also funds assessments and surveys which are disseminated to the public. However, federal datasets often have more stringent data requirements than the states, so the datasets may be less usable.

For data scientists in education, these reports and datasets can be analyzed to answer questions related to their field of interest. However, doing so is not always straightforward. Publicly available aggregate datasets are large and often suppressed to protect privacy. Sometimes they are already a couple of years old by the time they're released. Because of their coarseness, they can be difficult to interpret and use. Generally, aggregate data is used to surface broader trends and patterns in education as opposed to diagnosing underlying issues or making causal statements. It is very important that we consider the limitations of aggregate data *first* before analyzing it.

Analysis of aggregate data can help us identify patterns that may not have previously been known. When we have gained new insight, we can create research questions, craft hypotheses around our findings, and make recommendations on how to improve for the future.

We want to take time to explore aggregate data since it's so common in education but can also be challenging to meaningfully use. This chapter and the following one provide two different examples of cleaning an aggregate dataset and of using aggregate datasets to compare student experiences. In this chapter, we'll focus on educational equity by identifying and comparing patterns in student demographic groups. In the next chapter, we'll compare student counts longitudinally (or over time) in different states.

What is the difference between aggregate and student-level data?

Let's dig a little deeper into the differences between aggregate and student-level data. Publicly available data—like the data we'll use in this walkthrough—is a summary of student-level data. That means that student-level data is totaled to protect the identities of students before making the data publicly available. We can use R to demonstrate this concept.

Here are rows in a student-level dataset:

```
library(tidyverse)
# Create student-level data
tibble(
  student = letters[1:10],
  school = rep(letters[11:15], 2),
  test_score = sample(0:100, 10, replace = TRUE)
)
## # A tibble: 10 x 3
##    student school test_score
##    <chr>   <chr>       <int>
## 1  a       k              89
## 2  b       l              75
## 3  c       m              72
## 4  d       n              46
## 5  e       o              67
## 6  f       k              44
```

```
##   7 g          l                13
##   8 h          m                12
##   9 i          n                90
## 10 j          o                53
```

Aggregate data totals up a variable—the variable `test_score` in this case—to "hide" the student-level information. The rows of the resulting dataset represent a group. The group in our example is the `school` variable:

```
tibble(
  student = letters[1:10],
  school = rep(letters[11:15], 2),
  test_score = sample(0:100, 10, replace = TRUE)
) %>%
  # Aggregate by school
  group_by(school) %>%
  summarize(mean_score = mean(test_score))
## # A tibble: 5 x 2
##    school mean_score
##    <chr>       <dbl>
## 1 k              61
## 2 l              72
## 3 m              27
## 4 n            86.5
## 5 o              33
```

Notice that this dataset no longer identifies individual students.

Disaggregating aggregated data

Aggregated data can tell us many things, but in order for us to better examine subgroups (groups that share similar characteristics), we must have data *disaggregated* by the subgroups we hope to analyze. This data is still aggregated from row-level data but provides information on smaller components than the grand total (National Forum on Education Statistics 2016). Common disaggregations for students include gender, race/ethnicity, socioeconomic status, English learner designation, and whether they are served under the Individuals with Disabilities Education Act (IDEA) (The Glossary of Education Reform 2015).

Disaggregating data and equity

Disaggregated data is essential to monitor equity in educational resources and outcomes. If only aggregate data is provided, we are unable to distinguish how different groups of students are doing and what support they need. With disaggregated data, we can identify where solutions are needed to solve disparities in opportunity, resources, and treatment.

It is important to define what equity means to your team so you know whether you are meeting your equity goals.

Data sources

There are many publicly available aggregate datasets related to education. On the international level, perhaps the most well-known is PISA:

- *Programme for International Student Assessment (PISA)* (http://www.oecd.org/pisa/), which measures 15-year-old school pupils' scholastic performance in mathematics, science, and reading.

On the federal level, well-known examples include:

- *Civil Rights Data Collection (CRDC)* (https://www2.ed.gov/about/offices/list/ocr/data.html), which reports many different variables on educational program and services disaggregated by race/ethnicity, sex, limited English proficiency, and disability. This data is school-level.

- *Common Core of Data (CCD)* (https://www2.ed.gov/about/offices/list/ocr/data.html), which is the U.S. Department of Education's primary database on public elementary and secondary education.

- *EdFacts* (https://www2.ed.gov/about/inits/ed/edfacts/data-files/index.html), which includes state assessments and adjusted cohort graduation rates. This data is school- and district-level.

- *Integrated Postsecondary Education Data System (IPEDS)* (https://nces.ed.gov/ipeds/), which is the U.S. Department of Education's primary database on post-secondary education.

- *National Assessment for Educational Progress (NAEP) Data* (https://nces.ed.gov/nationsreportcard/researchcenter/datatools.aspx), which is an assessment of educational progress in the United States. Often called the "nation's report card", the NAEP reading and mathematics assessments are administered to a representative sample of fourth- and eighth-grade students in each state every two years.

At the state and district levels, two examples include:

- *California Department of Education* (https://www.cde.ca.gov/ds/), which is the state's Department of Education website. It includes both downloadable CSV files and "Data Quest", which lets you query the data online.

- *Minneapolis Public Schools* (https://mpls.k12.mn.us/reports_and_data), which is a district-level website with datasets beyond those listed in the state website.

Selecting data

For the purposes of this walkthrough, we will be looking at a particular school district's data; in the next, we will "zoom out" to look across states in the United States.

The district we focus on here reports their student demographics in a robust, complete way. Not only do they report the percentage of students in a subgroup, but they also include the number of students in each subgroup. This allows a deep look into their individual school demographics. Their reporting of the composition of their schools provides an excellent opportunity to explore inequities in a system.

Methods

In this chapter, we will walk through how running analyses on data from a single district can help education data practitioners understand and describe the landscape of needs and opportunities present there. As opposed to causal analyses, which aim to assess the root cause of an phenomenon or the effects of an intervention, we use descriptive analysis on an aggregate dataset to find out whether there *is* a phenomenon present, *what* it is, and *what* may be worth trying to address through future supports, reforms, or interventions (Loeb et al. 2017).

Load packages

As usual, we begin our code by calling the packages we will use. If you have not installed any of these packages yet, see the "Packages" section of the "Foundational Skills" chapter). Load the libraries, as they must be loaded each time we start a new project.

```
library(tidyverse)
library(here)
library(janitor)
library(dataedu)
```

ROpenSci created the {tabulizer} (https://github.com/ropensci/tabulizer) package (Leeper 2018) which provides R bindings to the Tabula java library, which can be used to computationally extract tables from PDF documents. {rJava} (Urbanek 2019) is a required package to load {tabulizer}. Unfortunately, installing {rJava} can be very tedious.

If you find yourself unable to install {rJava}, or would like to go straight to the data processing, you can skip the steps requiring {tabulizer}. We provide the raw and processed data in the {dataedu} package below.

```
library(tabulizer)
```

Import data

We have three options of getting the data:

1. We can use {tabulizer}, which pulls the PDF data into lists using `extract_tables()`.

2. We can get the data from the book's Github repository (https://github.com/data-edu/data-science-in-education/tree/master/data/agg_data). If you would

like to set up the folders in your working directory in the same way they are in the book, first create a folder called "data". Then, inside that folder, create a second folder called "agg_data" and place the `race_pdf.Rds` file in the "agg_data" folder. Then, you can run the code below and load the data using `here()`. Otherwise, you will have to change the file path inside of `here()` to match where the data is stored on your working directory.

3. Finally, you can get the data from the {dataedu} package.

```
# Get data using {tabulizer}
race_pdf <-
  extract_tables("https://studentaccounting.mpls.k12.mn.us/uploads/
mps_fall2018_racial_ethnic_by_school_by_grade.pdf")

# Get data from book repository
# The code below assumes you have set up folders data and agg_data
within your working directory
race_pdf <-
  readRDS(here("data", "agg_data", "race_pdf.Rds"))

# Get data using {dataedu}
race_pdf <-
  dataedu::race_pdf
```

We then transform the list to a data frame by, first, making the matrix version of the PDFs into a tibble by using `map(as_tibble())`. Then, we use the `map_df()` function then turns these tibbles into a single data frame. The `slice()` inside of `map_df()` removes unnecessary rows from the tibbles. Finally, we create readable column names using `set_names()` (otherwise, they look like `...1,` `...2`, etc.).

```
race_df <-
  race_pdf %>%
  # Turn each page into a tibble
  map(~ as_tibble(.x, .name_repair = "unique")) %>%
  # Make data frame and remove unnecessary rows
  map_df(~ slice(.,-1:-2)) %>%
  # Use descriptive column names
  set_names(
    c(
      "school_group",
      "school_name",
      "grade",
      "na_num", # Native American number of students
      "na_pct", # Native American percentage of students
      "aa_num", # African American number of students
      "aa_pct", # African American percentage
      "as_num", # Asian number of students
      "as_pct", # Asian percentage
      "hi_num", # Hispanic number of students
```

```
    "hi_pct",  # Hispanic percentage
    "wh_num",  # White number of students
    "wh_pct",  # White percentage
    "pi_pct",  # Pacific Islander percentage
    "blank_col",
    "tot" # Total number of students (from the Race PDF)
  )
)
```

For the Race/Ethnicity table, we want the totals for each district school as we won't be looking at grade-level variation. When analyzing the PDF, we see the school totals have "Total" in `school_name`.

   We clean up this dataset by:

1. Removing unnecessary or blank columns using `select()`. Negative selections means those columns will be removed.

2. Removing all "Grand Total" rows (otherwise they'll show up in our data when we just want district-level data) using `filter()`. We keep schools that have "Total" in the name but remove any rows that are "Grand Total".

3. Then we trim white space from strings using `trimws()`.

4. The data in the `percentage` columns are provided with a percentage sign. This means `percentage` was read in as a character. We will have to remove all of the non-numeric characters to be able to do math with these columns (for example, to add them together). Also, we want to divide the numbers by 100 so they are in decimal format.

Let's break this line down: `mutate_at(vars(contains("pct")), list( ~ as.numeric(str_replace(., "%", "")) / 100))`. We are telling `mutate_at()` to:

- Select the columns whose names contain the string "pct" by using `vars(contains("pct"))`.

- For the rows in those columns, replace the character "%" with blanks "" by using `str_replace(., "%", "")`.

- After doing that, make those rows numeric by using `as.numeric()`.

- Then, divide those numbers by 100 using `/100`.

```
race_df2 <-
  race_df %>%
  # Remove unnecessary columns
  select(-school_group, -grade, -pi_pct, -blank_col) %>%
  # Filter to get grade-level numbers
  filter(str_detect(school_name, "Total"),
         school_name != "Grand Total") %>%
  # Clean up school names
  mutate(school_name = str_replace(school_name, "Total", "")) %>%
```

```
# Remove white space
mutate_if(is.character, trimws) %>%
# Turn percentage columns into numeric and decimal format
mutate_at(vars(contains("pct")), list( ~ as.numeric(str_replace(.,
"%", "")) / 100))
```

Now, we will import the FRPL PDFs.

FRPL stands for Free/Reduced Price Lunch and is often used as a proxy for poverty (Snyder and Musu-Gillette 2015). Students from a household with an income up to 185% of the poverty threshold are eligible for free or reduced price lunch. (Sidenote: definitions are very important for disaggregated data. FRPL is used because it's ubiquitous but there is debate as to whether it actually reflects the level of poverty among students.)

```
# Get data using {tabulizer}
frpl_pdf <-
 extract_tables("https://studentaccounting.mpls.k12.mn.us/uploads/
fall_2018_meal_eligiblity_official.pdf")
# Get data from book repository
frpl_pdf <-
 readRDS(here("data", "agg_data", "frpl_pdf.Rds"))
# Get data using {dataedu}
frpl_pdf <-
  dataedu::frpl_pdf
```

Similar to the Race/Ethnicity PDF, we take the PDF matrix output, turn it into tibbles, then create a single data frame. There are rows that we don't need from each page, which we remove using `slice()`. Then, we create column names that can be easily understood.

```
frpl_df <-
  frpl_pdf %>%
  # Turn each page into a tibble
  map(~ as_tibble(.x, .name_repair = "unique")) %>%
  # Make data frame and remove unnecessary rows
  map_df( ~ slice(.,-1)) %>%
  # Use descriptive column names
  set_names(
    c(
      "school_name",
      "not_eligible_num", # Number of non-eligible students,
      "reduce_num", # Number of students receiving reduced price lunch
      "free_num",    # Number of students receiving free lunch
      "frpl_num",    # Total number of students (from the FRPL PDF)
      "frpl_pct" # Free/reduced price lunch percentage
    )
  )
```

To clean the dataset up further, we remove the rows that are blank. When looking at the PDF, we notice that there are aggregations inserted into the table that are not district-level. For example, the report includes "ELM K_08" as a value of the variable `school_name`, presumably to aggregate FRPL numbers up to the K–8 level. Although this is useful data, we don't need it for this district-level analysis. There are different ways we can remove these rows but we will just filter them out by using ! before the variable name.

```
frpl_df2 <-
  frpl_df %>%
  filter(
    # Remove blanks
    school_name != "",
    # Filter out the rows in this list
    !school_name %in% c(
      "ELM K_08",
      "Mid Schl",
      "High Schl",
      "Alt HS",
      "Spec Ed Total",
      "Cont Alt Total",
      "Hospital Sites Total",
      "Dist Total"
    )
  ) %>%
  # Turn percentage columns into numeric and decimal format
  mutate(frpl_pct = as.numeric(str_replace(frpl_pct, "%", "")) /
100)
```

Because we want to look at race/ethnicity data in conjunction with FPRL percentage, we join the two datasets by the name of the school. We want our student counts and percentages to be numeric, so apply `as.numeric` to multiple columns using `mutate_at()`.

```
# create full dataset, joined by school name
joined_df <-
  left_join(race_df2, frpl_df2, by = c("school_name")) %>%
  mutate_at(2:17, as.numeric)
```

Did you notice? The total number of students from the Race/Ethnicity table does **not** match the total number of students from the FRPL table, even though they're referring to the same districts in the same year. Why? Perhaps the two datasets were created by different people, who used different rules when aggregating the dataset. Perhaps the counts were taken at different times of the year, and students may have moved around in the meantime. We don't know, but it does require us to make strategic decisions about which data we consider the "truth" for our analysis.

Now we move on to the fun part of creating new columns based on the merged dataset using `mutate()`.

1. We want to calculate, for each race, the number of students in "high-poverty" schools. This is defined by NCES as schools that are over 75% FRPL (Education Statistics U.S. Department of Education 2019). When a school is over 75% FRPL, we count the number of students for that particular race under the variable `[racename]_povnum`.

2. The {janitor} package has a handy `adorn_totals()` function that sums columns for you. This is important because we want a weighted average of students in each category, so we need the total number of students in each group.

3. We create the weighted average of the percentage of each race by dividing the number of students by race by the total number of students.

4. To get FRPL percentage for all schools, we have to recalculate `frpl_pct` (otherwise, it would not be a weighted average).

5. To calculate the percentage of students by race who are in high-poverty schools, we must divide the number of students in high-poverty schools by the total number of students in that race.

```r
district_merged_df <-
  joined_df %>%
  # Calculate high-poverty numbers
  mutate(
    hi_povnum = case_when(frpl_pct > .75 ~ hi_num),
    aa_povnum = case_when(frpl_pct > .75 ~ aa_num),
    wh_povnum = case_when(frpl_pct > .75 ~ wh_num),
    as_povnum = case_when(frpl_pct > .75 ~ as_num),
    na_povnum = case_when(frpl_pct > .75 ~ na_num)
  ) %>%
  adorn_totals() %>%
  # Create percentage by demographic
  mutate(
    na_pct = na_num / tot,
    aa_pct = aa_num / tot,
    as_pct = as_num / tot,
    hi_pct = hi_num / tot,
    wh_pct = wh_num / tot,
    frpl_pct = (free_num + reduce_num) / frpl_num,
    # Create percentage by demographic and poverty
    hi_povsch = hi_povnum / hi_num[which(school_name == "Total")],
    aa_povsch = aa_povnum / aa_num[which(school_name == "Total")],
    as_povsch = as_povnum / as_num[which(school_name == "Total")],
    wh_povsch = wh_povnum / wh_num[which(school_name == "Total")],
    na_povsch = na_povnum / na_num[which(school_name == "Total")]
  )
```

To facilitate the creation of plots later on, we also put this data in tidy format using `pivot_longer()`.

```r
district_tidy_df <-
  district_merged_df %>%
  pivot_longer(
    cols = -matches("school_name"),
    names_to = "category",
    values_to = "value"
  )
```

Running the code above, particularly the download of the PDFs, takes a lot of time. We've saved copies of the merged and tidy data in the book's Github repository and {dataedu}. To access them, you can run the code below.

```r
# If reading in from book repository
district_tidy_df <-
  read_csv(here("data", "agg_data", "district_tidy_df.csv"))
district_merged_df <-
  read_csv(here("data", "agg_data", "district_merged_df.csv"))
# If using the {dataedu} package
district_tidy_df <- dataedu::district_tidy_df
district_merged_df <- dataedu::district_merged_df
```

View data

Discovering distributions

What do the racial demographics in this district look like? A barplot can quickly visualize the different proportion of subgroups.

```r
district_tidy_df %>%
  # Filter for Total rows, since we want district-level information
  filter(school_name == "Total",
         str_detect(category, "pct"),
         category != "frpl_pct") %>%
  # Reordering x-axis so bars appear by descending value
  ggplot(aes(x = reorder(category, -value), y = value)) +
  geom_bar(stat = "identity", aes(fill = category)) +
  labs(title = "Percentage of Population by Subgroup",
       x = "Subgroup",
       y = "Percentage of Population") +
  # Make labels more readable
  scale_x_discrete(
    labels = c(
      "aa_pct" = "Black",
      "wh_pct" = "White",
      "hi_pct" = "Hispanic",
      "as_pct" = "Asian",
      "na_pct" = "Native Am."
```

```
    )
) +
# Makes labels present as percentages
scale_y_continuous(labels = scales::percent) +
scale_fill_dataedu() +
theme_dataedu() +
theme(legend.position = "none")
```

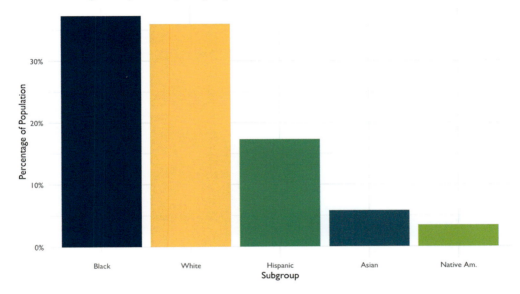

Figure 9.1: Percentage of Population by Subgroup

When we look at these data, the district has some racial diversity. Almost **40% of students are Black** and around **36% are White**. Note that this matches the percentages provided in the original PDFs. This shows our calculations above were accurate. Hooray!

`frpl_pct` is the percentage of the students in the district that are eligible for FRPL.

```
district_tidy_df %>%
  filter(category == "frpl_pct",
         school_name == "Total")
## # A tibble: 1 x 3
##   school_name category value
##   <chr>       <chr>    <dbl>
## 1 Total       frpl_pct 0.569
```

56.9% of the students are eligible for FRPL, compared to the US average of 52.1% (for Education Statistics 2018). This also matches the PDFs. Great!

Now, we dig deeper to see if there is more to the story.

Analyzing spread

Another view of the data is visualizing the distribution of students with different demographics across schools. Here is a histogram for the percentage of White students within the schools for which we have data.

```
district_merged_df %>%
  # Remove district totals
  filter(school_name != "Total") %>%
  # X-axis will be the percentage of White students within schools
  ggplot(aes(x = wh_pct)) +
  geom_histogram(breaks = seq(0, 1, by = .1),
                 fill = dataedu_colors("darkblue"))  +
  labs(title = "Count of Schools by White Population",
       x = "White Percentage",
       y = "Count") +
  scale_x_continuous(labels = scales::percent) +
  theme(legend.position = "none") +
  theme_dataedu()
```

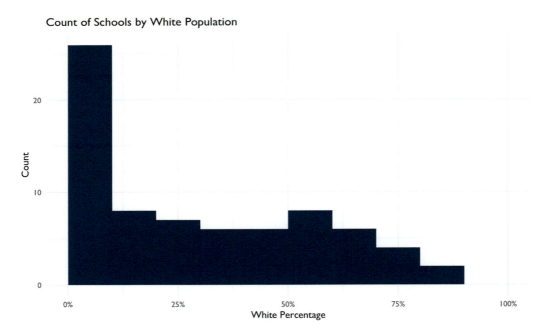

Figure 9.2: Count of Schools by White Population

26 of the 74 (35%) of schools have between 0 and 10% White students. This implies that even though the school district may be diverse, the demographics are not evenly distributed across the schools. More than half of schools enroll fewer than 30% of White students even though White students make up 35% of the district student population.

The school race demographics are not representative of the district populations but does that hold for socioeconomic status as well?

Analysis

Creating categories

High-poverty schools are defined as public schools where more than 75% of the students are eligible for FRPL. According to NCES, 24% of public school students attended high-poverty schools (Education Statistics U.S. Department of Education 2019). However, different subgroups are overrepresented and underrepresented within high-poverty schools. Is this the case for this district?

```
district_tidy_df %>%
  filter(school_name == "Total",
         str_detect(category, "povsch")) %>%
  ggplot(aes(x = reorder(category,-value), y = value)) +
  geom_bar(stat = "identity", aes(fill = factor(category))) +
  labs(title = "Distribution of Subgroups in High Poverty Schools",
       x = "Subgroup",
       y = "Percentage in High Poverty Schools") +
  scale_x_discrete(
    labels = c(
      "aa_povsch" = "Black",
      "wh_povsch" = "White",
      "hi_povsch" = "Hispanic",
      "as_povsch" = "Asian",
      "na_povsch" = "Native Am."
    )
  ) +
  scale_y_continuous(labels = scales::percent) +
  scale_fill_dataedu() +
  theme_dataedu() +
  theme(legend.position = "none")
```

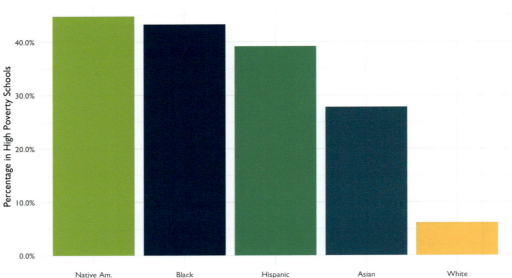

Figure 9.3: Distribution of Subgroups in High-Poverty Schools

8% of White students attend high-poverty schools, compared to **43% of Black students, 39% of Hispanic students, 28% of Asian students, and 45% of Native American students**. We can conclude that non-White students are disproportionally attending high-poverty schools.

Reveal relationships

Let's explore what happens when we correlate race and FRPL percentage by school.

```
district_merged_df %>%
  filter(school_name != "Total") %>%
  ggplot(aes(x = wh_pct, y = frpl_pct)) +
  geom_point(color = dataedu_colors("green")) +
  labs(title = "FRPL Percentage vs. White Percentage",
       x = "White Percentage",
       y = "FRPL Percentage") +
  scale_y_continuous(labels = scales::percent) +
  scale_x_continuous(labels = scales::percent) +
  theme_dataedu() +
  theme(legend.position = "none")
```

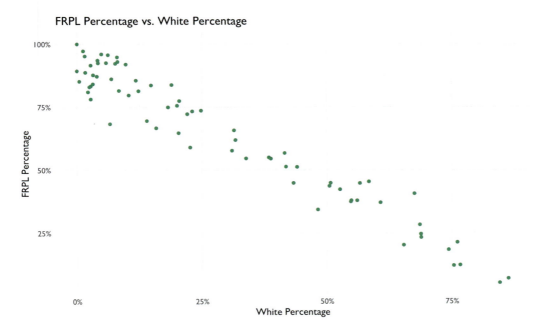

Figure 9.4: FRPL Percentage vs. White Percentage

Similar to the result in Creating Categories, there is a strong negative correlation between FRPL percentage and the percentage of White students in a school. That is, high-poverty schools appear to have a lower percentage of White students and low-poverty schools have a higher percentage of White students.

Results

Because of the disaggregated data this district provides, we can go deeper than the average of demographics across the district and see what it looks like on the school level. These distinct but closely related views demonstrate that:

1. There exists a distribution of race/ethnicity within schools that are not representative of the district.

2. Students of color are overrepresented in high-poverty schools.

3. There is a negative relationship between the percentage of White students in a school and the percentage of students eligible for FRPL.

Conclusion

This analysis, like all analyses, does not occur in a vacuum. According to the Urban Institute, the disproportionate percentage of students of color attending high-poverty schools "is a defining feature of almost all Midwestern and northeastern metropolitan school systems" (Jordan 2015). Among other issues, "low poverty schools tend to lack the educational resources - like highly qualified and experienced teachers, low student-teacher ratios, college prerequisite and advanced placement courses, and extracurricular activities - available in high-poverty schools". This has a huge impact on these students and their futures.

In addition, research shows that racial and socioeconomic diversity in schools can provide students with a range of cognitive and social benefits. Therefore, the deep segregation that exists in the district can have adverse effects on students.

As data scientists in education, we can use these data to showcase the inequity in a system and suggest interventions for what we can do to improve the situation in the district. In addition, we can advocate for more datasets such as these, which allow us to dig deep. In the next chapter, we discuss aggregate data further, focusing on how we can use them to understand changes over time.

Chapter 10

Walkthrough 4

Longitudinal analysis with federal students with disabilities data

Topics emphasized

- Importing data
- Tidying data
- Transforming data
- Visualizing data
- Modeling data
- Communicating results

Functions introduced

- `list.files()`
- `download.file()`
- `lubridate::ymd()`
- `identical()`
- `dplyr::top_n()`
- `ggplot2::geom_jitter()`
- `dplyr::arrange()`

Vocabulary

- aggregate data
- file path
- list

- read in

- tidy format

- statistical model

- student-level data

- longitudinal analysis

- ratio

- subset

- vector

Chapter overview

Data scientists working in education don't always have access to student level data, so knowing how to model publicly available datasets, as in the previous chapter, is a useful skill. This walkthrough builds upon and extends the focus on aggregate data from the last chapter to focus on a change over time in students with disabilities in each state. We note that analyses that involve time can go by a number of names, such as longitudinal analyses or time series analyses, or—less formally—analyses or studies of change over time.

Here, we primarily use the term longitudinal analysis to refer to analyses of data at multiple time points. While data from two time points would be included in this definition, our emphasis is on data from a greater number of time points, which can reveal more nuance in how change over time is happening.

Background

In this chapter, we'll be learning some ways to explore data over time. In addition, we'll be learning some techniques for exploring a publicly available dataset. Like most public datasets (see the previous chapter), this one contains aggregate data. This means that someone totaled up the student counts so that it doesn't reveal any private information.

You can download the datasets for this walkthrough on the United States Department of Education website (see Department of Education 2020),[1] though they are also available in the {dataedu} package that accompanies this book, as we describe in the "Importing the Data From the {dataedu} Package" section below.

Methods

In this walkthrough, we'll learn how to read multiple datasets in using the `map()` function. Next, we'll prepare our data for analysis by cleaning the variable names.

---

1 The documentation for the dataset is available here: https://www2.ed.gov/programs/osepidea/618-data/collection-documentation/data-documentation-files/part-b/child-count-and-educational-environment/idea-partb-childcountandedenvironment-2017-18.pdf

Finally, we'll explore this dataset by visualizing student counts and comparing male to female ratios over time.

Load packages

The function `here()` from the {here} package can cause conflicts with other functions called `here()`. We can prevent problems by loading that package last and including the package name for every call to `here()`, like this: `here::here()`. This is called "including the namespace".

If you have not installed any of these packages, then you will need to do so first, using the `install.packages()` function; see the "Packages" section of the "Foundational Skills" chapter for instructions (and an overview of what packages are and how they work).

You can load the packages needed in this walkthrough by running this code:

```
library(tidyverse)
library(dataedu)
library(lubridate)
library(here)
```

Import data

In this analysis we'll be importing and combining six datasets that describe the number of students with disabilities in a given year. Let's spend some time carefully reviewing how to get the `.csv` files we'll need downloaded and stored on your computer. If you want to run the code exactly as written here, you'll need to store the same datasets in the right location. As an alternate, we make these data files that are used in the walkthrough—like those in other walkthroughs—available through the {dataedu} package. Last, we note that while it's possible to use this walkthrough on different datasets or to store them in different locations on your computer, you'll need to make adjustments to your code based on the datasets you used and where you stored them. We suggest only doing this if you already have some experience using R.

What to download

In this walkthrough, we'll be using six separate datasets of child counts, one for each year between 2012 and 2017. If you're copying and pasting the code in this walkthrough, we recommend downloading the datasets from our GitHub repository for the most reliable results. As we note above, you can also access this data after they have been merged via the {dataedu} package; see the "Importing the Data From the {dataedu} Package" section of this chapter. Here's a link to each file; we also include a short URL via the URL-shortener website *bit.ly*:

- 2012 data (https://github.com/data-edu/data-science-in-education/raw/master/data/longitudinal_data/bchildcountandedenvironments2012.csv) (https://bit.ly/3dCtVtf)

- 2013 data (https://github.com/data-edu/data-science-in-education/raw/master/data/longitudinal_data/bchildcountandedenvironments2013.csv)(https://bit.ly/33WXnFX)

- 2014 data (https://github.com/data-edu/data-science-in-education/raw/master/data/longitudinal_data/bchildcountandedenvironments2014.csv)(https://bit.ly/2UvSwbx)

- 2015 data (https://github.com/data-edu/data-science-in-education/raw/master/data/longitudinal_data/bchildcountandedenvironments2015.csv)(https://bit.ly/39wQAUg)

- 2016 data (https://github.com/data-edu/data-science-in-education/raw/master/data/longitudinal_data/bchildcountandedenvironments2016.csv)(https://bit.ly/2JubWHC)

- 2017 data (https://github.com/data-edu/data-science-in-education/raw/master/data/longitudinal_data/bchildcountandedenvironments2017-18.csv)(https://bit.ly/2wPLu8w)

You can also find these files on the United States Department of Education website (https://www2.ed.gov/programs/osepidea/618-data/state-level-data-files/index.html)

A note on file paths

When you download these files, be sure to store them in a folder in your working directory. To get to the data in this walkthrough, we can use this file path in our working directory: "data/longitudinal_data". We'll be using the `here()` *function* from the {here} *package*, which conveniently fills in all the folders in the file path of your working directory all the way up to the folders you specify in the arguments. So, when referencing the file path "data/longitudinal_data", we'll use code like this:

```
here::here("data",
           "longitudinal_data",
           "bchildcountandedenvironments2012.csv")
```

You can use a different file path if you like, just take note of where your downloaded files are so you can use the correct file path when writing your code to import the data.

How to download the files

One way to download the files is manually, saving them to a working directory. Another way is to read them directly into R, using the `download.file()` function, and the same file path described in the previous section. This functionality works for any CSV files that you can download from webpages; the key is that the URL must be to the CSV file itself (one way to check is to ensure that the URL ends in `.csv`).

Here is how we would do it for the first dataset (from the year 2012), using the shortened URLs included along with the full URLs above.

```
download.file(
  # the url argument takes a URL for a CSV file
  url = 'https://bit.ly/3dCtVtf',
  # destfile specifies where the file should be saved
  destfile = here::here("data",
           "longitudinal_data",
           "bchildcountandedenvironments2012.csv"),
  mode = "wb")
```

We can do this for the remaining five datasets:

```
download.file(
  url = 'https://bit.ly/33WXnFX',
  destfile = here::here("data",
           "longitudinal_data",
           "bchildcountandedenvironments2013.csv"),
  mode = "wb")
download.file(
  url = 'https://bit.ly/2UvSwbx',
  destfile = here::here("data",
           "longitudinal_data",
           "bchildcountandedenvironments2014.csv"),
  mode = "wb")
download.file(
  url = 'https://bit.ly/39wQAUg',
  destfile = here::here("data",
           "longitudinal_data",
           "bchildcountandedenvironments2015.csv"),
  mode = "wb")
download.file(
  url = 'https://bit.ly/2JubWHC',
  destfile = here::here("data",
           "longitudinal_data",
           "bchildcountandedenvironments2016.csv"),
  mode = "wb")
download.file(
  url = 'https://bit.ly/2wPLu8w',
  destfile = here::here("data",
           "longitudinal_data",
           "bchildcountandedenvironments2017-18.csv"),
  mode = "wb")
```

Now that the files are downloaded (either through the above code or from GitHub), we're ready to proceed to reading the data into R. If you were unable to download these files for any reason, they are also available through the {dataedu} package, as we describe in the "Reading in Many Datasets" section.

Reading in one dataset

We'll be learning how to read in more than one dataset using the `map()` function. Let's try it first with one dataset, then we'll scale our solution up to multiple datasets. When you are analyzing multiple datasets that all have the same structure, you can read in each dataset using one code chunk. This code chunk will store each dataset as an element of a list.

Before doing that, you should explore one of the datasets to see what you can learn about its structure. Clues from this exploration inform how you read in all the datasets at once later on. For example, we can see that the first dataset has some lines at the top that contain no data:

```
## # A tibble: 16,234 x 31
##      `Extraction Dat… `6/12/2013` X3     X4     X5     X6     X7     X8
X9      X10
##      <chr>            <chr>       <chr>  <chr>  <chr>  <chr>  <chr>
<chr>  <chr>  <chr>
##  1 Updated:           2/12/2014   <NA>   <NA>   <NA>   <NA>   <NA>
<NA>   <NA>   <NA>
##  2 Revised:           <NA>        <NA>   <NA>   <NA>   <NA>   <NA>
<NA>   <NA>   <NA>
##  3 <NA>               <NA>        <NA>   <NA>   <NA>   <NA>   <NA>
<NA>   <NA>   <NA>
##  4 Year               State Name  SEA … SEA … Amer… Asia… Blac…
Hisp… Nati… Two …
##  5 2012               ALABAMA     Corr… All … -     -     -     -     -     -
##  6 2012               ALABAMA     Home  All … 1     1     57    12    0     2
##  7 2012               ALABAMA     Home… All … -     -     -     -     -     -
##  8 2012               ALABAMA     Insi… All … -     -     -     -     -     -
##  9 2012               ALABAMA     Insi… All … -     -     -     -     -     -
## 10 2012               ALABAMA     Insi… All … -     -     -     -     -     -
## # … with 16,224 more rows, and 21 more variables: X11 <chr>,
X12 <chr>,
## #   X13 <chr>, X14 <chr>, X15 <chr>, X16 <chr>, X17 <chr>, X18 <chr>,
## #   X19 <chr>, X20 <chr>, X21 <chr>, X22 <chr>, X23 <chr>, X24 <chr>,
## #    X25 <chr>, X26 <chr>, X27 <chr>, X28 <chr>, X29 <chr>, X30
<chr>, X31 <chr>
```

The rows containing "Extraction Date:", "Updated:", and "Revised:" aren't actually rows. They're notes the authors left at the top of the dataset to show when the dataset was changed.

`read_csv()` uses the first row as the variable names unless told otherwise, so we need to tell `read_csv()` to skip those lines using the `skip` argument. If we don't, `read_csv()` assumes the very first line—the one that says "Extraction Date:"—is the correct row of variable names. That's why calling `read_csv()` without the `skip` argument results in column names like X4. When there's no obvious column name to read in, `read_csv()` names them X[...] and lets you know in a warning message.

Try using `skip = 4` in your call to `read_csv()`:

```
read_csv(here::here(
  "data",
  "longitudinal_data",
  "bchildcountandedenvironments2012.csv"),
  skip = 4)
## # A tibble: 16,230 x 31
##      Year `State Name` `SEA Education ... `SEA Disability... `Amer-
ican India...
##     <dbl> <chr>        <chr>              <chr>              <chr>
##  1  2012 ALABAMA      Correctional Fa... All Disabilities  -
##  2  2012 ALABAMA      Home               All Disabilities  1
##  3  2012 ALABAMA      Homebound/Hospi... All Disabilities  -
##  4  2012 ALABAMA      Inside regular ... All Disabilities  -
##  5  2012 ALABAMA      Inside regular ... All Disabilities  -
##  6  2012 ALABAMA      Inside regular ... All Disabilities  -
##  7  2012 ALABAMA      Other Location ... All Disabilities  7
##  8  2012 ALABAMA      Other Location ... All Disabilities  1
##  9  2012 ALABAMA      Parentally Plac... All Disabilities  -
## 10  2012 ALABAMA      Residential Fac... All Disabilities  0
## # ... with 16,220 more rows, and 26 more variables: `Asian Age
3-5` <chr>, `Black
## #    or African American Age 3-5` <chr>, `Hispanic/Latino Age
3-5` <chr>,
## #   `Native Hawaiian or Other Pacific Islander Age 3-5` <chr>,
`Two or More
## #    Races Age 3-5` <chr>, `White Age 3-5` <chr>, `Female Age 3
to 5` <chr>,
## #   `Male Age 3 to 5` <chr>, `LEP Yes Age 3 to 5` <chr>, `LEP
No Age 3 to
## #    5` <chr>, `Age 3 to 5` <chr>, `Age 6-11` <chr>, `Age 12-17`
<chr>, `Age
## #    18-21` <chr>, `Ages 6-21` <chr>, `LEP Yes Age 6 to 21` <chr>,
`LEP No Age 6
## #    to 21` <chr>, `Female Age 6 to 21` <chr>, `Male Age 6 to
21` <chr>,
## #   `American Indian or Alaska Native Age 6 to21` <chr>, `Asian
Age 6
## #    to21` <chr>, `Black or African American Age 6 to21` <chr>,
`Hispanic/Latino
## #    Age 6 to21` <chr>, `Native Hawaiian or Other Pacific Is-
lander Age 6
## #    to21` <chr>, `Two or more races Age 6 to21` <chr>, `White
Age 6 to21` <chr>
```

The `skip` argument told `read_csv()` to make the line containing "Year", "State Name", and so on as the first line. The result is a dataset that has "Year", "State Name", and so on as variable names.

Reading in many datasets

Will the `read_csv()` and `skip = 4` combination work on all our datasets? To find out, we'll use this strategy:

- Store a vector of filenames and paths in a list. These paths point to our datasets

- Pass the list of filenames as arguments to `read_csv()` using `purrr::map()`, including `skip = 4`, in our `read_csv()` call

- Examine the new list of datasets to see if the variable names are correct

Imagine a widget-making machine that works by acting on raw materials it receives on a conveyer belt. This machine executes one set of instructions on each of the raw materials it receives. You are the operator of the machine and you design instructions to get a widget out of the raw materials. Your plan might look something like this:

- **Raw materials:** a list of filenames and their paths

- **Widget-making machine:** `purrr:map()`

- **Widget-making instructions:** `` `read_csv(path, skip = 4) ``

- **Expected widgets:** a list of datasets

Let's create the raw materials first. Our raw materials will be file paths to each of the CSVs we want to read. Use `list.files` to make a vector of filename paths and name that vector `filenames`. `list.files` returns a vector of file names in the folder specified in the `path` argument. When we set the `full.names` argument to "TRUE", we get a full path of these filenames. This will be useful later when we need the file names and their paths to read our data in.

```
# Get filenames from the data folder
filenames <-
   list.files(path = here::here("data", "longitudinal_data"),
              full.names = TRUE)
# A list of filenames and paths
filenames
```

That made a vector of six filenames, one for each year of child count data stored in the data folder. Now pass our raw materials, the vector called `filenames`, to our widget-making machine called `map()` and give the machine the instructions `read_csv(., skip = 4)`. Name the list of widgets it cranks out using `all_files`:

```
# Pass filenames to map and read_csv
all_files <-
  filenames %>%
  # Apply the function read_csv to each element of filenames
  map(., ~ read_csv(., skip = 4))
```

It is important to think ahead here. The goal is to combine the datasets in `all_files` into one dataset using `bind_rows()`. But that will only work if all the datasets in our list have the same number of columns and the same column names. We can check our column names by using `map()` and `names()`:

We can use `identical()` to see if the variables from two datasets match. We see that the variable names of the first and second datasets don't match, but the variables from the second and third do.

```
# Variables of first and second dataset don't match
identical(names(all_files[[1]]), names(all_files[[2]]))
## [1] FALSE
# Variables of third and second files match
identical(names(all_files[[2]]), names(all_files[[3]]))
## [1] TRUE
```

And we can check the number of columns by using `map()` and `ncol()`:

```
all_files %>%
  # apply the function ncol to each element of all_files
  map(ncol)
## [[1]]
## [1] 31
##
## [[2]]
## [1] 50
##
## [[3]]
## [1] 50
##
## [[4]]
## [1] 50
##
## [[5]]
## [1] 50
##
## [[6]]
## [1] 50
```

We have just encountered an extremely common problem in education data! Neither the number of columns nor the column names match. This is a problem because with different column names, we won't be able to combine the datasets in a later step. As we can see, when we try, `bind_rows()` returns a dataset with 100 columns, instead of the expected 50.

```
# combining the datasets at this stage results in the incorrect
# number of columns
bind_rows(all_files) %>%
  # check the number of columns
  ncol()
## [1] 100
```

We'll correct this in the next section by selecting and renaming our variables, but it's good to notice this problem early in the process so you know to work on it later.

Loading the data from {dataedu}

After all of the hard work we've done above, it may seem painful to simply read in the final result! But, if you were unable to download the files because you do not have Internet access (or for any other reason!), you can read in the `all_files` list of six data frames through the {dataedu} package with the following line of code:

```
all_files <- dataedu::all_files
```

Process data

Transforming your dataset before visualizing it and fitting models is critical. It's easier to write code when variable names are concise and informative. Many functions in R, especially those in the {ggplot2} package, work best when datasets are in a "tidy" format. It's easier to do an analysis when you have just the variables you need. Any unused variables can confuse your thought process.

Let's preview the steps we'll be taking:

1. Fix the variable names in the 2016 data

2. Combine the datasets

3. Pick variables

4. Filter for the desired categories

5. Rename the variables

6. Standardize the state names

7. Transform the column formats from wide to long using `pivot_longer`

8. Change the data types of variables

9. Explore NAs

In real life, data scientists don't always know the cleaning steps until they dive into the work. Learning what cleaning steps are needed requires exploration, trial and error, and clarity on the analytic questions you want to answer.

After a lot of exploring, we settled on these steps for this analysis. When you do your own, you will find different things to transform. As you do more and more data analysis, your instincts for what to transform will improve.

Fix the variable names in the 2016 data

When we print the 2016 dataset, we notice that the variable names are incorrect. Let's verify that by looking at the first ten variable names of the 2016 dataset, which is the fifth element of `all_files`:

```
# Look at the first 10 column names of 2016
names(all_files[[5]])[1:10]
##    [1] "2016"                     "Alabama"
##    [3] "Correctional Facilities"  "All Disabilities"
##    [5] "-"                        "-_1"
##    [7] "-_2"                      "-_3"
##    [9] "-_4"                      "-_5"
```

We want the variable names to be `Year` and `State Name`, not `2016` and `Alabama`. But first, let's go back and review how to get at the 2016 dataset from `all_files`. We need to identify which element the 2016 dataset was in the list. The order of the list elements was set all the way back when we fed `map()` our list of filenames. If we look at `filenames` again, we see that its fifth element is the 2016 dataset. Try looking at the first and fifth elements of `filenames`:

```
filenames[[1]]
filenames[[5]]
```

Once we know the 2016 dataset is the fifth element of our list, we can pluck it out by using double brackets:

```
all_files[[5]]
## # A tibble: 16,230 x 50
##      `2016` Alabama `Correctional F... `All Disabiliti... `-`      `-_1`
  `-_2`  `-_3`
##       <dbl> <chr>   <chr>              <chr>              <chr>
  <chr> <chr> <chr>
## 1    2016 Alabama Home               All Disabilities     43 30 35 0
## 2    2016 Alabama Homebound/Hospi... All Disabilities   -  -   -  -
## 3    2016 Alabama Inside regular  ... All Disabilities   -  -   -  -
## 4    2016 Alabama Inside regular  ... All Disabilities   -  -   -  -
## 5    2016 Alabama Inside regular  ... All Disabilities   -  -   -  -
## 6    2016 Alabama Parentally Plac ... All Disabilities   -  -   -  -
## 7    2016 Alabama Residential Fac ... All Disabilities    5  3   4  0
## 8    2016 Alabama Residential Fac... All Disabilities   -  -   -  -
```

```
## 9   2016 Alabama Separate Class   All Disabilities 58   58   98   0
## 10  2016 Alabama Separate School… All Disabilities 11   20   19   0
## # … with 16,220 more rows, and 42 more variables: `-_4` <chr>,
`-_5` <chr>,
## #   `-_6` <chr>, `-_7` <chr>, `-_8` <chr>, `-_9` <chr>, `-_10` <chr>,
## #   `-_11` <chr>, `-_12` <chr>, `-_13` <chr>, `-_14` <chr>, `0` <chr>,
## #   `0_1` <chr>, `0_2` <chr>, `0_3` <chr>, `0_4` <chr>, `0_5` <chr>,
## # `0_6` <chr>, `0_7` <chr>, `0_8` <chr>, `1` <chr>, `2` <chr>, `4` <chr>,
## # `14` <chr>, `22` <chr>, `30` <chr>, `4_1` <chr>, `0_9` <chr>, `7` <chr>,
## #   `70` <chr>, `77` <chr>, `0_10` <chr>, `77_1` <chr>, `1_1` <chr>,
## #   `76` <chr>, `0_11` <chr>, `0_12` <chr>, `68` <chr>, `0_13` <chr>,
## #    `0_14` <chr>, `0_15` <chr>, `9` <chr>
```

We used `skip` = 4 when we read in the datasets in the list. That worked for all datasets except the fifth one. In that one, skipping four lines left out the variable name row. To fix it, we'll read the 2016 dataset again using `read_csv()` and the fifth element of `filenames` but this time will use the argument `skip` = 3. We'll assign the newly read dataset to the fifth element of the `all_files` list:

```
all_files[[5]] <-
# Skip the first 3 lines instead of the first 4
read_csv(filenames[[5]], skip = 3)
```

Try printing `all_files` now. You can confirm we fixed the problem by checking that the variable names are correct.

Pick variables

Now that we know all our datasets have the correct variable names, we simplify our datasets by picking the variables we need. This is a good place to think carefully about which variables to pick. This usually requires a fair amount of trial and error, but here is what we found we needed:

- Our analytic questions are about gender, so let's pick the gender variable

- Later, we'll need to filter our dataset by disability category and program location so we'll want SEA Education Environment and SEA Disability Category

- We want to make comparisons by state and reporting year, so we'll also pick State Name and Year

Combining `select()` and `contains()` is a convenient way to pick these variables without writing a lot of code. Knowing that we want variables that contain the acronym "SEA" and variables that contain "male" in their names, we can pass those characters to `contains()`:

```
all_files[[1]] %>%
  select(
    Year,
```

```
      contains("State", ignore.case = FALSE),
      contains("SEA", ignore.case = FALSE),
      contains("male")
  )
## # A tibble: 16,230 x 8
##    Year `State Name` `SEA Education ... `SEA Disability... `Female Age 3 t...
##    <dbl> <chr>        <chr>              <chr>              <chr>
##  1  2012 ALABAMA      Correctional Fa... All Disabilities  -
##  2  2012 ALABAMA      Home               All Disabilities  63
##  3  2012 ALABAMA      Homebound/Hospi... All Disabilities  -
##  4  2012 ALABAMA      Inside regular ... All Disabilities  -
##  5  2012 ALABAMA      Inside regular ... All Disabilities  -
##  6  2012 ALABAMA      Inside regular ... All Disabilities  -
##  7  2012 ALABAMA      Other Location ... All Disabilities  573
##  8  2012 ALABAMA      Other Location ... All Disabilities  81
##  9  2012 ALABAMA      Parentally Plac... All Disabilities  -
## 10  2012 ALABAMA      Residential Fac... All Disabilities  6
## # ... with 16,220 more rows, and 3 more variables: `Male Age 3
to 5` <chr>,
## #   `Female Age 6 to 21` <chr>, `Male Age 6 to 21` <chr>
```

That code chunk verifies that we got the variables we want, so now we will turn the code chunk into a function called `pick_vars()`. We will then use `map()` to apply `pick_vars()` to each dataset of our list, `all_files`, to the function. In this function, we'll use a special version of `select()` called `select_at()`, which conveniently picks variables based on criteria we give it. The argument `vars(Year, contains("State", ignore.case = FALSE), contains("SEA", ignore.case = FALSE), contains("male"))` tells R we want to keep any column whose name has "State" in upper or lower case letters, has "SEA" in the title, and has "male" in the title. This will result in a newly transformed `all_files` list that contains six datasets, all with the desired variables.

```
# build the function
pick_vars <-
  function(df) {
    df %>%
      select_at(vars(
        Year,
        contains("State", ignore.case = FALSE),
        contains("SEA", ignore.case = FALSE),
        contains("male")
      ))
  }
# use the function with `all_files`
all_files <-
  all_files %>%
  map(pick_vars)
```

Combine six datasets into one

Now we'll turn our attention to combining the datasets in our list `all_files` into one. We'll use `bind_rows()`, which combines datasets by adding each one to the bottom of the one before it. The first step is to check and see if our datasets have the same number of variables and the same variable names. When we use `names()` on our list of newly changed datasets, we see that each dataset's variable names are the same:

```
# check variable names
all_files %>%
  map(names)
## [[1]]
## [1] "Year"                     "State Name"
## [3] "SEA Education Environment" "SEA Disability Category"
## [5] "Female Age 3 to 5"        "Male Age 3 to 5"
## [7] "Female Age 6 to 21"       "Male Age 6 to 21"
##
## [[2]]
## [1] "Year"                     "State Name"
## [3] "SEA Education Environment" "SEA Disability Category"
## [5] "Female Age 3 to 5"        "Male Age 3 to 5"
## [7] "Female Age 6 to 21"       "Male Age 6 to 21"
##
## [[3]]
## [1] "Year"                     "State Name"
## [3] "SEA Education Environment" "SEA Disability Category"
## [5] "Female Age 3 to 5"        "Male Age 3 to 5"
## [7] "Female Age 6 to 21"       "Male Age 6 to 21"
##
## [[4]]
## [1] "Year"                     "State Name"
## [3] "SEA Education Environment" "SEA Disability Category"
## [5] "Female Age 3 to 5"        "Male Age 3 to 5"
## [7] "Female Age 6 to 21"       "Male Age 6 to 21"
##
## [[5]]
## [1] "Year"                     "State Name"
## [3] "SEA Education Environment" "SEA Disability Category"
## [5] "Female Age 3 to 5"        "Male Age 3 to 5"
## [7] "Female Age 6 to 21"       "Male Age 6 to 21"
##
## [[6]]
## [1] "Year"                     "State Name"
## [3] "SEA Education Environment" "SEA Disability Category"
## [5] "Female Age 3 to 5"        "Male Age 3 to 5"
## [7] "Female Age 6 to 21"       "Male Age 6 to 21"
```

That means that we can combine all six datasets into one using `bind_rows()`. We'll call this newly combined dataset `child_counts`:

```
child_counts <-
  all_files %>%
  # combine all datasets in `all_files`
  bind_rows()
```

Since we know the following, we can conclude that all our rows combined together correctly:

1. each of our six datasets had eight variables

2. our combined dataset also has eight variables,

But, let's use `str()` to verify:

```
str(child_counts)
## tibble [97,387 × 8] (S3: spec_tbl_df/tbl_df/tbl/data.frame)
## $ Year                   : num [1:97387] 2012 2012 2012 2012 2012 ...
## $ State Name             : chr [1:97387] "ALABAMA" "ALABAMA" "AL-
ABAMA" "ALABAMA" ...
## $ SEA Education Environment: chr [1:97387] "Correctional Fa-
cilities" "Home" "Homebound/Hospital" "Inside regular class 40%
through 79% of day" ...
## $ SEA Disability Category : chr [1:97387] "All Disabilities"
"All Disabilities" "All Disabilities" "All Disabilities" ...
## $ Female Age 3 to 5   : chr [1:97387] "-" "63" "-" "-" ...
## $ Male Age 3 to 5     : chr [1:97387] "-" "174" "-" "-" ...
## $ Female Age 6 to 21  : chr [1:97387] "4" "-" "104" "1590" ...
## $ Male Age 6 to 21    : chr [1:97387] "121" "-" "130" "3076" ...
```

Importing the data from the {dataedu} package

If you would like to load this processed dataset (`child_counts`), then you can run the following code to load it directly from the {dataedu} package:

```
longitudinal_data <- dataedu::child_counts
```

Filter for the desired disabilities and age groups

We want to explore gender-related variables, but our dataset has additional aggregate data for other subgroups. For example, we can use `count()` to explore all the different disability groups in the dataset. Here's the number of times an SEA Disability Category appears in the dataset:

```
child_counts %>%
  # count number of times the category appears in the dataset
  count(`SEA Disability Category`)
```

```
## # A tibble: 16 x 2
##    `SEA Disability Category`                                    n
##    <chr>                                                    <int>
## 1 All Disabilities                                          6954
## 2 Autism                                                    6954
## 3 Deaf-blindness                                            6954
## 4 Developmental delay                                       4636
## 5 Developmental delay (valid only for children ages 3-9 when
defined by …  2318
## 6 Emotional disturbance                                     6954
## 7 Hearing impairment                                        6954
## 8 Intellectual disability                                   6954
## 9 Multiple disabilities                                     6954
## 10 Orthopedic impairment                                    6954
## 11 Other health impairment                                  6954
## 12 Specific learning disability                             6954
## 13 Speech or language impairment                            6954
## 14 Traumatic brain injury                                   6954
## 15 Visual impairment                                        6954
## 16 <NA>                                                       31
```

Since we will be visualizing and modeling gender variables for all students in the dataset, we'll filter out all subgroups except "All Disabilities" and the age totals:

```
child_counts <-
  child_counts %>%
  filter(
    # filter all but the All Disabilities category
    `SEA Disability Category` == "All Disabilities",
    # filter all but the age totals
    `SEA Education Environment` %in% c("Total, Age 3-5", "Total,
      Age 6-21")
  )
```

Rename the variables

In the next section we'll prepare the dataset for visualization and modeling by "tidying" it. When we write code to transform datasets, we'll be typing the column names a lot, so it's useful to change them to ones with more convenient names.

```
child_counts <-
  child_counts %>%
  rename(
    # change these columns to more convenient names
    year = Year,
    state = "State Name",
    age = "SEA Education Environment",
    disability = "SEA Disability Category",
```

```
    f_3_5 = "Female Age 3 to 5",
    m_3_5 = "Male Age 3 to 5",
    f_6_21 = "Female Age 6 to 21",
    m_6_21 = "Male Age 6 to 21"
)
```

Clean state names

You might have noticed that some state names in our dataset are in uppercase letters, and some are in lowercase letters:

```
child_counts %>%
  count(state) %>%
  head()
## # A tibble: 6 x 2
##   state              n
##   <chr>          <int>
## 1 Alabama            8
## 2 ALABAMA            4
## 3 Alaska             8
## 4 ALASKA             4
## 5 American Samoa     8
## 6 AMERICAN SAMOA     4
```

If we leave it like this, R will treat state values like "CALIFORNIA" and "California" as two different states. We can use `mutate` and `tolower` to transform all the state names to lowercase letters.

```
child_counts <-
  child_counts %>%
  mutate(state = tolower(state))
```

Tidy the dataset

Visualizing and modeling our data will be much easier if our dataset is in a "tidy" format. *Tidy Data* (Wickham 2014) defines tidy datasets as possessing the following characteristics:

1. Each variable forms a column

2. Each observation forms a row

3. Each type of observational unit forms a table

A note on the gender variable in this dataset

This dataset uses a binary approach to data collection about gender. Students are described as either male or female. The need for an inclusive approach to documenting gender identity is discussed in a paper by ("Reachable: Data Collection

Methods for Sexual Orientation and Gender Identity" 2016) of The Williams Institute at UCLA.

The gender variables in our dataset are spread across four columns, with each one representing a combination of gender and age range. We can use `pivot_longer()` to bring the gender variable into one column. In this transformation, we create two new columns: a `gender` column and a `total` column. The `total` column will contain the number of students in each row's gender and age category.

```
child_counts <-
  child_counts %>%
    pivot_longer(cols = f_3_5:m_6_21,
                 names_to = "gender",
                 values_to = "total")
```

To make the values of the `gender` column more intuitive, we'll use `case_when()` to transform the values to either "f" or "m":

```
child_counts <-
  child_counts %>%
  mutate(
    gender = case_when(
      gender == "f_3_5" ~ "f",
      gender == "m_3_5" ~ "m",
      gender == "f_6_21" ~ "f",
      gender == "m_6_21" ~ "m",
      TRUE ~ as.character(gender)
    )
  )
```

Convert data types

The values in the `total` column represent the number of students from a specific year, state, gender, and age group. We know from the `chr` under their variable names that R is treating these values like characters instead of numbers. While R does a decent job of treating numbers like numbers when needed, it's much safer to prepare the dataset by changing these character columns to numeric columns. We'll use `mutate()` to change the count columns.

```
child_counts <-
  child_counts %>%
  mutate(total = as.numeric(total))
## Warning: NAs introduced by coercion
child_counts
## # A tibble: 2,928 x 6
##      year state   age           disability        gender total
##     <dbl> <chr>   <chr>         <chr>             <chr>  <dbl>
## 1    2012 alabama Total, Age 3-5  All Disabilities f      2228
## 2    2012 alabama Total, Age 3-5  All Disabilities m      5116
```

```
##  3   2012 alabama Total, Age 3-5   All Disabilities f        NA
##  4   2012 alabama Total, Age 3-5   All Disabilities m        NA
##  5   2012 alabama Total, Age 6-21  All Disabilities f        NA
##  6   2012 alabama Total, Age 6-21  All Disabilities m        NA
##  7   2012 alabama Total, Age 6-21  All Disabilities f     23649
##  8   2012 alabama Total, Age 6-21  All Disabilities m     48712
##  9   2012 alaska  Total, Age 3-5   All Disabilities f       676
## 10   2012 alaska  Total, Age 3-5   All Disabilities m      1440
## # … with 2,918 more rows
```

Converting these count columns from character classes to number classes resulted in two changes. First, the chr under these variable names has now changed to dbl, short for "double-precision". This lets us know that R recognizes these values as numbers with decimal points. Second, the blank values changed to NA. When R sees a character class value like "4", it knows to change it to numeric class 4. But there is no obvious number represented by a value like "" or -, so it changes it to NA:

```
# Convert a character to a number
as.numeric("4")
## [1] 4
# Convert a blank character or a symbol to a number
as.numeric("")
## [1] NA
as.numeric("-")
## Warning: NAs introduced by coercion
## [1] NA
```

Similarly, the variable year needs to be changed from the character format to the date format. Doing so will make sure R treats this variable like a point in time when we plot our dataset. The package {lubridate} has a handy function called ymd that can help us. We just have to use the truncated argument to let R know we don't have a month and date to convert.

```
child_counts <-
  child_counts %>%
  mutate(year = ymd(year, truncated = 2))
```

Explore and address NAs

You'll notice that some rows in the total column contain an NA. When we used pivot_longer() to create a gender column, R created unique rows for every year, state, age, disability, and gender combination. Since the original dataset had both gender and age range stored in a column like Female Age 3 to 5, R made rows where the total value is NA . For example, there is no student count for the age value "Total, Age 3–5" that also has the gender value for female students who were age 6–21. You can see that more clearly by sorting the dataset by year, state, and gender.

In our "Foundational Skills" chapter, we introduced a {dplyr} function called arrange() to sort the rows of a dataset by the values in a column. Let's use arrange() here to sort the dataset by the year, state and gender columns. When you pass arrange() a variable, it will sort by the order of the values in that variable. If you pass it multiple variables, arrange() will sort by the first variable, then by the second, and so on. Let's see what it does on child_counts when we pass it the year, state, and gender variables:

```
child_counts %>%
  arrange(year, state, gender)
## # A tibble: 2,928 x 6
##    year       state   age             disability         gender total
##    <date>     <chr>   <chr>           <chr>              <chr>  <dbl>
##  1 2012-01-01 alabama Total, Age 3-5  All Disabilities f       2228
##  2 2012-01-01 alabama Total, Age 3-5  All Disabilities f         NA
##  3 2012-01-01 alabama Total, Age 6-21 All Disabilities f         NA
##  4 2012-01-01 alabama Total, Age 6-21 All Disabilities f      23649
##  5 2012-01-01 alabama Total, Age 3-5  All Disabilities m       5116
##  6 2012-01-01 alabama Total, Age 3-5  All Disabilities m         NA
##  7 2012-01-01 alabama Total, Age 6-21 All Disabilities m         NA
##  8 2012-01-01 alabama Total, Age 6-21 All Disabilities m      48712
##  9 2012-01-01 alaska  Total, Age 3-5  All Disabilities f        676
## 10 2012-01-01 alaska  Total, Age 3-5  All Disabilities f         NA
## # … with 2,918 more rows
```

We can simplify our dataset by removing the rows with NA s, leaving us with one row for each category:

- females age 3–5

- females age 6–21

- males age 3–5

- males age 6–21

Each of these categories will be associated with a state and reporting year:

```
child_counts <-
  child_counts %>%
  filter(!is.na(total))
```

We can verify we have the categories we want by sorting again:

```
child_counts %>%
  arrange(year, state, gender)
## # A tibble: 1,390 x 6
##    year       state      age             disability         gender total
##    <date>     <chr>      <chr>           <chr>              <chr>  <dbl>
## 1 2012-01-01 alabama     Total, Age 3-5  All Disabilities f       2228
## 2 2012-01-01 alabama     Total, Age 6-21 All Disabilities f      23649
## 3 2012-01-01 alabama     Total, Age 3-5  All Disabilities m       5116
## 4 2012-01-01 alabama     Total, Age 6-21 All Disabilities m      48712
```

```
##  5 2012-01-01 alaska         Total, Age 3-5  All Disabilities f      676
##  6 2012-01-01 alaska         Total, Age 6-21 All Disabilities f     5307
##  7 2012-01-01 alaska         Total, Age 3-5  All Disabilities m     1440
##  8 2012-01-01 alaska         Total, Age 6-21 All Disabilities m    10536
##  9 2012-01-01 american samoa Total, Age 3-5  All Disabilities f       45
## 10 2012-01-01 american samoa Total, Age 6-21 All Disabilities f      208
## # … with 1,380 more rows
```

Analysis

In the last section, we focused on importing our dataset. In this section, we will ask, "How have child counts changed over time?" First, we'll use visualization to explore the number of students in special education over time. In particular, we'll compare the count of male and female students. Next, we'll use what we learn from our visualizations to quantify any differences that we see.

Visualize the dataset

Showing this many states in a plot can be overwhelming, so to start we'll make a subset of the dataset. We can use a function in the {dplyr} package called `top_n()` to help us learn which states have the highest mean count of students with disabilities:

```
child_counts %>%
  group_by(state) %>%
  summarize(mean_count = mean(total)) %>%
  # which six states have the highest mean count of students with
disabilities
  top_n(6, mean_count)
## # A tibble: 6 x 2
##    state                                                mean_count
##    <chr>                                                     <dbl>
## 1 california                                             180879.
## 2 florida                                                 92447.
## 3 new york                                               121751.
## 4 pennsylvania                                            76080.
## 5 texas                                                  115593.
## 6 us, outlying areas, and freely associated states      1671931.
```

These six states have the highest mean count of students in special education over the six years we are examining. For reasons we will see in a later visualization, we are going to exclude outlying areas and freely associated states. That leaves us with five states: California, Florida, New York, Pennsylvania, and Texas. We can remove all other states but these by using `filter()`. We'll call this new dataset `high_count`:

```
high_count <-
  child_counts %>%
  filter(state %in% c("california", "florida", "new york", "pennsyl-
vania", "texas"))
```

Now we can use `high_count` to do some initial exploration. Our analysis is about comparing counts of male and female students in special education, but visualization is also a great way to explore related curiosities. You may surprise yourself with what you find when visualizing your datasets. You might come up with more interesting hypotheses, find that your initial hypothesis requires more data transformation, or find interesting subsets of the data—we saw a little of that in the surprisingly high `mean_count` of freely associated states in the `state` column. Let your curiosity and intuition drive this part of the analysis. It's one of the activities that makes data analysis a creative process.

In that spirit, we'll start by visualizing specific genders and age groups. Feel free to try these, but also try the other student groups for practice and more exploration.

Start by copying and running this code in your console to see what it does:

```
high_count %>%
  filter(gender == "f", age == "Total, Age 6-21") %>%
  ggplot(aes(x = year, y = total, color = state)) +
  geom_freqpoly(stat = "identity", size = 1) +
  labs(title = "Count of Female Students in Special Education Over
       Time", subtitle = "Ages 6-21") +
  scale_color_dataedu() +
  theme_dataedu()
```

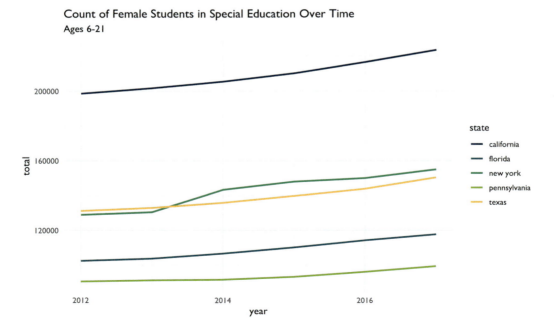

Figure 10.1: Count of Female Students in Special Education over Time

That gives us a plot that has the years on the x-axis and a count of female students on the y-axis. Each line takes a different color based on the state it represents.

Let's look at that closer: we used `filter()` to subset our dataset for students who are female and ages 6 to 21. We used `aes` to connect visual elements of our plot to our data. We connected the x-axis to `year`, the y-axis to `total`, and the color of the line to `state`.

It's worth calling out one more thing since it's a technique we'll be using as we explore further. Note here that, instead of storing our new dataset in a new variable, we filter the dataset then use the pipe operator `%>%` to feed it to {ggplot2}. Since we're exploring freely, we don't need to create a lot of new variables we probably won't need later.

We can also try the same plot, but subsetting for male students instead. We can use the same code we used for the last plot, but filter for the value "m" in the gender field:

```
high_count %>%
  filter(gender == "m", age == "Total, Age 6-21") %>%
  ggplot(aes(x = year, y = total, color = state)) +
  geom_freqpoly(stat = "identity", size = 1) +
  labs(title = "Count of Male Students in Special Education Over
       Time", subtitle = "Ages 6-21") +
  scale_color_dataedu() +
  theme_dataedu()
```

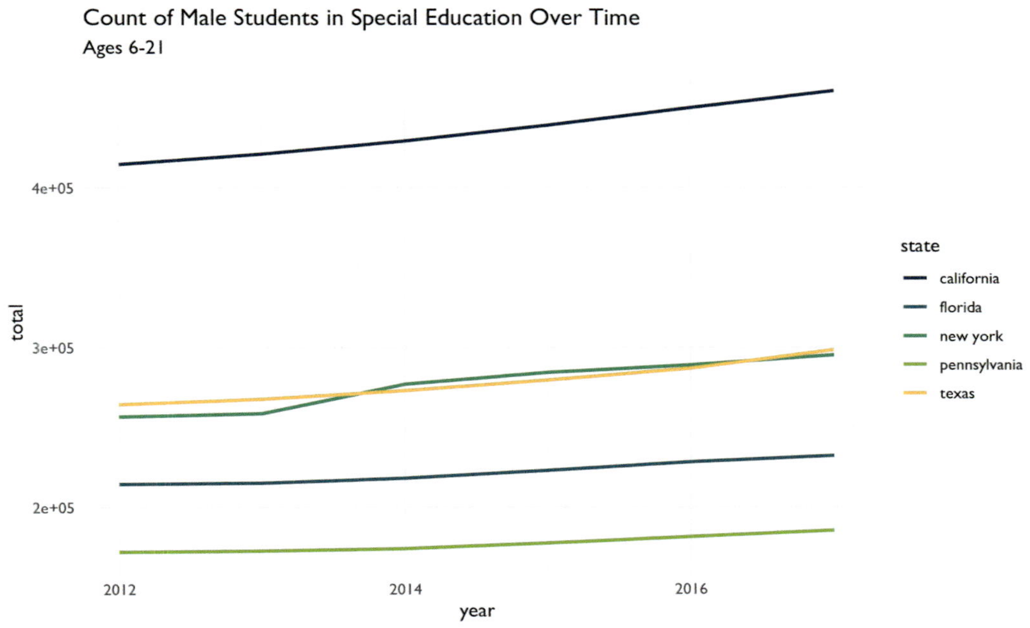

Figure 10.2: Count of Male Students in Special Education over Time

We've looked at each gender separately. What do these lines look like if we visualized the total amount of students each year per state? To do that, we'll need to add both gender values together and both age group values together. We'll do this using a very common combination of functions: `group_by()` and `summarize()`.

```
high_count %>%
  group_by(year, state) %>%
  summarize(n = sum(total)) %>%
  ggplot(aes(x = year, y = n, color = state)) +
  geom_freqpoly(stat = "identity", size = 1) +
  labs(title = "Total Count of Students in Special Education Over
        Time", subtitle = "Ages 3-21") +
  scale_color_dataedu() +
  theme_dataedu()
```

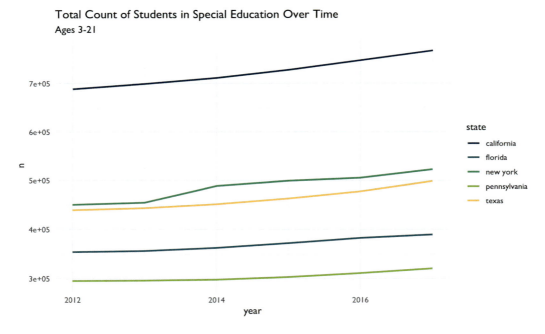

Figure 10.3: Total Count of Students in Special Education over Time

So far we've looked at a few ways to count students over time. In each plot, we see that while counts have grown overall for all states, each state has different sized populations. Let's see if we can summarize that difference by looking at the median student count for each state over the years:

```
high_count %>%
    group_by(year, state) %>%
    summarize(n = sum(total)) %>%
    ggplot(aes(x = state, y = n)) +
    geom_boxplot(fill = dataedu_colors("yellow")) +
    labs(title = "Median Students with Disabilities Count",
         subtitle = "All ages and genders, 2012-2017") +
    theme_dataedu()
```

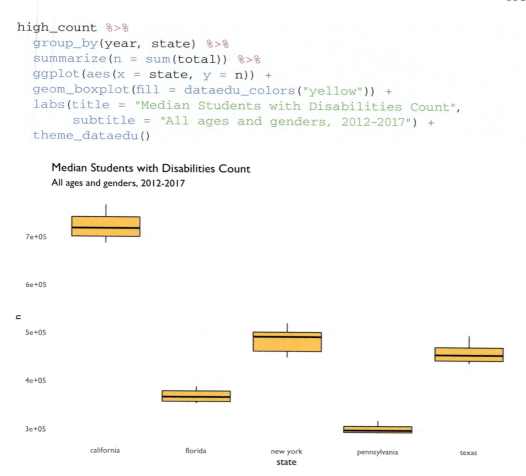

Figure 10.4: Median Students with Disabilities Count

The boxplots show us what we might have expected from our `freqpoly` plots before it. The highest median student count over time is California and the lowest is Pennsylvania.

What have we learned about our data so far? The five states in the US with the highest total student counts (not including outlying areas and freely associated states) do not have similar counts to each other. The student counts for each state also appear to have grown over time.

But how can we start comparing the male student count to the female student count? One way is to use a "ratio", the number of times the first number contains the second. For example, if Variable A is equal to 14, and Variable B is equal to 7, the ratio between Variable A and Variable B is 2.00, indicating that the first number contains twice the number of the second.

We can use the count of male students in each state and divide it by the count of each female student. The result is the number of times male students are in special education more or less than the female students in the same state and year. Our coding strategy will be to:

- Use `pivot_wider()` to create separate columns for male and female students.

- Use `mutate()` to create a new variable called `ratio`. The values in this column will be the result of dividing the count of male students by the count of female students

Note here that we can also accomplish this comparison by dividing the number of female students by the number of male students. In this case, the result would be the number of times female students are in special education more or less than male students.

```
high_count %>%
  group_by(year, state, gender) %>%
  summarize(total = sum(total)) %>%
  # Create new columns for male and female student counts
  pivot_wider(names_from = gender,
              values_from = total) %>%
  # Create a new ratio column
  mutate(ratio = m / f) %>%
  ggplot(aes(x = year, y = ratio, color = state)) +
  geom_freqpoly(stat = "identity", size = 1) +
  scale_y_continuous(limits = c(1.5, 2.5)) +
  labs(title = "Male Student to Female Student Ratio Over Time",
       subtitle = "Ages 6-21") +
  scale_color_dataedu() +
  theme_dataedu()
```

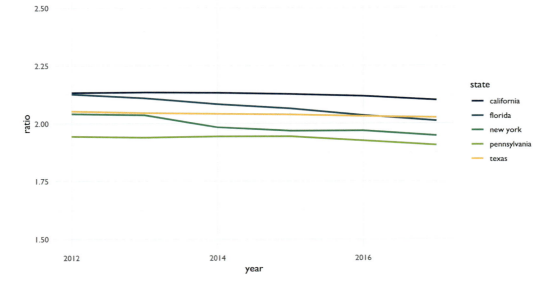

Figure 10.5: Male Student to Female Student Ratio over Time

By visually inspecting, we can hypothesize that there was no significant change in the male to female ratio between the years 2012 and 2017. But very often we want to understand the underlying properties of our education dataset. We can do this by quantifying the relationship between two variables. In the next section, we'll explore ways to quantify the relationship between male student counts and female student counts.

Model the dataset

When you visualize your datasets, you are exploring possible relationships between variables. But sometimes visualizations can be misleading because of the way we perceive graphics. In his book *Data Visualization: A Practical Introduction*, Healy (2019) teaches us that

> Visualizations encode numbers in lines, shapes, and colors. That means that our interpretation of these encodings is partly conditional on how we perceive geometric shapes and relationships generally.

What are some ways we can combat these errors of perception and at the same time draw substantive conclusions about our education dataset? When you spot a possible relationship between variables, the relationship between female and male counts for example, you'll want to quantify it by fitting a statistical model. Practically speaking, this means you are selecting a distribution that represents your dataset reasonably well. This distribution will help you quantify and predict relationships between variables. This is an important step in the analytic process because it acts as a check on what you saw in your exploratory visualizations.

In this example, we'll follow our intuition about the relationship between male and female student counts in our special education dataset. In particular, we'll test the hypothesis that this ratio has decreased over the years. Fitting a linear regression model that estimates the year as a predictor of the male to female ratio will help us do just that.

In the context of modeling the dataset, we note that there are techniques available (other than a linear regression model) for longitudinal analyses that are helpful for accounting for the way that individual data points over time can be modeled as grouped within units (such as individual students). Such approaches, like those involving structural equation models (Grimm, Ram, and Estabrook 2016) and multi-level models (West, Welch, and Galecki 2014), are especially helpful for analyzing patterns of change over time—and what predicts those patterns. Both of the references cited above include R code for carrying out such analyses.

Do we have enough information for our model?

At the start of this section, we chose to exclude outlying areas and freely associated states. This visualization suggests that there are some states that have a child count so high it leaves a gap in the x-axis values. This can be problematic when we try to interpret our model later. Here's a plot of female students compared to male students. Note that the relationship appears linear, but there is a large gap in the distribution of female student counts somewhere between the values of 250,000 and 1,750,000:

```
child_counts %>%
  filter(age == "Total, Age 6-21") %>%
  pivot_wider(names_from = gender,
              values_from = total) %>%
  ggplot(aes(x = f, y = m)) +
  geom_point(size = 3, alpha = .5, color = dataedu_colors("green")) +
  geom_smooth() +
  labs(
     title = "Comparison of Female Students to Male Students in
Special Education",
     subtitle = "Counts of students in each state, ages 6-21",
     x = "Female students",
     y = "Male students",
     caption = "Data: US Dept of Education"
  ) +
  theme_dataedu()
```

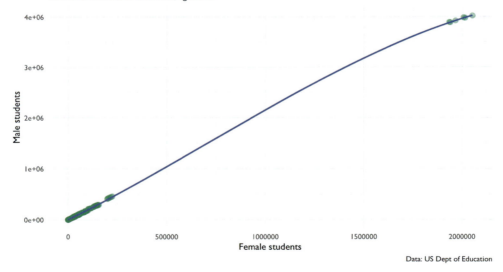

Figure 10.6: Comparison of Female Students to
Male Students in Special Education

If you think of each potential point on the linear regression line as a ratio of male to female students, you'll notice that we don't know a whole lot about what happens in states where there are between 250,000 and 1,750,000 female students in any given year.

To learn more about what's happening in our dataset, we can filter it for only states that have more than 500,000 female students in any year:

```
child_counts %>%
  filter(age == "Total, Age 6-21") %>%
  pivot_wider(names_from = gender,
              values_from = total) %>%
  filter(f > 500000) %>%
  select(year, state, age, f, m)
## # A tibble: 6 x 5
##   year       state                                age       f    m
##   <date>     <chr>                                <chr>   <dbl> <dbl>
## 1 2012-01-01 us, outlying areas, and freely associ… Total, Age
6… 1933619 3.89e6
## 2 2013-01-01 us, outlying areas, and freely associ… Total, Age
6… 1937726 3.88e6
## 3 2014-01-01 us, outlying areas, and freely associ… Total, Age
6… 1965204 3.92e6
## 4 2015-01-01 us, outlying areas, and freely associ… Total, Age
6… 2007174 3.98e6
## 5 2016-01-01 us, outlying areas, and freely associ… Total, Age
6… 2014120 3.97e6
## 6 2017-01-01 us, outlying areas, and freely associ… Total, Age
6… 2051438 4.02e6
```

This is where we discover that each of the data points in the upper right hand corner of the plot are from the state value "us, us, outlying areas, and freely associated states". If we remove these outliers, we have a distribution of female students that looks more complete.

```
child_counts %>%
  filter(age == "Total, Age 6-21") %>%
  pivot_wider(names_from = gender,
              values_from = total) %>%
  # Filter for female student counts less than 500,000
  filter(f <= 500000) %>%
  ggplot(aes(x = f, y = m)) +
  geom_point(size = 3, alpha = .5, color = dataedu_colors("green")) +
  labs(
    title = "Comparison of Female Students to Male Students with
Disabilities",
    subtitle = "Counts of students in each state, ages 6-21.\nDoes
not include outlying areas and freely associated states",
    x = "Female students",
    y = "Male students",
    caption = "Data: US Dept of Education"
  ) +
  theme_dataedu()
```

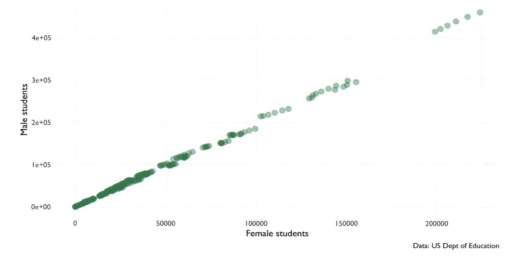

Figure 10.7: Comparison of Female Students to Male Students with Disabilities

This should allow us to fit a better model for the relationship between male and female student counts, albeit only the ones where the count of female students takes a value between 0 and 500,000.

Male to female ratio over time

Earlier, we asked the question, "Do we have enough data points for the count of female students to learn about the ratio of female to male students?" Similarly, we should ask ourselves, "Do we have enough data points across our year variable to learn about how this ratio has changed over time?"

To answer that, let's start by making a new dataset that includes any rows where the f variable has a value that is less than or equal to 500,000. We'll convert the year variable to a factor data type—we'll see how this helps in a bit. We'll also add a column called ratio that contains the male to female count ratio.

```
model_data <- child_counts %>%
  filter(age == "Total, Age 6-21") %>%
  mutate(year = as.factor(year(year))) %>%
  pivot_wider(names_from = gender,
              values_from = total) %>%
  # Exclude outliers
  filter(f <= 500000) %>%
  # Compute male student to female student ratio
  mutate(ratio = m / f) %>%
  select(-c(age, disability))
```
We can see how much data we have per year by using count():

```
model_data %>%
  count(year)
## # A tibble: 6 x 2
##   year        n
##   <fct> <int>
## 1 2012       59
## 2 2013       56
## 3 2014       56
## 4 2015       58
## 5 2016       57
## 6 2017       55
```

Let's visualize the ratio values across all years as an additional check. Note the use of `geom_jitter()` to spread the points horizontally so we can estimate the quantities better:

```
ggplot(data = model_data, aes(x = year, y = ratio)) +
  geom_jitter(alpha = .5, color = dataedu_colors("green")) +
  labs(title = "Male to Female Ratio Across Years (Jittered)") +
  theme_dataedu()
```

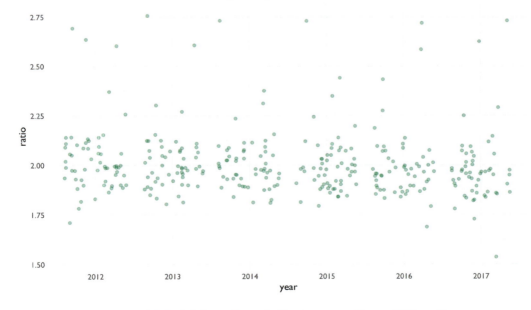

Figure 10.8: Male to Female Ratio across Years (Jittered)

Each year seems to have data points that can be considered when we fit the model. This means that there are enough data points to help us learn how the year variable predicts the ratio variable.

We fit the linear regression model by passing the argument ratio ~ year to
the function lm(). In R, the ~ usually indicates a formula. In this case, the formula
is the variable year as a predictor of the variable ratio. The final argument we
pass to lm is data = model_data, which tells R to look for the variables ratio
and year in the dataset model_data. The results of the model are called a "model
object". We'll store the model object in ratio_year:

```
ratio_year <-
   lm(ratio ~ year, data = model_data)
```

Each model object is filled with all sorts of model information. We can look at this
information using the function summary():

```
summary(ratio_year)
##
## Call:
## lm(formula = ratio ~ year, data = model_data)
##
## Residuals:
##       Min        1Q    Median        3Q       Max
## -0.44025  -0.10138  -0.02810   0.05343   0.75737
##
## Coefficients:
##               Estimate Std. Error t value Pr(>|t|)
## (Intercept)    2.03356    0.02200  92.418   <2e-16 ***
## year2013      -0.01205    0.03153  -0.382   0.7027
## year2014      -0.02372    0.03153  -0.752   0.4524
## year2015      -0.03104    0.03125  -0.993   0.3213
## year2016      -0.03964    0.03139  -1.263   0.2075
## year2017      -0.05760    0.03168  -1.818   0.0699 .
## ---
## Signif. codes:  0 '***' 0.001 '**' 0.01 '*' 0.05 '.' 0.1 ' ' 1
##
## Residual standard error: 0.169 on 335 degrees of freedom
## Multiple R-squared:  0.01215,    Adjusted R-squared:  -0.002594
## F-statistic: 0.8241 on 5 and 335 DF,  p-value: 0.5332
```

Here's how we can interpret the Estimate column: The estimate of the (Intercept) is 2.03, which is the estimated value of the ratio variable when the year
variable is "2012". Note that the value year2012 isn't present in the in the list of
rownames. That's because the (Intercept) row represents year2012. In linear
regression models that use factor variables as predictors, the first level of the factor
is the intercept. Sometimes this level is called a "dummy variable". The remaining
rows of the model output show how much each year differs from the intercept,
2012. For example, year2013 has an estimate of −0.012, which suggests that on
average the value of ratio is 0.012 less than 2.03. On average, the ratio of year2014
is 0.02 less than 2.03. The t value column tells us the size of difference between

the estimated value of the ratio for each year and the estimated value of the ratio of the intercept. Generally speaking, the larger the t value, the larger the chance that any difference between the coefficient of a factor level and the intercept are significant.

Though the relationship between `year` as a predictor of `ratio` is not linear (recall our previous plot), the linear regression model still gives us useful information. We fit a linear regression model to a factor variable, like `year`, as a predictor of a continuous variable, like `ratio`. In doing so, we got the average `ratio` at every value of `year`. We can verify this by taking the mean `ratio` of ever `year`:

```
model_data %>%
  group_by(year) %>%
  summarize(mean_ratio = mean(ratio))
## # A tibble: 6 x 2
##    year  mean_ratio
##    <fct>      <dbl>
## 1 2012        2.03
## 2 2013        2.02
## 3 2014        2.01
## 4 2015        2.00
## 5 2016        1.99
## 6 2017        1.98
```

This verifies that our intercept, the value of `ratio` during the year 2012, is 2.03 and the value of `ratio` for 2013 is 0.012 less than that of 2012 on average. Fitting the model gives us more details about these mean ratio scores—namely the coefficient, t-value, and p-value. These values help us apply judgement when deciding if differences in `ratio` values suggest an underlying difference between years or simply differences you can expect from randomness. In this case, the absence of "*" in all rows except the Intercept row suggest that any differences occurring between years are within the range you'd expect by chance.

If we use `summary()` on our `model_data` dataset, we can verify the intercept again:

```
model_data %>%
  filter(year == "2012") %>%
  summary()
##     year           state                 f                m              ratio
## 2012:59    Length:59          Min.  : 208    Min.   :  443    Min.   :1.710
## 2013: 0    Class :character   1st Qu.: 5606  1st Qu.: 11467   1st Qu.:1.927
## 2014: 0    Mode :character    Median : 22350 Median : 44110   Median :1.994
## 2015: 0                       Mean   : 32773 Mean   : 65934   Mean   :2.034
## 2016: 0                       3rd Qu.: 38552 3rd Qu.: 77950   3rd Qu.:2.093
## 2017: 0                       Max.   : 198595 Max.  :414466   Max.   :2.692
```

The mean value of the `ratio` column when the `year` column is 2012 is 2.03, just like in the model output's intercept row.

Lastly, we may want to communicate to a larger audience that there were roughly twice the number of male students in this dataset than there were female students, and this did not change significantly between the years 2012 and 2017. When you are not communicating to an audience of other data scientists, it's helpful to illustrate your point without the technical details of the model output. Think of yourself as an interpreter: since you can speak the language of model outputs and the language of data visualization, your challenge is to take what you learned from the model output and tell that story in a way that is meaningful to your non-data scientist audience.

There are many ways to do this, but we'll choose boxplots to show our audience that there was roughly twice as many male students in special education than female students between 2012 and 2017. For our purposes, let's verify this by looking at the median male to female ratio for each year:

```
model_data %>%
  group_by(year) %>%
  summarize(median_ratio = median(ratio))
## # A tibble: 6 x 2
##    year   median_ratio
##    <fct>          <dbl>
## 1 2012            1.99
## 2 2013            1.99
## 3 2014            1.98
## 4 2015            1.98
## 5 2016            1.97
## 6 2017            1.96
```

Now let's visualize this using our boxplots:

```
model_data %>%
  pivot_longer(cols = c(f, m),
               names_to = "gender",
               values_to = "students") %>%
  ggplot(aes(x = year, y = students, color = gender)) +
  geom_boxplot() +
  scale_y_continuous(labels = scales::comma) +
  labs(
     title = "Median Male and Female Student Counts in Special
Education",
     subtitle = "Ages 6-21. Does not include outlying areas and
freely associated states",
     x = "",
     y = "",
     caption = "Data: US Dept of Education"
  ) +
  scale_color_dataedu() +
  theme_dataedu()
```

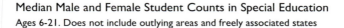

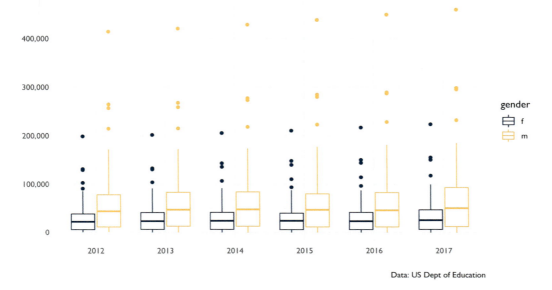

Figure 10.9: Median Male and Female Student Counts in Special Education

Once we learned from our model that male to female ratios did not change in any meaningful way from 2012 to 2017 and that the median ratio across states was about two male students to every female student, we can present these two ideas using this plot. When discussing the plot, it helps to have your model output in your notes so you can reference specific coefficient estimates when needed.

Results

We learned that each state has a different count of students with disabilities—so different that we need to use statistics like ratios or visualizations to compare across states. Even when we narrow our focus to the five states with the highest counts of students with disabilities, we see that there are differences in these counts.

When we look at these five states over time, we see that, despite the differences in total count each year, all five increased their student counts. We also learned that though the male to female ratios for students with disabilities appears to have gone down slightly over time, our model suggests that these decreases do not represent a big difference.

The comparison of student counts across each state is tricky because there is a lot of variation in total enrollment across all 50 states. While we explored student counts across each state and verified that there is variation in the counts, a good next step would be to combine this data with total enrollment data. This would allow us to compare counts of students with disabilities as a percentage of total enrollment. Comparing proportions like this is a common way to compare subgroups of a population across states when each state's population varies in size.

Conclusion

Education data science is about using data science tools to learn about and improve the lives of our students. So why choose a publicly available aggregate dataset instead of a student-level dataset? We chose to use an aggregate dataset because it reflects an analysis that a data scientist in education would typically do.

Using student-level data requires that the data scientist be either an employee of the school agency or someone who works under a memorandum of understanding (MOU) that allows her to access this data. Without either of these conditions, the education data scientist learns about the student experience by working on publicly available datasets, almost all of which are aggregated student-level datasets.

Student-level data for analysis of local populations: aggregate data for base rate and context

Longitudinal analysis is typically done with student-level data because educators are interested in what happens to students over time. So if you cannot access student-level data, how do we use aggregate data to offer value to the analytic conversation?

Aggregate data is valuable because it allows us to learn from populations that are larger or different from the local student-level population. Think of it as an opportunity to learn from totaled up student data from other states or the whole country.

In the book *Thinking Fast and Slow*, Kahneman (2011) discusses the importance of learning from larger populations, a context he refers to as the "base rate". The base rate fallacy is the tendency to only focus on conclusions we can draw from immediately available information. It's the difference between computing how often a student at one school is identified for special education services (student-level data) and how often students are identified for special educations services nationally (base rate data). We can use aggregate data to combat the base rate fallacy by putting what we learn from local student data in the context of surrounding populations.

For example, consider an analysis of student-level data in a school district over time. Student-level data allows us to ask questions about our local population. One such question is, "Are the rates of special education identification for male students different from other gender identities *in our district*?" This style of question looks *inward* at your own educational system.

Taking a cue from Kahneman, we should also ask what this pattern looks like in other states or in the country. Aggregate data allows us to ask questions about a larger population. One such question is, "Are the rates of special education identification for male students different from other gender identities *in the United States*?" This style of question looks for answers *outside* your own educational system. The combination of the two lines of inquiry is a powerful way to generate new knowledge about the student experience.

So education data scientists should not despair in situations where they cannot access student-level data. Aggregate data is a powerful way to learn from state-level or national-level data when a data sharing agreement for student-level data is not possible. In situations where student-level data *is* available, including aggregate data is an excellent way to combat the base rate fallacy.

Chapter 11

Walkthrough 5

Text analysis with social media data

Topics emphasized

- Tidying data

- Transforming data

- Visualizing data

Functions introduced

- `sample_n()`
- `set.seed()`
- `tidytext::unnest_tokens()`
- `nrc::get_sentiments()`
- `tidytext::inner_join()`

Functions introduced in the appendix

- `readr::read_delim()`
- `rtweet::lookup_statuses()`

Vocabulary

- RDS files

- Text analysis

- Stop words

- Tokenize

Chapter overview

The ability to work with many kinds of datasets is one of the great features of doing data science with programming. So far we've analyzed data in `.csv` files, but that's not the only way data is stored. If we can learn some basic techniques for analyzing text, we increase the number of places we can find information to learn about the student experience.

In this chapter, we focus on analyzing textual data from Twitter. We focus on this particular data source because we think it is relevant to a number of educational topics and questions, including how newcomers learn to visualize data. In addition, Twitter data is complex and includes not only information about who posted a tweet (and when—and a great deal of additional information (see Kearney 2020)) but also the text of the tweet. This makes it especially well-suited for exploring the uses of text analysis, which is broadly part of a group of techniques involving the analysis of text as data—Natural Language Processing (often abbreviated NLP) (Hirschberg and Manning 2015).

We note that while we focused on #tidytuesday because we think it exemplifies the new kinds of learning-related data that a data science toolkit allows an analyst to try to understand, we also chose this because it is straightforward to access data from Twitter and—due to the presence of an interactive Shiny application—it is particularly easy to access data on #tidytuesday. While this chapter dives deeply into the analysis of the *text* of tweets, Appendix B elaborates on a number of techniques for accessing data from Twitter—including data from #tidytuesday—and Chapter 12 explores the nature of the interactions that take place between individuals through #tidytuesday.

Background

When we think about data science in education, our minds tend to go to data stored in spreadsheets. But what can we learn about the student experience from during which data? Take a moment to mentally review all the moments in your work day during which you generated or consumed text data. In education, we're surrounded by it. We do our lessons in word-processing documents, our students submit assignments online, and the school community expresses themselves on public social media platforms. The text we generate can be an authentic reflection of reality in schools, so how might we learn from it?

Even the most basic text analysis techniques will expand your data science toolkit. For example, you can use text analysis to count the number of key words that appear in open-ended survey responses. You can analyze word patterns in student responses or message board posts.

Analyzing a collection of text is different from analyzing large numerical datasets because words don't have agreed upon values the way numbers do. The number 2 will always be more than 1 and less than 3. The word "fantastic", on the other hand, has multiple ambiguous levels of degree depending on interpretation and context.

Using text analysis can help to broadly estimate what is happening in the text. When paired with observations, interviews, and close review of the text, this approach can help education staff learn from text data. In this chapter, we'll learn how to count the frequency of words in a dataset and associate those words with common feelings like positivity or joy.

We'll show these techniques using a dataset of tweets. We encourage you to complete the walkthrough, then reflect on how the skills learned can be applied to other texts, like word-processing documents or websites.

Data source

It's useful to learn text analysis techniques from datasets that are available for download. Take a moment to do an online search for "download tweet dataset" and note the abundance of Twitter datasets available. Since there's so many, it's useful to narrow the tweets to only those that help you answer your analytic questions. Hashtags are text within a tweet that act as a way to categorize content. Here's an example:

> RT @CKVanPay: I'm trying to recreate some Stata code in R, anyone have a good resource for what certain functions in Stata are doing? #RStats #Stata

Twitter recognizes any words that start with a "#" as a hashtag. The hashtags "#RStats" and "#Stata" make this tweets conveniently searchable. If Twitter uses search for "#RStats", Twitter returns all the Tweets containing that hashtag.

In this example, we'll be analyzing a dataset of tweets that have the hashtag #tidytuesday (https://twitter.com/hashtag/tidytuesday). #tidytuesday is a community sparked by the work of one of the *Data Science in Education Using R* co-authors, Jesse Mostipak, who created the (related) #r4ds community from which #tidytuesday was created. #tidytuesday is a weekly data visualization challenge. A great place to see examples from past #tidytuesday challenges is an interactive Shiny application (https://github.com/nsgrantham/tidytuesdayrocks).

The #tidytuesday hashtag (search Twitter for the hashtag, or see the results here: http://bit.ly/tidytuesday-search) returns tweets about the weekly TidyTuesday practice, where folks learning R create and tweet data visualizations they made while learning to use tidyverse R packages.

Methods

In this walkthrough, we'll be learning how to count words in a text dataset. We'll also use a technique called sentiment analysis to count and visualize the appearance of words that have a positive association. Lastly, we'll learn how to get more context by selecting random rows of tweets for closer reading.

Load packages

For this analysis, we'll be using the {tidyverse}, {here}, and {dataedu} packages. We will also use the {tidytext} package for working with textual data (Robinson and Silge 2020). As it has not been used previously in the book, you may need to install the {tidytext} package (and—if you haven't just yet—the other packages) first. For instructions on and an overview about installing packages, see the "Packages" section of the "Foundational Skills" chapter.

Let's load our packages before moving on to importing the data:

```
library(tidyverse)
library(here)
library(dataedu)
library(tidytext)
```

Import data

Let's start by getting the data into our environment so we can start analyzing it. In Chapter 12 and in Appendix B, we describe how we accessed this data through Twitter's Application Programming Interface, or API (and how you can access data from Twitter on other hashtags or terms, too).

We've included the raw dataset of TidyTuesday tweets in the {dataedu} package. You can see the dataset by typing `tt_tweets`. Let's start by assigning the name `raw_tweets` to this dataset:

```
raw_tweets <- dataedu::tt_tweets
```

View data

Let's return to our `raw_tweets` dataset. Run `glimpse(raw_tweets)` and notice the number of variables in this dataset. It's good practice to use functions like `glimpse()` or `str()` to look at the data type of each variable. For this walkthrough, we won't need all 90 variables so let's clean the dataset and keep only the ones we want.

Process data

In this section we'll select the columns we need for our analysis and we'll transform the dataset so each row represents a word. After that, our dataset will be ready for exploring.

First, let's use `select()` to pick the two columns we'll need: `status_id` and `text`. `status_id` will help us associate interesting words with a particular tweet and `text` will give us the text from that tweet. We'll also change `status_id` to the character data type since it's meant to label tweets and doesn't actually represent a numerical value.

```
tweets <-
  raw_tweets %>%
  #filter for English tweets
  filter(lang == "en") %>%
  select(status_id, text) %>%
  # Convert the ID field to the character data type
  mutate(status_id = as.character(status_id))
```

Now the dataset has a column to identify each tweet and a column that shows the text that users tweeted. But each row has the entire tweet in the `text` variable, which makes it hard to analyze. If we kept our dataset like this, we'd need to use functions on each row to do something like count the number of times the word "good" appears. We can count words more efficiently if each row represented a single word. Splitting sentences in a row into single words in a row is called "tokenizing". In their book *Text Mining With R*, Silge and Robinson (2017) describe tokens this way:

> A token is a meaningful unit of text, such as a word, that we are interested in using for analysis, and tokenization is the process of splitting text into tokens. This one-token-per-row structure is in contrast to the ways text is often stored in current analyses, perhaps as strings or in a document-term matrix.

Let's use `unnest_tokens()` from the {tidytext} package to take our dataset of tweets and transform it into a dataset of words.

```
tokens <-
  tweets %>%
  unnest_tokens(output = word, input = text)
tokens
## # A tibble: 131,233 x 2
##      status_id            word
##      <chr>                <chr>
##  1 1163154266065735680 first
##  2 1163154266065735680 tidytuesday
##  3 1163154266065735680 submission
##  4 1163154266065735680 roman
##  5 1163154266065735680 emperors
##  6 1163154266065735680 and
##  7 1163154266065735680 their
##  8 1163154266065735680 rise
##  9 1163154266065735680 to
## 10 1163154266065735680 power
## # … with 131,223 more rows
```

We use `output = word` to tell `unnest_tokens()` that we want our column of tokens to be called `word`. We use `input = text` to tell `unnest_tokens()` to tokenize the tweets in the `text` column of our `tweets` dataset. The result is a new dataset where each row has a single word in the `word` column and a unique ID in the `status_id` column that tells us which tweet the word appears in.

Notice that our `tokens` dataset has many more rows than our `tweets` dataset. This tells us a lot about how `unnest_tokens()` works. In the `tweets` dataset, each row has an entire tweet and its unique ID. Since that unique ID is assigned to the entire tweet, each unique ID only appears once in the dataset. When we used `unnest_tokens()`, we put each word on its own row and broke each tweet into many words. This created additional rows in the dataset. And since each word in a single tweet shares the same ID for that tweet, an ID now appears multiple times in our new dataset.

We're almost ready to start analyzing the dataset! There's one more step we'll take—removing common words that don't help us learn what people are tweeting about. Words like "the" or "a" are in a category of words called "stop words". Stop words serve a function in verbal communication, but don't tell us much on their own. As a result, they clutter our dataset of useful words and make it harder to manage the volume of words we want to analyze. The {tidytext} package includes a dataset called `stop_words` that we'll use to remove rows containing stop words. We'll use `anti_join()` on our `tokens` dataset and the `stop_words` dataset to keep only rows that have words *not* appearing in the `stop_words` dataset.

```
data(stop_words)
tokens <-
  tokens %>%
  anti_join(stop_words, by = "word")
```

Why does this work? Let's look closer. `inner_join()` matches the observations in one dataset to another by a specified common variable. Any rows that don't have a match get dropped from the resulting dataset. `anti_join()` does the same thing as `inner_join()` except it drops matching rows and keeps the rows that *don't* match. This is convenient for our analysis because we want to remove rows from `tokens` that contain words in the `stop_words` dataset. When we call `anti_join()`, we're left with rows that *don't* match words in the `stop_words` dataset. These remaining words are the ones we'll be analyzing.

One final note before we start counting words: Remember when we first tokenized our dataset and we passed `unnest_tokens()` the argument `output = word`? We conveniently chose `word` as our column name because it matches the column name `word` in the `stop_words` dataset. This makes our call to `anti_join()` simpler because `anti_join()` knows to look for the column named `word` in each dataset.

Analysis: counting words

Now it's time to start exploring our newly cleaned dataset of tweets. Computing the frequency of each word and seeing which words showed up the most often is a good start. We can pipe `tokens` to the `count` function to do this:

```
tokens %>%
    count(word, sort = TRUE)
## # A tibble: 15,335 x 2
##    word                n
##    <chr>           <int>
##  1 t.co             5432
##  2 https            5406
##  3 tidytuesday      4316
##  4 rstats           1748
##  5 data             1105
##  6 code              988
##  7 week              868
```

```
##  8 r4ds               675
##  9 dataviz            607
## 10 time               494
## # … with 15,325 more rows
```

We pass count() the argument sort = TRUE to sort the n variable from the highest value to the lowest value. This makes it easy to see the most frequently occurring words at the top. Not surprisingly, "tidytuesday" was the third most frequent word in this dataset.

We may want to explore further by showing the frequency of words as a percent of the whole dataset. Calculating percentages like this is useful in a lot of education scenarios because it helps us make comparisons across different sized groups. For example, you may want to calculate what percentage of students in each classroom receive special education services.

In our tokens dataset, we'll be calculating the count of words as a percentage of all tweets. We can do that by using mutate() to add a column called percent. percent will divide n by sum(n), which is the total number of words. Finally, will multiply the result by 100.

```
tokens %>%
  count(word, sort = TRUE) %>%
  # n as a percent of total words
  mutate(percent = n / sum(n) * 100)
## # A tibble: 15,335 x 3
##     word              n percent
##     <chr>         <int>   <dbl>
##  1 t.co           5432    7.39
##  2 https          5406    7.36
##  3 tidytuesday    4316    5.87
##  4 rstats         1748    2.38
##  5 data           1105    1.50
##  6 code            988    1.34
##  7 week            868    1.18
##  8 r4ds            675    0.919
##  9 dataviz         607    0.826
## 10 time            494    0.672
## # … with 15,325 more rows
```

Even at 4,316 appearances in our dataset, "tidytuesday" represents only about 6% of the total words in our dataset. This makes sense when you consider our dataset contains 15,335 unique words.

Analysis: sentiment analysis

Now that we have a sense of the most frequently appearing words, it's time to explore some questions in our tweets dataset. Let's imagine that we're education consultants trying to learn about the community surrounding the TidyTuesday data visualization ritual. We know from the first part of our analysis that the token "dataviz" (a short name for data visualization) appeared frequently relative to other words, so maybe we can explore that further. A good start would be to see how the appearance of that token in a tweet is associated with other positive words.

We'll need to use a technique called "sentiment analysis" to get at the "positivity" of words in these tweets. Sentiment analysis tries to evaluate words for their emotional association. If we analyze words by the emotions they convey, we can start to explore patterns in large text datasets like our `tokens` data.

Earlier we used `anti_join()` to remove stop words in our dataset. We're going to do something similar here to reduce our `tokens` dataset to only words that have a positive association. We'll use a dataset called "the NRC Word-Emotion Association Lexicon" to help us identify words with a positive association. This dataset was published by Mohammad and Turney (2013).

We need to install a package called {textdata} to make sure we have the NRC Word-Emotion Association Lexicon dataset available to us. Note that you only need to have this package installed. You do not need to load it with the `library(textdata)` command.

If you don't already have it, let's install {textdata}:

```
install.packages("textdata")
```

To explore this dataset further, we'll use a {tidytext} function called `get_sentiments()` to view some words and their associated sentiment. If this is your first time using the NRC Word-Emotion Association Lexicon, you'll be prompted to download the NRC lexicon. Respond "yes" to the prompt and the NRC lexicon will download. Note that you'll only have to do this the first time you use the NRC lexicon.

```
get_sentiments("nrc")
## # A tibble: 13,901 x 2
##      word         sentiment
##      <chr>        <chr>
##   1 abacus        trust
##   2 abandon       fear
##   3 abandon       negative
##   4 abandon       sadness
##   5 abandoned     anger
##   6 abandoned     fear
##   7 abandoned     negative
##   8 abandoned     sadness
##   9 abandonment   anger
## 10 abandonment   fear
## # … with 13,891 more rows
```

This returns a dataset with two columns. The first is `word` and contains a list of words. The second is the `sentiment` column, which contains an emotion associated with each word. This dataset is similar to the `stop_words` dataset. Note that this dataset also uses the column name `word`, which will again make it easy for us to match this dataset to our `tokens` dataset.

Count positive words

Let's begin working on reducing our `tokens` dataset down to only words that the NRC dataset associates with positivity. We'll start by creating a new dataset, `nrc_pos`, which contains the NRC words that have the positive sentiment. Then we'll match that new dataset to `tokens` using the `word` column that is common to both datasets. Finally, we'll use `count()` to total up the appearances of each positive word.

```r
# Only positive in the NRC dataset
nrc_pos <-
  get_sentiments("nrc") %>%
  filter(sentiment == "positive")
# Match to tokens
pos_tokens_count <-
  tokens %>%
  inner_join(nrc_pos, by = "word") %>%
  # Total appearance of positive words
  count(word, sort = TRUE)
pos_tokens_count
## # A tibble: 644 x 2
##      word         n
##      <chr>     <int>
##   1 fun         173
##   2 top         162
##   3 learn       131
##   4 found       128
##   5 love        113
##   6 community   110
##   7 learning     97
##   8 happy        95
##   9 share        90
## 10 inspired      85
## # … with 634 more rows
```

We can visualize these words nicely by using {ggplot2} to show the positive words in a bar chart. There are 644 words total, which is hard to convey in a compact chart. We'll solve that problem by filtering our dataset to only words that appear 75 times or more.

```r
pos_tokens_count %>%
  # only words that appear 75 times or more
  filter(n >= 75) %>%
  ggplot(., aes(x = reorder(word, -n), y = n)) +
  geom_bar(stat = "identity", fill = dataedu_colors("darkblue")) +
  labs(
    title = "Count of Words Associated with Positivity",
    subtitle = "Tweets with the hashtag #tidytuesday",
```

```
  caption = "Data: Twitter and NRC",
  x = "",
  y = "Count"
) +
theme_dataedu()
```

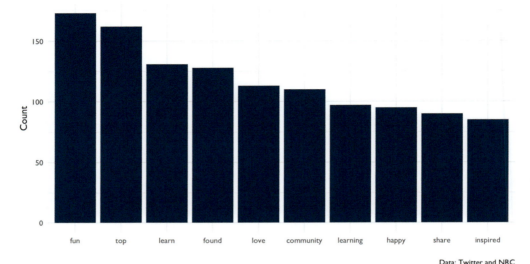

Figure 11.1: Count of Words Associated with Positivity

Note the use of `reorder()` when mapping the `word` variable to the x aesthetic. Using `reorder()` here sorts our x-axis in descending order by the variable n. Sorting the bars from highest frequency to lowest makes it easier for the reader to identify and compare the most and least common words in the visualization.

"Dataviz" and other positive words

Earlier in the analysis we learned that "dataviz" was among the most frequently occurring words in this dataset. We can continue our exploration of TidyTuesday tweets by seeing how many tweets with "dataviz" also had at least one positive word from the NRC dataset. Looking at this might give us some clues about how people in the TidyTuesday learning community view dataviz as a tool.

There are a few steps to this part of the analysis, so let's review our strategy. We'll need to use the `status_id` field in the `tweets` dataset to filter the tweets that have the word dataviz in them. Then we need to use the `status_id` field in this new bunch of dataviz tweets to identify the tweets that include at least one positive word.

How do we know which `status_id` values contain the word "dataviz" and which ones contain a positive word? Recall that our `tokens` dataset only has one word per row, which makes it easy to use functions like `filter()` and `inner_join()` to make two new datasets: one of `status_id` values that have "dataviz" in the `word` column and one of `status_id` values that have a positive word in the `word` column.

We'll explore the combinations of "dataviz" and any positive words in our `tweets` dataset using these three ingredients: our `tweets` dataset, a vector of `status_ids` for tweets that have "dataviz" in them, and a vector of `status_ids` for tweets that have positive words in them. Now that we have our strategy, let's write some code and see how it works.

First, we'll make a vector of `status_ids` for tweets that have "dataviz" in them. This will be used later to identify tweets that contain "dataviz" in the text. We'll use `filter()` on our `tokens` dataset to keep only the rows that have "dataviz" in the `word` column. Let's name that new dataset `dv_tokens`.

```
dv_tokens <-
  tokens %>%
  filter(word == "dataviz")
dv_tokens
## # A tibble: 607 x 2
##      status_id              word
##      <chr>                  <chr>
##  1 1116518351147360257 dataviz
##  2 1098025772554612738 dataviz
##  3 1161454327296339968 dataviz
##  4 1110711892086001665 dataviz
##  5 1151926405162291200 dataviz
##  6 1095854400004853765 dataviz
##  7 1157111441419395074 dataviz
##  8 1154958378764046336 dataviz
##  9 1105642831413239808 dataviz
## 10 1108196618464047105 dataviz
## # … with 597 more rows
```

The result is a dataset that has IDs in one column and the word "dataviz" in the other column. We can use `$` to extract a vector of IDs for tweets that have "dataviz" in the text. This vector has hundreds of values, so we'll use `head` to view just the first ten.

```
# Extract status_id
head(dv_tokens$status_id)
## [1] "1116518351147360257" "1098025772554612738" "1161454327296339968"
## [4] "1110711892086001665" "1151926405162291200" "1095854400004853765"
```

Now let's do this again, but this time, we'll make a vector of IDs for tweets that have positive words in them. This will be used later to identify tweets that contain a positive word in the text. We'll use `filter()` on our `tokens` dataset to keep only the rows that have any of the positive words in the in the `word` column. If you've been running all the code up to this point in the walkthrough, you'll notice that you already have a dataset of positive words called `nrc_pos`, which can be turned into a vector of positive words by typing `nrc_pos$word`. We can use the `%in%` operator in our call to `filter()` to find only words that are in this vector of positive words. Let's name this new dataset `pos_tokens`.

```
pos_tokens <-
  tokens %>%
  filter(word %in% nrc_pos$word)
pos_tokens
## # A tibble: 4,925 x 2
##     status_id            word
##     <chr>                <chr>
##  1 1163154266065735680  throne
##  2 1001412196247666688  honey
##  3 1001412196247666688  production
##  4 1001412196247666688  increase
##  5 1001412196247666688  production
##  6 1161638973808287746  found
##  7 991073965899644928   community
##  8 991073965899644928   community
##  9 991073965899644928   trend
## 10 991073965899644928   white
## # … with 4,915 more rows
```

The result is a dataset that has IDs in one column and a positive word from `tokens` in the other column. We'll again use $ to extract a vector of IDs for these tweets.

```
# Extract status_id
head(pos_tokens$status_id)
## [1] "1163154266065735680" "1001412196247666688" "1001412196247666688"
## [4] "1001412196247666688" "1001412196247666688" "1161638973808287746"
```

That's a lot of IDs, many of which are duplicates. Let's try and make the vector of IDs a little shorter. We can use `distinct()` to get a data frame of IDs, where each ID only appears once:

```
pos_tokens <-
  pos_tokens %>%
  distinct(status_id)
```

Note that `distinct()` drops all variables except for `status_id`. For good measure, let's use `distinct()` on our `dv_tokens` data frame too:

```
dv_tokens <-
  dv_tokens %>%
  distinct(status_id)
```

Now we have a data frame of `status_id` for tweets containing "dataviz" and another for tweets containing a positive word. Let's use these to transform our

tweets dataset. First we'll filter `tweets` for rows that have the "dataviz" sta-
tus_id. Then we'll create a new column called `positive` that will tell us if the
ID is from the group of IDs associated with positive words. We'll name this filtered
dataset `dv_pos`.

```
dv_pos <-
  tweets %>%
  # Only tweets that have the dataviz status_id
  filter(status_id %in% dv_tokens$status_id) %>%
  # Is the status_id from our vector of positive word?
  mutate(positive = if_else(status_id %in% pos_tokens$status_id,
1, 0))
```

Let's take a moment to dissect how we use `if_else()` to create our `positive` column. We gave `if_else()` three arguments:

- `status_id %in% pos_tokens$status_id`: a logical statement

- `1`: the value of `positive` if the logical statement is true

- `0`: the value of `positive` if the logical statement is false

So our new `positive` column will take the value 1 if the `status_id` was in our
`pos_tokens` dataset and the value 0 if the `status_id` was not in our `pos_tokens`
dataset. Practically speaking, `positive` is 1 if the tweet has a positive word and 0
if it does not have a positive word.

And finally, let's see what percent of tweets that had "dataviz" in them also had
at least one positive word:

```
dv_pos %>%
  count(positive) %>%
  mutate(perc = n / sum(n))
## # A tibble: 2 x 3
##   positive     n  perc
##      <dbl> <int> <dbl>
## 1        0   272 0.450
## 2        1   333 0.550
```

About 55% of tweets that have "dataviz" in them also had at least one positive
word, and about 45% of them did not have at least one positive word. It's worth
noting here that this finding doesn't necessarily mean users didn't have anything
good to say about 45% of the "dataviz" tweets. We can't know precisely why some
tweets had positive words and some didn't, we just know that more dataviz tweets
had positive words than not. To put this in perspective, we might have a different
impression if 5% or 95% of the tweets had positive words.

Since the point of exploratory data analysis is to explore and develop questions,
let's continue to do that. In this last section we'll review a random selection of
tweets for context.

Taking a close read of randomly selected tweets

Let's review where we are so far as we work to learn more about the TidyTuesday learning community through tweets. So far we've counted frequently used words and estimated the number of tweets with positive associations. This dataset is large, so we need to zoom out and find ways to summarize the data. But it's also useful to explore by zooming in and reading some of the tweets. Reading tweets helps us to build intuition and context about how users talk about TidyTuesday in general. Even though this doesn't lead to quantitative findings, it helps us to learn more about the content we're studying and analyzing. Instead of reading all 4,418 tweets, let's write some code to randomly select tweets to review.

First, let's make a dataset of tweets that had positive words from the NRC dataset. Remember earlier when we made a dataset of tweets that had "dataviz" and a column that had a value of 1 for containing positive words and 0 for not containing positive words? Let's reuse that technique, but instead of applying to a dataset of tweets containing "dataviz", let's use it on our dataset of all tweets.

```
pos_tweets <-
  tweets %>%
  mutate(positive = if_else(status_id %in% pos_tokens$status_id,
1, 0)) %>%
  filter(positive == 1)
```

Again, we're using `if_else` to make a new column called `positive` that takes its value based on whether `status_id %in% pos_tokens$status_id` is true or not.

We can use `slice()` to help us pick the rows. When we pass `slice()` a row number, it returns that row from the dataset. For example, we can select the 1st and 3rd row of our `tweets` dataset this way:

```
tweets %>%
  slice(1, 3)
## # A tibble: 2 x 2
##   status_id          text
##   <chr>              <chr>
## 1 1163154266065735... "First #TidyTuesday submission! Roman emperors
and their ri...
## 2 1001412196247666... "My #tidytuesday submission for week 8.
Honey production da...
```

Randomly selecting rows from a dataset is great technique to have in your toolkit. Random selection helps us avoid some of the biases we all have when we pick rows to review ourselves.

Here's one way to do that using base R:

```
sample(x = 1:10, size = 5)
## [1]  7  6  8  1 10
```

Passing `sample()` a vector of numbers and the size of the sample you want returns a random selection from the vector. Try changing the value of `x` and `size` to see how this works.

{dplyr} has a version of this called `sample_n()` that we can use to randomly select rows in our tweets dataset. Using `sample_n()` looks like this:

```
set.seed(2020)

pos_tweets %>%
  sample_n(., size = 10)
## # A tibble: 10 x 3
##    status_id       text                                    positive
##    <chr>           <chr>                                        <dbl>
##  1 113347244173969… "Today is the day - excited to be leading
this Bos…        1
##  2 114436276456938… "UFO sightings with gganimate - need to tidy
up so…        1
##  3 996745975124430… "This week's #TidyTuesday dataset looks too
fun to…        1
##  4 108681181347857… "This week: 2019-01-15 #TidyTuesday #rstats
my foc…        1
##  5 103451450126419… "#TidyTuesday week 22.\nInteresting patterns
in ho…        1
##  6 113597645318988… ".@broadwym is kicking off the #TidyTuesday
colear…        1
##  7 114881375394674… "Night everyone i am heading to bed now i
love you…        1
##  8 107466544430342… "@sebastianhwells @jspairani Hi Sebastian
- every …        1
##  9 115468388823039… "Have you signed up for our next #rladies
event? \…        1
## 10 112789066770597… "Better late than never. My first #TidyTues-
day plo…        1
```

That returned ten randomly selected tweets that we can now read through and discuss. Let's look a little closer at how we did that. We used `sample_n()`, which returns randomly selected rows from our tweets dataset. We also specified that `size = 10`, which means we want `sample_n()` to give us 10 randomly selected rows. A few lines before that, we used `set.seed(2020)`. This helps us ensure that, while `sample_n()` theoretically plucks 10 random numbers, our readers can run this code and get the same result we did. Using `set.seed(2020)` at the top of your code makes `sample_n()` pick the same ten rows every time. Try changing 2020 to another number and notice how `sample_n()` picks a different set of ten numbers, but repeatedly picks those numbers until you change the argument in `set.seed()`.

Conclusion

The purpose of this walkthrough is to share code with you so you can practice some basic text analysis techniques. Now it's time to make your learning more meaningful by adapting this code to text-based files you regularly see at work. Trying reading in some of these and doing a similar analysis:

- News articles

- Procedure manuals

- Open-ended responses in surveys

There are also advanced text analysis techniques to explore. Consider trying topic modeling (https://www.tidytextmining.com/topicmodeling.html) or finding correlations between terms (https://www.tidytextmining.com/ngrams.html), both described in *Text Mining With R* (Silge and Robinson 2017).

Finally, if you feel like there is more to analyze where it comes to this particular hashtag, we agree! We use this dataset further in the next chapter on social network analysis. Moreover, if you want to collect your own Twitter data, head to Appendix B to read about and consider some potential strategies.

Chapter 12

Walkthrough 6

Exploring relationships using social network analysis with social media data

Topics emphasized

- Transforming data
- Visualizing data

Functions introduced

- `rtweet::search_tweets()`
- `randomNames::randomNames()`
- `tidyr::unnest()`
- `tidygraph::as_tbl_graph()`
- `ggraph::ggraph()`

Vocabulary

- Application Programming Interface (API)
- edgelist
- edge
- influence model
- regex
- selection model

- social network analysis

- sociogram

- vertex

Chapter overview

This chapter builds on Walkthrough 5 in Chapter 11, where we worked with #ti-dytuesday data. In the previous chapter we focused on using text analysis to understand the *content* of tweets. In this chapter, we focus on the *interactions* between #tidytuesday participants using social network analysis (sometimes referred to as network analysis) techniques.

While social network analysis is increasingly common, it remains challenging to carry out. For one, cleaning and tidying the data can be even more challenging than for most other data sources because net data for social network analysis (or network data) often includes variables about both individuals (such as information on students or teachers) and their relationships (whether they have a relationship at all, for example, or how strong or of what type their relationship is). This chapter is designed to take you from not having carried out social network analysis to visualizing network data.

Like the previous chapter, we've also included an appendix (Appendix C) to introduce some social network-related ideas for further exploration. These focus on modeling social network processes, particularly, the processes of who chooses (or selects) to interact with whom, and of influence, or how relationships can impact individuals' behaviors.

You will need a Twitter account to complete *all* of the code outlined in this chapter in order to access your own Twitter data (through the Twitter Application Interface [API]; see Chapter 11 for an in-depth description of what this means and how to access it).

If you do not have a Twitter account, you can create one and keep it private, or even delete the account once you're done with this walkthrough. Additionally, you can get data that has already been accessed from the Twitter API via the {dataedu} package (as we describe below).

Background

There are a few reasons to be interested in social media. For example, if you work in a school district, you may want to know who is interacting with the content you share. If you are a researcher, you may want to investigate what teachers, administrators, and others do through state-based hashtags (e.g., Rosenberg et al. 2016). Social media-based data also provides new contexts for learning to take place, like in professional learning networks (Trust, Krutka, and Carpenter 2016).

In the past, if a teacher wanted advice about how to plan a unit or to design a lesson, they would turn to a trusted peer in their building or district (Spillane, Kim, and Frank 2012). Today they are as likely to turn to someone in a social media network. Social media interactions like the ones tagged with the #tidytuesday hashtag are increasingly common in education. Using data science tools to learn from these interactions is valuable for improving the student experience.

Packages

In this chapter, we access data using the {rtweet} package (Kearney 2016). Through {rtweet} and a Twitter account, it is easy to access data from Twitter. We will load the {tidyverse} and {rtweet} packages to get started.

We will also load other packages that we will be using in this analysis, including two packages related to social network analysis (Pedersen 2019, 2020) as well as one that will help us to use not-anonymized names in a savvy way (Betebenner 2019). As always, if you have not installed any of these packages before (which may particularly be the case for the {rtweet}, {randomNames}, {tidygraph}, and {ggraph} packages, which we have not yet used in the book), do so using the `install.packages()` function. More on installing packages is included in the "Packages" section of the "Foundational Skills" chapter.

Let's load the packages with the following calls to the `library()` function:

```
library(tidyverse)
library(rtweet)
library(dataedu)
library(randomNames)
library(tidygraph)
library(ggraph)
```

Data sources and import

Here is an example of searching the most recent 1,000 tweets which include the hashtag #rstats. When you run this code, you will be prompted to authenticate your access via Twitter.

```
rstats_tweets <-
  search_tweets("#rstats")
```

You can change the search term to other hashtags terms. For example, to search for #tidytuesday tweets, we can replace #rstats with #tidytuesday:

```
tt_tweets   <-
  search_tweets("#tidytuesday")
```

You can find a greater number of tweets by adding a greater value to the n argument of the `search_tweets()` function, as follows, to collect the most recent 500 tweets:

```
tt_tweets   <-
  search_tweets("#tidytuesday", n = 500)
```

You may notice that the most recent tweets containing the #tidytuesday hashtag are returned. What if you wanted to go further back in time? We'll discuss this topic in the next section and in Appendix B.

Using an Application Programming Interface (or API)

It's worth taking a short detour to talk about how you can obtain a dataset spanning a longer period of time. A common way to import data from websites, including social media platforms, is to use something called an Application Programming Interface (API). In fact, if you ran the code above, you just accessed an API!

Think of an API as a special door a home builder made for a house that has a lot of cool stuff in it. The home builder doesn't want everyone to be able to walk right in and use a bunch of stuff in the house. But they also don't want to make it too hard because, after all, sharing is caring! Imagine the home builder made a door just for folks who know how to use doors. In order to get through this door, users need to know where to find it along the outside of the house. Once they're there, they have to know the code to open. And, once they're through the door, they have to know how to use the stuff inside. An API for social media platforms like Twitter and Facebook are the same way. You can download datasets of social media information, like tweets, using some code and authentication credentials organized by the website.

There are some advantages to using an API to import data at the start of your education dataset analysis. Every time you run the code in your analysis, you'll be using the API to contact the social media platform and download a fresh dataset. Now your analysis is not just a one-off product, but, rather, is one that can be updated with the most recent data (in this case, tweets), every time you run it. By using an API to import new data every time you run your code, you create an analysis that can be used again and again on future datasets. However, a key point—and limitation—is that Twitter allows access to their data via their API only for (approximately) the seven most recent days. There are a number of *other* ways to access older data, though we focus on one way here: having access to the URLs of (or the status IDs for) tweets.

As a result, we used this technique—described in-depth in Appendix B—to collect older (historical) data from Twitter about the #tidytuesday hashtag, using a different function than the one described above (`rtweet::lookup_statuses()` instead of `rtweet::search_tweets()`). This was important for this chapter because having access to a greater number of tweets allows us to better understand the interactions between a larger number of the individuals participating in #tidytuesday. The data that we prepared from accessing historical data for #tidytuesday is available in the {dataedu} R package as the `tt_tweets` dataset, as we describe next.

Accessing the data from {dataedu}

Don't have Twitter or don't wish to access the data via Twitter? Then, you can load the data from the {dataedu} package (just as we did in the last chapter, Chapter 11), as follows:

```
tt_tweets <- dataedu::tt_tweets
```

View data

We can see that there are *many* rows for the data:

```
nrow(tt_tweets)
## [1] 4418
```

Methods: process data

Network data requires some processing before it can be used in subsequent analyses. The network dataset needs a way to identify each participant's role in the interaction. We need to answer questions like: Did someone reach out to another for help? Was someone contacted by another for help? We can process the data by creating an "edgelist". An edgelist is a dataset where each row is a unique interaction between two parties. Each row (which represents a single relationship) in the edgelist is referred to as an "edge". We note that one challenge facing data scientists beginning to use network analysis is the different terms that are used for similar (or the same!) aspects of analyses: Edges are sometimes referred to as "ties" or "relations", but these generally refer to the same thing, though they may be used in different contexts.

An edgelist looks like the following, where the `sender` (sometimes called the "nominator") column identifies who is initiating the interaction and the `receiver` (sometimes called the "nominee") column identifies who is receiving the interaction:

```
## # A tibble: 12 x 2
##    sender            receiver
##    <chr>             <chr>
##  1 Songer, Preston   Muya, Kensie
##  2 Wilson, Braedon   Waltonallen, Kayla
##  3 Wilson, Braedon   White, Kimberly
##  4 Toy, Li           Waltonallen, Kayla
##  5 Toy, Li           Muya, Kensie
##  6 Toy, Li           Mekonnen, Steffi
##  7 Lee, Monina       White, Kimberly
##  8 Lee, Monina       Bauste, Samuel
##  9 Lee, Monina       Mekonnen, Steffi
## 10 Hernandez, Kaylee Mizokami, Srida
## 11 Vincent, Fredric  White, Kimberly
## 12 Vincent, Fredric  Mizokami, Srida
```

In this edgelist, the `sender` column might identify someone who nominates another (the receiver) as someone they go to for help. The sender might also identify someone who interacts with the receiver in other ways, like "liking" or "mentioning" their tweets. In the following steps, we will work to create an edgelist from the data from #tidytuesday on Twitter.

Extracting mentions

Let's extract the mentions. There is a lot going on in the code below; let's break it down line-by-line, starting with `mutate()`:

- `mutate(all_mentions = str_extract_all(text, regex))`: this line uses a regex, or regular expression, to identify all of the usernames in the tweet (*note*: the regex comes from this Stack Overflow page (https://stackover-flow.com/questions/18164839/get-twitter-username-with-regex-in-r)).

- `unnest(all_mentions)`: this line uses a {tidyr} function, `unnest()`, to move every mention to its own line, while keeping all of the other information the same (see more about `unnest()` here: https://tidyr.tidyverse.org/reference/unnest.html)).

Now let's use these functions to extract the mentions from the dataset. Here's how all the code looks in action:

```
regex <- "@([A-Za-z]+[A-Za-z0-9_]+)(?![A-Za-z0-9_]*\\.)"
tt_tweets <-
  tt_tweets %>%
  # Use regular expression to identify all the usernames in a tweet
  mutate(all_mentions = str_extract_all(text, regex)) %>%
  unnest(all_mentions)
```

Let's put these into their own data frame, called `mentions`.

```
mentions <-
  tt_tweets %>%
  mutate(all_mentions = str_trim(all_mentions)) %>%
  select(sender = screen_name, all_mentions)
```

Putting the edgelist together

Recall that an edgelist is a data structure that has columns for the "sender" and "receiver" of interactions. Someone "sends" the mention to someone who is mentioned, who can be considered to "receive" it. To make the edgelist, we'll need to clean it up a little by removing the "@" symbol. Let's look at our data as it is now.

```
mentions
## # A tibble: 2,447 x 2
##     sender   all_mentions
##     <chr>    <chr>
##  1 cizzart  @eldestapeweb
##  2 cizzart  @INDECArgentina
##  3 cizzart  @ENACOMArgentina
##  4 cizzart  @tribunalelecmns
##  5 cizzart  @CamaraElectoral
##  6 cizzart  @INDECArgentina
```

```
##   7 cizzart @tribunalelecmns
##   8 cizzart @CamaraElectoral
##   9 cizzart @AgroMnes
## 10 cizzart @AgroindustriaAR
## # … with 2,437 more rows
```

Let's remove that "@" symbol from the columns we created and save the results to a new tibble, edgelist.

```
edgelist <-
  mentions %>%
  # remove "@" from all_mentions column
  mutate(all_mentions = str_sub(all_mentions, start = 2)) %>%
  # rename all_mentions to receiver
  select(sender, receiver = all_mentions)
```

Analysis and results

Now that we have our edgelist, let's plot the network. We'll use the {tidygraph} and {ggraph} packages to visualize the data. We note that network visualizations are often referred to as "sociograms" or a representation of the relationships between individuals in a network. We use this term and the term network visualization interchangeably in this chapter.

Plotting the network

Large networks like this one can be hard to work with because of their size. We can get around that problem by only including some individuals. Let's explore how many interactions each individual in the network sent by using count():

```
interactions_sent <- edgelist %>%
  # this counts how many times each sender appears in the data frame,
effectively counting how many interactions each individual sent
  count(sender) %>%
  # arranges the data frame in descending order of the number of
interactions sent
  arrange(desc(n))

interactions_sent
## # A tibble: 618 x 2
##     sender            n
##     <chr>         <int>
##  1 thomas_mock     347
##  2 R4DScommunity    78
##  3 WireMonkey       52
##  4 CedScherer       41
##  5 allison_horst    37
##  6 mjhendrickson    34
```

```
##   7 kigtembu           27
##   8 WeAreRLadies       25
##   9 PBecciu            23
## 10 sil_aarts           23
## # … with 608 more rows
```

618 senders of interactions is a lot! What if we focused on only those who sent more than one interaction?

```
interactions_sent <-
  interactions_sent %>%
  filter(n > 1)
```

That leaves us with only 349, which will be much easier to work with.

We now need to filter the edgelist to only include these 349 individuals. The following code uses the filter() function combined with the %in% operator to do this:

```
edgelist <- edgelist %>%
  # the first of the two lines below filters to include only senders
in the interactions_sent data frame
  # the second line does the same, for receivers
  filter(sender %in% interactions_sent$sender,
         receiver %in% interactions_sent$sender)
```

We'll use the as_tbl_graph() function, which identifies the first column as the "sender" and the second as the "receiver". Let's look at the object it creates:

```
g <-
  as_tbl_graph(edgelist)
g
## # A tbl_graph: 267 nodes and 975 edges
## #
## # A directed multigraph with 7 components
## #
## # Node Data: 267 x 1 (active)
##    name
##    <chr>
## 1 dgwinfred
## 2 datawookie
## 3 jvaghela4
## 4 FournierJohanie
## 5 JonTheGeek
## 6 jakekaupp
## # … with 261 more rows
## #
## # Edge Data: 975 x 2
##    from    to
```

```
##      <int>  <int>
## 1        1     32
## 2        1     36
## 3        2    120
## # … with 972 more rows
```

We can see that the network now has 267 individuals, all of whom sent more than one interaction. The individuals in a network are often referred to as "nodes" (and this terminology is used in the {ggraph} functions for plotting the individuals—the nodes—in a network). We note that nodes are sometimes referred to as "vertices" or "actors"; like the different names for edges, these generally mean the same thing.

Next, we'll use the `ggraph()` function:

```
g %>%
    # we chose the kk layout as it created a graph which was
easy-to-interpret, but others are available; see ?ggraph
  ggraph(layout = "kk") +
  # this adds the points to the graph
  geom_node_point() +
  # this adds the links, or the edges; alpha = .2 makes it so that
the lines are partially transparent
  geom_edge_link(alpha = .2) +
   # this last line of code adds a ggplot2 theme suitable for
network graphs
  theme_graph()
```

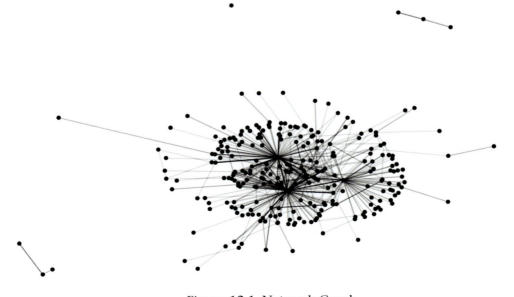

Figure 12.1 Network Graph

Finally, let's size the points based on a measure of centrality. A common way to do this is to measure how influential an individual may be based on the interactions observed.

```
g %>%
  # this calculates the centrality of each individual using the
built-in centrality_authority() function
  mutate(centrality = centrality_authority()) %>%
  ggraph(layout = "kk") +
  geom_node_point(aes(size = centrality, color = centrality)) +
  # this line colors the points based upon their centrality
  scale_color_continuous(guide = 'legend') +
  geom_edge_link(alpha = .2) +
  theme_graph()
```

Figure 12.2 Network Graph with Centrality

There is much more you can do with {ggraph} (and {tidygraph}); check out the {ggraph} tutorial here: https://ggraph.data-imaginist.com/.

Conclusion

In this chapter, we used social media data from the #tidytuesday hashtag to prepare and visualize social network data. Sociograms are a useful visualization tool to reveal who is interacting with whom—and, in some cases, to suggest why. In our applications of data science, we have found that the individuals (such as teachers or students) who are represented in a network often like to see what the network (and the relationships in it) *look like*. It can be compelling to think about why networks are the way they are, and how changes could be made to—for example—foster more connections between individuals who have few opportunities to interact. In this way, social network analysis can be useful to the data scientist in education because it provides a technique to communicate with other educational stakeholders in a compelling way.

Social network analysis is a broad (and growing) domain, and this chapter was intended to present some of its foundation. Fortunately for R users, many recent developments are implemented first in R (e.g., Hoff et al. 2017). If you are interested in some of the additional steps that you can take to model and analyze network data, consider the appendix on two types of models (for selection and influence processes), Appendix C.

Chapter 13

Walkthrough 7

The role (and usefulness) of multilevel models

Topics emphasized

- Transforming data
- Modeling data
- Communicating results

Functions introduced

- `dummies::dummy()`
- `dplyr::bind_cols()`
- `lme4::lmer()`
- `performance::icc()`

Vocabulary

- dummy coding
- Hierarchical Linear Model (HLM)
- intra-class correlation
- multilevel model

Chapter overview

The *purpose* of this walkthrough is to explore students' performance in these on-line courses. While this and the analysis in Walkthrough 1 in Chapter 7 focus on the time students spent in the course, this walkthrough focuses on the effects of being in a particular course. To do that, we'll use multilevel models, which can help us consider the idea that the students in our dataset shared classes. While the conceptual details underlying multilevel models can be complex, they do address a basic problem that is relatable to educators: how can we include variables, like cases, and student grouping levels, like classes or schools, in our model? We note that while carrying out multilevel models is very accessible through R, some of the concepts remain challenging, and, in such cases, we think it can be helpful to try running such a model with data that you have collected; later, the technical details (described here and in other, recommended resources) can help you go deeper with analyses and further your understanding of multilevel models.

Background

Using multilevel models helps us account for the way in which individual students are "grouped" together into higher-level units, like classes. Multilevel models do something different than a simple linear regression like the ones described in Walkthrough 1 in Chapter 7 and Walkthrough 4 in Chapter 10—they estimate the effect of being a student in a particular group. A multilevel model uses a different way to standardize the estimates for each group based on how systematically different the groups are from the other groups, relative to the effect on the dependent variable.

Though these conceptual details are complex, fitting them is fortunately straightforward and should be familiar if you have used R's `lm()` function before. So, let's get started!

Data source

We'll use the same data source on students' motivation in online science classes that we processed in Walkthrough 1 in Chapter 7.

Methods

Does the amount of time students spend on a course depend on the specific course they're in? Does the amount of time students spend on a course affect the points they earn? There are a number of ways to approach these questions. Let's use our linear model.

To do this, we'll assign codes to the groups so we can include them in our model. We'll use a technique called "dummy coding". This means transforming a variable with multiple categories into new variables, where each variable indicates the presence and absence of each category.

Load packages

We will load the tidyverse and a few other packages specific to using multilevel models: {lme4} (Bates et al. 2019) and {performance} (Lüdecke et al. 2020).

If you have not before—as for other packages used for the first time—you'll need to install {lme4}, {performance}, and {dummies} once to do the rest of this walkthrough. If helpful, head to the "Packages" section of the "Foundational Skills" chapter for an overview of installing packages.

The remaining packages ({tidyverse}, {sjPlot}, and {dataedu}) are used in other chapters, but, if you have not installed these before, you will have to install them too, using the `install.packages()` function, with the name of the package included (in quotations), just like for the previous three packages.

```
library(tidyverse)
library(dummies)
library(sjPlot)
library(lme4)
library(performance)
library(dataedu)
```

The role of dummy codes

Before we import our data, let's spend some time learning about dummy coding. In this discussion, we'll see how dummy coding works through using the {dummies} package, though you often do not need to manually dummy code variables like this. A note that the {dummies} package tends to work better with base R as opposed to the {tidyverse}. In this section, we will use base R and data.frame instead of the {tidyverse} and tibbles.

Let's look at the `iris` data that comes built into R.

```
str(iris)
## 'data.frame':    150 obs. of  5 variables:
##  $ Sepal.Length: num  5.1 4.9 4.7 4.6 5 5.4 4.6 5 4.4 4.9 ...
##  $ Sepal.Width : num  3.5 3 3.2 3.1 3.6 3.9 3.4 3.4 2.9 3.1 ...
##  $ Petal.Length: num  1.4 1.4 1.3 1.5 1.4 1.7 1.4 1.5 1.4 1.5 ...
##  $ Petal.Width : num  0.2 0.2 0.2 0.2 0.2 0.4 0.3 0.2 0.2 0.1 ...
##  $ Species     : Factor w/ 3 levels "setosa","versicolor",..: 1
1 1 1 1 1 1 1 1 1 ...
```

As we can see above, the `Species` variable is a factor. Recall that factor data types are categorical variables. They associate a row with a specific category, or level, of that variable. So how do we consider factor variables in our model? `Species` seems to be made up of, well, words, such as "setosa".

A common way to approach this is through dummy coding, where you create new variables for each of the possible values of `Species` (such as "setosa"). These new variables will have a value of 1 when the row is associated with that level (i.e., the first row in the data frame above would have a 1 for a column named `setosa`).

Let's put the {dummies} package to work on this task. How many possible values are there for `Species`? We can check with the `levels` function:

```
levels(iris$Species)
## [1] "setosa"     "versicolor" "virginica"
```

The function `dummy.data.frame()` takes a data frame and creates a `data.frame` where all the specified columns are given dummy attributes. We use it to turn `iris` into a dummy data frame. Then we run the `get.dummy()` function specifically on the `Species` variable. It returns *three* variables, one for each of the three levels of Species—`setosa`, `versicolor`, and `virginica`.

Please note that the code below will trigger a warning. A warning will run the code but alert you that something should be changed. This warning is because of an outdated parameter in the `dummy.data.frame()` function that hasn't been updated. R 3.6 and above triggers a warning when this happens. This is a good reminder that packages evolve (or don't) and you have to be aware of any changes when using them for analysis.

```
d_iris <-
  dummy.data.frame(iris)
## Warning in model.matrix.default(~x - 1, model.frame(~x - 1),
contrasts = FALSE):
## non-list contrasts argument ignored
get.dummy(d_iris, name = "Species") %>%
  head()
##   Speciessetosa Speciesversicolor Speciesvirginica
## 1             1                 0                0
## 2             1                 0                0
## 3             1                 0                0
## 4             1                 0                0
## 5             1                 0                0
## 6             1                 0                0
```

Let's confirm that every row associated with a specific species has a 1 in the column it corresponds to. We can do this by binding together the dummy codes and the `iris` data and then counting how many rows were coded with a "1" for each dummy code. For example, when the `Species` is "setosa", the variable `Speciessetosa` always equals 1—as is the case for the other species.

Now we need to combine the dummy coded variables with the `iris` dataset. `bind_cols()` is a useful {tidyverse} function for binding together data frames by column.

```
# create matrix of dummy-coded variables
species_dummy_coded <-
  get.dummy(d_iris, name = "Species")
# add dummy coded variables to iris
iris_with_dummy_codes <-
  bind_cols(iris, species_dummy_coded)
Let's look at the results.
iris_with_dummy_codes %>%
  count(Species, Speciessetosa, Speciesversicolor, Speciesvirginica)
## # A tibble: 3 x 5
##   Species   Speciessetosa Speciesversicolor Speciesvirginica     n
##   <fct>             <int>             <int>             <int> <int>
```

```
## 1 setosa            1            0            0      50
## 2 versicolor        0            1            0      50
## 3 virginica         0            0            1      50
```

Now that we have a basic understanding of how dummy codes work, let's explore how we use them in our model. When fitting models in R that include factor variables, R displays coefficients for all but one level in the model output. The factor level that's not explicitly named is called the "reference group". The reference group is the level that all other levels are compare to.

So why can't R explicitly name every level of a dummy-coded column? It has to do with how the dummy codes are used to facilitate comparison of groups. The purpose of the dummy code is to show how different the dependent variable is for all of the observations that are in one group. Let's go back to our iris example. Consider all the flowers that are in the "setosa" group. To represent how different those flowers are, they have to be compared to another group of flowers. In R, we would compare all the flowers in the "setosa" group to the reference group of flowers. Recall that the reference group of flowers would be the group that is not explicitly named in the model output.

However, if every level of flower groups is dummy coded, there would be no single group to compare to. For this reason, one group is typically selected as the reference group to which every other group is compared.

Import data

Now that we have some background on dummy codes, let's return to the online science class data. We'll be using the same dataset that we used in Chapter 7. Let's load that dataset now from the {dataedu} package.

```
dat <- dataedu::sci_mo_processed
```

To wrap up our discussion about factor variables, levels, and dummy codes, let's look at how many classes are represented in the course_id variable. These classes will be our factor levels that we'll be using in our model soon. We can use the count() function to see how many courses there are:

```
dat %>%
  count(course_id)
## # A tibble: 26 x 2
##    course_id         n
##    <chr>         <int>
## 1 AnPhA-S116-01    43
## 2 AnPhA-S116-02    29
## 3 AnPhA-S216-01    43
## 4 AnPhA-S216-02    17
## 5 AnPhA-T116-01    11
## 6 BioA-S116-01     34
## 7 BioA-S216-01      7
```

```
##   8 BioA-T116-01        2
##   9 FrScA-S116-01       70
## 10 FrScA-S116-02       12
## # … with 16 more rows
```

Analysis

Regression (linear model) analysis with dummy codes

Before we fit our model, let's talk about our dataset. We will keep the variables we used in our last set of models—TimeSpent and course_id—as independent variables. Recall that TimeSpent is the amount of time in minutes that a student spent in a course and course_id is a unique identifier for a particular course. In this walkthrough we'll predict students' final grade rather than the percentage_ earned variable that we created in Walkthrough 1 in Chapter 7.

Since we will be using the final grade variable a lot, let's rename it to make it easier to type.

```
dat <-
  dat %>%
  rename(final_grade = FinalGradeCEMS)
```

Now we can fit our model. We will save the model object to m_linear_dc, where the dc stands for dummy code. Later we'll be working with course_id as a factor variable, so we can expect to see lm() treat it as a dummy coded variable. This means that the model output will include a reference variable for course_id that all other levels of course_id will be compared against.

```
m_linear_dc <-
  lm(final_grade ~ TimeSpent_std + course_id, data = dat)
```

The output from the model will be long. This is because each course in the course_ id variable will get its own line in the model output. We can see that using tab_ model() from {sjPlot}:

```
tab_model(m_linear_dc,
          title = "Table 13.1")
```

	Final Grade		
Predictors	Estimates	CI	p
(Intercept)	73.20	67.20–79.20	<0.001
TimeSpent_std	9.66	7.91–11.40	<0.001
course_id [AnPhA-S116-02]	−1.59	−10.88–7.70	0.737
course_id [AnPhA-S216-01]	−9.05	−17.44–−0.67	0.034
course_id [AnPhA-S216-02]	−4.51	−16.41–7.40	0.457
course_id [AnPhA-T116-01]	7.24	−6.34–20.82	0.296
course_id [BioA-S116-01]	−3.56	−12.67–5.55	0.443

course_id [BioA-S216-01]	−14.67	−31.61–2.26	0.089
course_id [BioA-T116-01]	9.18	−18.84–37.20	0.520
course_id [FrScA-S116-01]	12.02	4.33–19.70	0.002
course_id [FrScA-S116-02]	−3.14	−17.36–11.08	0.665
course_id [FrScA-S116-03]	3.51	−5.43–12.46	0.441
course_id [FrScA-S116-04]	5.23	−14.98–25.43	0.612
course_id [FrScA-S216-01]	9.92	2.41–17.43	0.010
course_id [FrScA-S216-02]	7.37	−2.70–17.45	0.151
course_id [FrScA-S216-03]	2.38	−25.65–30.40	0.868
course_id [FrScA-S216-04]	15.40	−2.92–33.72	0.099
course_id [FrScA-T116-01]	8.12	−12.08–28.33	0.430
course_id [OcnA-S116-01]	4.06	−5.67–13.79	0.413
course_id [OcnA-S116-02]	2.02	−9.89–13.93	0.739
course_id [OcnA-S116-03]	−18.75	−57.86–20.36	0.347
course_id [OcnA-S216-01]	−6.41	−15.04–2.22	0.145
course_id [OcnA-S216-02]	−2.76	−13.47–7.95	0.613
course_id [OcnA-T116-01]	−2.05	−16.97–12.87	0.787
course_id [PhysA-S116-01]	15.35	6.99–23.71	<0.001
course_id [PhysA-S216-01]	5.40	−6.01–16.82	0.353
course_id [PhysA-T116-01]	20.73	−7.23–48.70	0.146
Observations	573		
R^2 / R^2 adjusted	0.252 / 0.216		

Table 13.1 Time Spent (Standardized) and Course ID (Dummy Coded)
Regressed on Final Grade

Wow! Those are a lot of effects. The model estimates the effects of being in each class, accounting for the time students spent on a course and the class they were in. We know this because the model output includes the time spent (TimeSpent_std) variable and subject variables (like course_id[AnPhA-S116-02]).

If we count the number of classes, we see that there are 25—and not 26! One has been automatically selected as the reference group, and every other class's coefficient represents how different each class is from it. The intercept's value of 73.20 represents the number of percentage points that students in the reference group class are expected to earn. lm() automatically picks the first level of the course_ id variable as the reference group when it is converted to a factor. In this case, the course associated with course ID course_idAnPhA-S116-01, a first semester physiology course, is picked as the reference variable.

What if we want to pick another class as the reference variable? For example, say that we want course_idPhysA-S116-01 (the first section of the physics class offered during this semester and year) to be the reference group. We can do this by using the fct_relevel() function, which is a part of the {tidyverse} suite of packages. Note that before using fct_relevel(), the variable course_id was a character data type, which lm() coerced into a factor data type when we included it as a predictor variable. Using fct_relevel() will explicitly convert course_id to a factor data type. It's important to note that the actual *value* of the variable is what is in square brackets in the output, whereas course_id is the variable *name*; in the output, these are just combined to make it easier to tell what the values represent (e.g., "PhysA-S116-01" is an ID for a course).

Now let's use fct_relevel() and mutate() to re-order the levels within a factor so that the "first" level will change:

```
dat <-
  dat %>%
  mutate(course_id = fct_relevel(course_id, "PhysA-S116-01"))
```

We can now see that "PhysA-S116-01" is no longer listed as an independent variable. Now every coefficient listed in this model is in comparison to the new reference variable, "PhysA-S116-01". We also see that `course_id` is now recognized as a factor data type.

Now let's fit our model again with the newly releveled `course_id` variable. We'll give it a different name, `m_linear_dc_1`:

```
m_linear_dc_1 <-
  lm(final_grade ~ TimeSpent_std + course_id, data = dat)

tab_model(m_linear_dc_1,
          title = "Table 13.2")
```

	Final Grade		
Predictors	Estimates	CI	p
(Intercept)	88.55	82.83–94.27	<0.001
TimeSpent_std	9.66	7.91–11.40	<0.001
course_id [AnPhA-S116-01]	−15.35	−23.71–−6.99	<0.001
course_id [AnPhA-S116-02]	−16.94	−26.20–−7.67	<0.001
course_id [AnPhA-S216-01]	−24.40	−32.77–−16.04	<0.001
course_id [AnPhA-S216-02]	−19.86	−31.71–−8.01	0.001
course_id [AnPhA-T116-01]	−8.11	−21.64–5.42	0.240
course_id [BioA-S116-01]	−18.91	−27.72–−10.09	<0.001
course_id [BioA-S216-01]	−30.02	−46.80–−13.24	<0.001
course_id [BioA-T116-01]	−6.17	−34.09–21.75	0.664
course_id [FrScA-S116-01]	−3.33	−10.76–4.10	0.379
course_id [FrScA-S116-02]	−18.49	−32.58–−4.39	0.010
course_id [FrScA-S116-03]	−11.84	−20.59–−3.08	0.008
course_id [FrScA-S116-04]	−10.12	−30.32–10.08	0.326
course_id [FrScA-S216-01]	−5.43	−12.62–1.75	0.138
course_id [FrScA-S216-02]	−7.97	−17.85–1.90	0.113
course_id [FrScA-S216-03]	−12.97	−40.89–14.95	0.362
course_id [FrScA-S216-04]	0.05	−18.15–18.25	0.996
course_id [FrScA-T116-01]	−7.22	−27.47–13.02	0.484
course_id [OcnA-S116-01]	−11.29	−20.98–−1.60	0.022
course_id [OcnA-S116-02]	−13.33	−25.16–−1.49	0.027
course_id [OcnA-S116-03]	−34.10	−73.17–4.97	0.087
course_id [OcnA-S216-01]	−21.76	−30.29–−13.23	<0.001
course_id [OcnA-S216-02]	−18.11	−28.66–−7.56	0.001
course_id [OcnA-T116-01]	−17.40	−32.22–−2.58	0.021
course_id [PhysA-S216-01]	−9.94	−21.16–1.28	0.082
course_id [PhysA-T116-01]	5.39	−22.55–33.32	0.705
Observations	573		
R^2 / R^2 adjusted	0.252 / 0.216		

Table 13.2 Time Spent (Standardized) and Course ID (Dummy Coded) Regressed on Final Grade with a Different Reference Group ("PhysA-S116-01")

Using dummy codes is very common—they are used in nearly every case where you need to fit a model with variables that are factors. We've already seen one benefit of using R functions like `lm()` or the `lme4::lmer()` function we discuss later: these functions automatically convert character data types into factor data types.

For example, imagine you include a variable for courses that has values like "mathematics", "science", "english language" (typed like that!), "social studies", and "art" as an argument in `lm()`. `lm()` will automatically dummy code these for you. You'll just need to decide if you want to use the default reference group or if you should use `fct_revel()` to pick a different one.

Lastly, it's worth noting that there may be some situations where you do not want to dummy code a factor variable. These are situations where you don't want a single factor level to act as a reference group. In such cases, no intercept is estimated. This can be done by passing a –1 as the first value after the tilde, as follows:

```r
# specifying the same linear model as the previous example, but
# using a "-1" to indicate that there should not be a reference group
m_linear_dc_2 <-
   lm(final_grade ~ -1 + TimeSpent_std + course_id, data = dat)
tab_model(m_linear_dc_2,
          title = "Table 13.3")
```

| | Final Grade | | |
Predictors	Estimates	CI	p
TimeSpent_std	9.66	7.91–11.40	<0.001
course_id [PhysA-S116-01]	88.55	82.83–94.27	<0.001
course_id [AnPhA-S116-01]	73.20	67.20–79.20	<0.001
course_id [AnPhA-S116-02]	71.61	64.38–78.83	<0.001
course_id [AnPhA-S216-01]	64.15	58.12–70.17	<0.001
course_id [AnPhA-S216-02]	68.69	58.35–79.04	<0.001
course_id [AnPhA-T116-01]	80.44	68.20–92.67	<0.001
course_id [BioA-S116-01]	69.64	62.89–76.40	<0.001
course_id [BioA-S216-01]	58.53	42.74–74.32	<0.001
course_id [BioA-T116-01]	82.38	55.04–109.72	<0.001
course_id [FrScA-S116-01]	85.22	80.46–89.98	<0.001
course_id [FrScA-S116-02]	70.06	57.18–82.94	<0.001
course_id [FrScA-S116-03]	76.71	70.08–83.34	<0.001
course_id [FrScA-S116-04]	78.43	59.08–97.78	<0.001
course_id [FrScA-S216-01]	83.12	78.72–87.52	<0.001
course_id [FrScA-S216-02]	80.57	72.51–88.64	<0.001
course_id [FrScA-S216-03]	75.58	48.23–102.92	<0.001
course_id [FrScA-S216-04]	88.60	71.31–105.89	<0.001
course_id [FrScA-T116-01]	81.32	61.94–100.71	<0.001
course_id [OcnA-S116-01]	77.26	69.49–85.03	<0.001
course_id [OcnA-S116-02]	75.22	64.88–85.56	<0.001
course_id [OcnA-S116-03]	54.45	15.80–93.10	0.006
course_id [OcnA-S216-01]	66.79	60.50–73.07	<0.001
course_id [OcnA-S216-02]	70.44	61.57–79.31	<0.001

course_id [OcnA-T116-01]	71.15	57.48–84.81	<0.001
course_id [PhysA-S216-01]	78.60	68.94–88.27	<0.001
course_id [PhysA-T116-01]	93.93	66.60–121.27	<0.001
Observations	573		
R^2 / R^2 adjusted	0.943 / 0.940		

Table 13.3 Time Spent (Standardized) and Course ID (Dummy Coded)
Regressed on Final Grade with No Intercept

In the vast majority of cases, you'll *want* to dummy code your factor variables so you probably won't be using it very often.

A deep-dive into multilevel models

Let's discuss multilevel models a little more by exploring some of the nuances of using them with education data.

Dummy coding variables and ease of interpretation

Analyzing the effect of multiple levels is a trade-off between considering more than one variable and how easy it is to interpret your model's output. A technique like dummy coding is a very helpful strategy for working with a small number of groups as predictors. In this walkthrough, we estimated the effects of being in one of the five online science courses. Dummy coding can help us analyze even further by accounting for multiple course sections or classes for each subject. But consider the challenge of interpreting the effect of being a student in a particular class, where each class and section becomes its own line of the model output. Interpreting the effects in comparison to the intercept can get complicated.

Multilevel models and the assumption of independent data points

Including a group in our model can help us meet the assumption of independent data points. Linear regression models assume that each data point is not correlated with another. This is what is meant by the "assumption of independence" or of "independently and identically distributed" (*i.i.d.*) residuals (Field, Miles, and Field 2012). A linear regression model that considers students in different sections (i.e., for an introductory life science class, different laboratory sections) as a single sample will assume that the outcome of each of those students is not correlated with the outcome of any other student in their section. This is a tough assumption when you consider that students who are in the same section may perform similarly when it comes to the outcome being measured (because of what the instructor of the section does, when the section happened to be scheduled, or the fact that students in a section helped one another study). Adding a section group to the model helps us meet the assumption of independent data points by considering the effect of being in a particular section. Generally speaking, analysts often have the goal of accounting for the fact that students share a class. This is very different from determining the effect of any one particular class on the outcome.

Regularization

It's helpful to introduce more vocabulary you're likely to see if you explore multi-level modeling more. So far we've learned that multilevel models help us meet the assumption of independent data points by considering groups in the model. Multi-level models do this by estimating the effect of being a student in each group, but with a key distinction from linear models: instead of determining how different the observations in a group are from those in the reference group, the multilevel model "regularizes" the difference based on how systematically different the groups are. You may also see the term "shrink" to describe this. The term "shrinkage" is occasionally used because the group-level estimates (e.g., for classes) obtained through multilevel modeling can never be larger than those from a linear regression model. As described earlier, when there are groups included in the model, a regression effectively estimates the effect for each group independent of all of the others.

Through regularization, groups that comprise individuals who are consistently higher or lower than individuals on average are not regularized very much. Their estimated difference may be close to the estimate from a multilevel model. Whereas groups with only a few individuals, or a lot of variability within individuals, would be regularized a lot. The way that a multilevel model does this "regularizing" is by considering the groups to be samples from a larger population of classes. By considering the effects of groups to be samples from a larger population, the model not only uses information particular to each group, but also information across all of the data.

Intra-class correlation coefficient

Multilevel models are very common in educational research because they help account for the way in which students take the same classes, or even go to the same school (see Raudenbush and Bryk 2002). Using multilevel models means that the assumption of independence can be addressed. Their use also means that individual coefficients for classes do not need to be included (or interpreted, thankfully!), though they are still included in and accounted for in the model.

So what's the most useful way to report the importance of groups in a model? The way that information about the groups is reported is usually in the form of the "intra-class correlation coefficient" (ICC), which explains the proportion of variation in the dependent variable that the groups explain. Smaller ICCs (such as ICCs with values of 0.05, representing 5% of the variation in the dependent variable) mean that the groups are not very important; larger ICCs, such as ICCs with values of 0.10 or larger (values as high as 0.50 are not uncommon!) suggest that groups are indeed important. When groups are important, not including them in the model may ignore the assumption of independence.

We wanted to include this as multilevel models *are* common. Consider how often in the data you collect students are grouped in classes, or classes are grouped in schools. Educational data is complex, and so it is not surprising that multilevel models may be encountered in educational data science analyses, reports, and articles.

Multilevel model analysis

Fortunately, for all of the complicated details, multilevel models are relatively easy to use in R. We'll need a new package for this next example. One of the most common for estimating these types of models is {lme4}. We use `lme4::lmer()` very similarly to the `lm()` function, but we pass it an additional argument for the *groups* we want to include in the model. This model is often referred to as a "varying intercepts" multilevel model. The difference between the groups is the effect of being a student in a class: the intercepts between the groups vary.

Now we can fit our multilevel model using the `lmer()` function:

```
m_course <-
    lmer(final_grade ~ TimeSpent_std + (1|course_id), data = dat)
```

You'll notice something here that we didn't see when we used `lm()`. We use a new term—`(1|course_id)`. We use this to model the group (in this case, courses) in the data. With `lmer()`, these group terms are in parentheses and to the right of the bar. That is what the `|course_id` part means—it is telling `lmer()` that courses are groups in the data that we want to include in the model. The `1` on the left side of the bar tells `lmer()` that we want varying intercepts for each group (1 is used to denote the intercept).

If you're familiar with Bayesian methods, you'll appreciate a connection here (Gelman and Hill 2006). Regularizing in a multilevel model takes data across all groups into account when generating estimates for each group. The data for all of the classes can be interpreted as a Bayesian *prior* for the group estimates.

There's more you can do with `lmer()`. For example, you can include different effects for each group in your model output, so each as its own slope. To explore techniques like this and more, we recommend the book by West, Welch, and Galecki (2014), which provides an excellent walkthrough on how to specify varying slopes using `lmer()`.

Results

Let's view the results using the `tab_model()` function from {sjPlot} again.

```
tab_model(m_course,
          title = "Table 13.4")
```

	Final Grade		
Predictors	Estimates	CI	p
(Intercept)	75.63	72.41–78.84	<0.001
TimeSpent_std	9.45	7.74–11.16	<0.001
Random Effects			
σ^2	385.33		
$\tau_{00\ course\_id}$	38.65		
ICC	0.09		
N_{course_id}	26		
Observations	573		
Marginal R^2 / Conditional R^2	0.170 / 0.246		

Table 13.4 Time Spent (Standardized) Regressed on Final Grade with Course ID as a Grouping Variable (Using a Multilevel Model)

For `lm()` models, `tab_model()` provides the output, including some fit statistics, coefficients and their standard errors and estimates. There are two things to note about `lmer()` output:

1. p-values are not automatically provided, due to debates in the wider field about how to calculate the degrees of freedom for coefficients[1]

2. In addition to the coefficients, there are also estimates for how much variability there is between the groups.

A common way to understand how much variability is at the group level is to calculate the *intra-class* correlation. This value is the proportion of the variability in the outcome (the y-variable) that is accounted for solely by the groups identified in the model. There is a useful function in the {performance} package for doing this.

You can install the {performance} package by typing this code in your console:

```
install.packages("performance")
```
After that, try this function:
```
icc(m_course)
## # Intraclass Correlation Coefficient
##
##          Adjusted ICC: 0.091
##     Conditional ICC: 0.076
```

This shows that 9.1% of the variability in the percentage of points students earned can be explained simply by knowing what class they are in can be explained simply by knowing what class they are in. The adjusted ICC is what is typically reported: This value is for the proportion of the variability in the dependent variable that is explained by the groups (courses). See the documentation for `icc()` for details on the interpretation of the conditional ICC.

Adding additional levels

Now let's add some additional levels. The data that we are using is all from one school, and so we cannot estimate a "two-level" model. Imagine, however, that instead of 26 classes, we had student data from 230 classes and that these classes were from 15 schools. We could estimate a two-level, varying intercepts (where there are now two groups with effects) model similar to the model we estimated above, but with another group added for the school. The model will automatically account for the way that the classes are nested within the schools (Bates et al. 2019).

We don't have a variable containing the name of different schools. If we did we could fit the model like this, where `school_id` is the variable containing different schools:
```
# this model would specify a group effect for both the course and
school
```

---

1 Run `?lme4::pvalues` to see a discussion of the issue and solutions. We have found {lmerTest} to be helpful for an easy solution, though some of the recommendations available through `?lme4::pvalues` may be preferable because the technique {lmerTest} implements has some known issues.

```
m_course_school <-
    lmer(final_grade ~ TimeSpent + (1|course_id) + (1|school_id),
data = dat)
```

Were we to estimate this model (and then use the `icc()` function), we would see two ICC values representing the proportion of the variation in the dependent variable explained by the course and the school. Note that as long as the courses are uniquely labelled, it is not necessary to explicitly nest the courses within schools.

The {lme4} package was designed for complex multilevel models, so you can add even more levels, even those with not nested but crossed random effects. For more on advanced multilevel techniques like these see West, Welch, and Galecki (2014).

Conclusion

In this walkthrough, the groups in our multilevel model are classes. But multilevel models can be used for other cases where data is associated with a common group. For example, if students respond to repeated measures (such as quizzes) over time, then the multiple quiz responses for each student are "grouped" within students. In such a case, we'd specify students as the "grouping factor" instead of courses. Moreover, multilevel models can include multiple groups even if the groups are of very different kinds (i.e., if students from multiple classes responded to multiple quizzes).

We note that the groups in multilevel models do not need to be nested. They can also be "crossed", as may be the case for data from teachers in different schools who attended different teacher preparation programs. Not every teacher in a school necessarily attended the same teacher preparation program, and graduates from every teacher preparation program are highly unlikely to all teach in the same school!

Finally, as noted earlier, multilevel models have similarities to the Bayesian methods which are becoming more common among some R users—and educational data scientists. There are also references to recommended books on Bayesian methods in the additional resources chapter.

There is much more that can be done with multilevel models; we have more recommendations in the "Additional Resources" chapter.

Chapter 14

Walkthrough 8

Predicting students' final grades using machine learning methods with online course data

Topics emphasized

- Transforming data
- Modeling data

Functions introduced

- `caret::nearZeroVar()`
- `caret::createDataPartition()`
- `caret::train()`
- `caret::trainControl()`
- `caret::varImp()`

Vocabulary

- listwise deletion
- machine learning
- parameters
- random forest
- research question
- resampling
- Root Mean Square Error (RMSE)

- rsquared

- training data

- test data

- tuning parameter

- variable importance

Chapter overview

In this chapter, we use the same dataset used in Walkthrough 1 in Chapter 7 and Walkthrough 7 in Chapter 13 but pursue a new aim. We focus on *predicting* an outcome, final grade, more than *explaining* how variables relate to an outcome, such as how the amount of time students spend on the course relates to their final grade. We illustrate a common but powerful machine learning method, random forest modeling. We'll explore its use in-depth rather than providing a more general overview of other machine learning methods. Though we focus on the use of random forests, many of the ideas explored in this chapter will likely extend and prove useful for other machine learning methods. Our goal is for you to finish this final walkthrough with the confidence to explore using machine learning to answer a question or to solve a problem of your own with respect to teaching, learning, and educational systems.

Background

One area of interest for data scientists in education is the delivery of online instruction, which is becoming more prevalent: in 2007, over 3.9 million U.S. students were enrolled in one or more online courses (Allen and Seaman 2008). With the growth of online learning comes an abundance of new educational tools to facilitate that learning. Online learning platforms are used to submit assignments and quizzes in courses in which students and instructor meet face-to-face, but these interfaces are also used in fully online courses to deliver instruction and assessment.

In a face-to-face classroom, an educator might count on behavioral cues to help them effectively deliver instruction. Online, educators do not readily have access to the behavioral cues essential for effective face-to-face instruction. For example, in a face-to-face classroom, cues such as a student missing class repeatedly or many students seeming distracted during a lecture can trigger a shift in the delivery of instruction. Many educators find themselves looking for ways to understand and support students online in the same way that face-to-face instructors would. Educational technology affords unique opportunities to support student success online because it provides new methods of collecting and storing data.

Online learning management systems often automatically track several types of student interactions with the system and feed that data back to the course instructor. For example, an instructor might be able to quickly see how many students logged into their course on a certain day, or they might see how long students engaged with a posted video before pausing it or logging out. The collection of this data is met with mixed reactions from educators. Some are concerned that data collection in this manner is intrusive, but others see a new opportunity to support students in online contexts in new ways. As long as data is collected and utilized responsibly, data collection can support student success.

One meaningful perspective from which to consider students' engagement with online courses is related to their motivation to achieve. It is important to consider how and why students are engaging with the course. Considering the psychological mechanisms behind achievement is valuable because they may help identify meaningful points of intervention. Educators, researchers, and administrators in both online and face-to-face courses can analyze and use the intersection between behavioral measures and students' motivational and emotional experiences in courses.

In this walkthrough, we examine the educational experiences of students attending online science courses at a virtual middle school in order to characterize their motivation to achieve and their tangible engagement with the course. We use a dataset that includes self-reported motivation as well as behavioral trace data collected from a learning management system (LMS) to identify predictors of final course grade. Our work examines educational success in terms of student interactions with an online science course.

We explore the following four questions:

1. Is motivation more predictive of course grades as compared to other online indicators of engagement?

2. Which types of motivation are most predictive of achievement?

3. Which types of trace measures are most predictive of achievement?

4. How does a random forest compare to a simple linear model (regression)?

Data sources

This dataset comes from 499 students who were enrolled in online middle school science courses in 2015–2016. The data was originally collected for use as a part of a research study, though the findings have not been published yet.

The setting of this study was a public provider of individual online courses in a Midwestern state. In particular, the context was two semesters (Fall and Spring) of offerings of five online science courses (Anatomy & Physiology, Forensic Science, Oceanography, Physics, and Biology), with a total of 36 classes.

Specific information in the dataset included:

1. A self-report survey assessing three aspects of students' motivation

2. Log-trace data, such as data output from the learning management system

3. Discussion board data

4. Academic achievement data

For discussion board responses, we were interested in calculating the number of posts per student and understanding the emotional tone of the discussion board posts. We used the Linguistic Inquiry and Word Count (LIWC; Pennebaker et al. 2015) tool to calculate the number of posts per student and to categorize the emotional tone (positive or negative) and topics of those posts. That linguistic categorization was conducted after the data was gathered from the discussion posts but is not replicated here to protect the privacy of the students' posts. Instead, we present the already-categorized discussion board data, in its ready-to-use format. In the dataset used in this walkthrough, we will see pre-created variables for the mean levels of students' cognitive processing, positive emotions, negative emotions, and social-related discourse.

At the beginning of the semester, students were asked to complete the pre-course survey about their perceived competence, utility value, and interest. At the end of the semester, the time students spent on the course, their final course grades, and the contents of the discussion forums were collected.

Methods

Defining a research question

When you begin a new project, there are often many approaches to analyzing data and answering questions you might have about it. Some projects have a clearly defined scope and question to answer. This type of project is characterized by (1) a defined number of variables (data inputs) and (2) specific directional hypotheses. For example, if we are studying the effect of drinking coffee after dinner on ability to quickly fall asleep, we might have a very specific directional hypothesis: we expect that drinking coffee after dinner would decrease the ability to fall asleep quickly. In this case, we might collect data by having some people drink coffee and having other people drink nothing or an herbal tea before bed. We could monitor how quickly people from each group fall asleep. Since we collected data from two clearly defined groups, we can then do a statistical analysis that compares the amount of time it takes to fall asleep for each group. One option would be a test called a t-test, which we could use to see if there is a significant difference in the average amount of minutes to fall asleep for the group. This approach works very well in controlled experimental situations, especially when we can change only one thing at a time (in our coffee example, the only thing we changed was the coffee-drinking behavior of our participants—all other life conditions were held equal for both groups). Rarely are educational data projects as clear-cut and simple.

For this walkthrough, we have many sources of data—survey data, learning management system data, discussion forum data, and academic achievement data as measured by final course grades. Luckily, having too much data is what we call a "good problem". In our coffee example above, we had one really specific idea that we wanted to investigate—does coffee affect time taken to fall asleep? In this walkthrough we have many ideas we are curious to explore: the relationships among motivation, engagement in the course (discussion boards, time spent online in the course site), and academic achievement. If we wanted to tackle a simpler problem, we could choose just one of these relationships. For example, we could measure whether students with high motivation earn higher grades than students with low motivation. However, we are being a bit more ambitious than that here—we are interested in understanding the complex relationships among the different types of motivation. Rather than simply exploring whether A affects B, we are interested in the nuances. We suspect that many factors affect B, and we would like to see which of those factors has most relative importance. To explore this idea, we will use a machine learning approach.

Predictive analytics and machine learning

A buzzword in education software spheres these days is "predictive analytics". Administrators and educators alike are interested in applying the methods long utilized by marketers and other business professionals to try to determine what a person will want, need, or do next. "Predictive analytics" is a blanket term that can be used to describe any statistical approach that yields a prediction. We could ask a predictive model: "What is the likelihood that my cat will sit on my keyboard today?" and, given enough past information about your cat's computer-sitting behavior, the model could give you a probability of that computer-sitting happening today. Under the hood, some predictive models are not very complex. If we have an outcome with two possibilities, a logistic regression model could be fit to the data in order to help us answer the cat-keyboard question. In this chapter, we'll compare a machine learning model to another type of regression: multiple regression. We want to make sure to fit the simplest model as possible to our data. After all, the effectiveness in predicting the outcome is really the most important thing, not the fanciness of the model.

Data collection is an essential first step in any type of machine learning or predictive analytics. It is important to note here that machine learning only works effectively when (1) a person selects variables to include in the model that are anticipated to be related to the outcome and (2) a person correctly interprets the model's findings. There is an adage that goes, "garbage in, garbage out". This holds true here. If we do not feel confident that the data we collected are accurate, we will not be able to be confident in our conclusions no matter what model we build. To collect good data, we must first clarify what it is that we want to know (i.e., what question are we really asking?) and what information we would need in order to effectively answer that question. Sometimes, people approach analysis from the opposite direction—they might look at the data they have and ask what questions could be answered based on that data. That approach is okay, as long as you are willing to acknowledge that sometimes the pre-existing dataset may *not* contain all the information you need, and you might need to go out and find additional information to add to your dataset to truly answer your question.

When people talk about "machine learning", you might get the image in your head of a desktop computer learning how to spell. You might picture your favorite social media site showing you advertisements that are just a little too accurate. At its core, machine learning is the process of "showing" your statistical model only some of the data at once and training the model to predict accurately on that training dataset (this is the "learning" part of machine learning). Then, the model as developed on the training data is shown new data—data you had all along, but hid from your computer initially—and you see how well the model that you developed on the training data performs on this new testing data. Eventually, you might use the model on entirely new data.

Random forest

For our analyses, we use random forest modeling (Breiman 2001). Random forest is an extension of decision tree modeling, whereby a collection of decision trees are simultaneously "grown" and are evaluated based on out-of-sample predictive accuracy (Breiman 2001). Random forest is random in two main ways: first, each tree is only allowed to "see" and split on a limited number of predictors instead of all the predictors available; second, a random subsample of the data is used to grow each individual tree, such that no individual case is weighted too heavily in the final prediction.

One thing about random forest that makes it quite different from other types of analysis we might do is that here, we are giving the computer a large amount of information and asking it to find connections that might not be immediately visible to the naked human eye. This is great for a couple of reasons. First, while humans are immensely creative and clever, we are not immune to biases. If we are exploring a dataset, we usually come in with some predetermined notions about what we think is true, and we might (consciously or unconsciously) seek evidence that supports the hypothesis we privately hold. By setting the computer loose on some data, we can learn that there are connections between areas that we did not expect. We must also be ready for our hypotheses to not be supported! Random forest is particularly well-suited to the research questions explored here because we do not have specific directional hypotheses. Machine learning researchers talk about this as "exploring the parameter space"—we want to see what connections exist, and we acknowledge that we might not be able to accurately predict all the possible connections. Indeed, we expect—and hope—that we will find surprising connections.

Whereas some machine learning approaches (e.g., boosted trees) use an iterative model-building approach, random forest estimates all the decision trees at once. This way, each tree is independent of every other tree. The random forest algorithm provides a regression approach that is distinct from other modeling approaches. The final random forest model aggregates the findings across all the separate trees in the forest in order to offer a collection of "most important" variables as well as a percent variance explained for the final model.

Five hundred trees are grown as part of our random forest. We partitioned the data before conducting the main analysis so that neither the training nor the testing dataset would be disproportionately representative of high-achieving or low-achieving students. The training dataset consisted of 80% of the original data ($n = 400$ cases), whereas the testing dataset consisted of 20% of the original data ($n = 99$ cases). We built our random forest model on the training dataset, and then evaluated the model on the testing dataset. Three variables were tried at each node.

Note that the random forest algorithm does not accept cases with missing data, so we delete cases listwise (that is, an entire row is deleted if any single value is missing). This decision eliminated 60 cases from our original dataset to bring us to our final sample size of 464 unique students. If you have a very small dataset with a lot of missing data, the random forest approach may not be well suited for your goals—you might consider a linear regression instead.

A random forest is well suited to the research questions that we had here because it allows for nonlinear modeling. We hypothesized complex relationships between students' motivation, their engagement with the online courses, and their achievement. For this reason, a traditional regressive or structural equation model would have been insufficient to model the parameter space we were interested in modeling. Our random forest model had one outcome and 11 predictors.

One term you will hear used in machine learning is "tuning parameter". People often think of tuning parameters as knobs or dials on a radio: they are features of the model that can be adjusted to get the clearest signal. A common tuning parameter for machine learning models is the number of variables considered at each split (Kuhn and others 2008); we considered three variables at each split for this analysis.

The outcome was the final course grade that the student earned. The predictor variables included motivation variables (interest value, utility value, and science perceived competence) and trace variables (the amount of time spent in the course, the course name, the number of discussion board posts over the course of the semester, the mean level of cognitive processing evident in discussion board posts, the positive emotions evident in discussion board posts, the negative emotions evident in discussion board posts, and the social-related discourse evident in their discussion board posts). We used this random forest model to address all three of our research questions.

To interpret our findings, we will consider three main factors: (1) predictive accuracy of the random forest model, (2) variable importance, and (3) variance explained by the final random forest model. In this walkthrough, we will use the R package {caret} (Kuhn 2020) to carry out the analysis. We also use the {tidylog} package (Elbers 2020) to help us to understand how the data processing steps we take have the desired effect. This is a handy package that tells us in words what our previously executed code changed in our dataset.

Load packages

As always, if you have not installed any of these packages before, do so first using the `install.packages()` function. For a description of packages and their installation, review the "Packages" section of the "Foundational Skills" chapter.

```r
# load the packages
library(tidyverse)
library(caret)
library(ranger)
library(e1071)
library(tidylog)
library(dataedu)
```

First, we will load the data. Our data is stored in the {dataedu} package that is part of this book. Within that package, the data is stored as an `.rda` file. We note that this data is augmented to have some other—and additional—variables that the `sci_mo_processed` data used in Chapter 7 does not.

Import and view data

```
# Loading the data from the .rda file and storing it as an object
named 'data'
df <- dataedu::sci_mo_with_text
```

It's a good practice to take a look at the data and make sure it looks the way you expect it to look. R is pretty smart, but sometimes we run into issues like column headers being read as data points. By using the `glimpse()` function from the {dplyr} package, we can quickly skim our data and see whether we have all the right variables and values. Remember that the {dplyr} package loads automatically when we load the {tidyverse} library, so there is no need to call the {dplyr} package separately. Run the code below to glimpse the data, but note we won't show the output here (there are a lot of variables!).

```
glimpse(df)
```

Scanning the data we glimpsed, we see that we have 606 observations and 74 variables. Many of these variables—everything below *WC* except the variable *n*—are related to the text content of the discussion board posts. Our analysis here is not focused on the specifics of the discussion board posts, so we will select just a few variables from the LIWC analysis. If you're interested in learning more about analyzing text, the text analysis walkthrough in Chapter 11 would be a good place to start.

As is the case with many datasets you'll work with in education contexts, there is lots of great information in this dataset—but we won't need all of it. Even if your dataset has many variables, for most analyses you will find that you are only interested in some of them. There are statistical reasons not to include 20 or more variables in a data analysis as well. At a certain point, adding more variables will *appear* to make your analysis more accurate, but will in fact obscure the truth from you. It's generally a good practice to select a few variables you are interested in and go from there. As we discussed above, the way to do this is to start with the research questions you are trying to answer.

Process data

Since we are interested in data from one specific semester, we'll need to narrow down the data to make sure that we only include data points relevant to that semester. For each step, we save over the previous version of the `df` object so that our working environment doesn't get cluttered with each new version of the dataset. Keep in mind that the original data will stay intact, and that any changes we make to it within R will not overwrite that original data (unless we tell R to specifically save out a new file with exactly the same name as the original file). Changes we make within our working environment are all totally reversible.

Below, we will *select* only the variables we are interested in: motivation, time spent in the course, grade in the course, subject, enrollment information, positive and negative emotions, cognitive processing, and the number of discussion board posts. After this step, we see that 60 variables have been removed from the dataset.

```r
# selecting only the variables we are interested in:
df <-
    df %>%
    select(
        int,
        uv,
        pc,
        time_spent,
        final_grade,
        subject,
        enrollment_reason,
        semester,
        enrollment_status,
        cogproc,
        social,
        posemo,
        negemo,
        n
    )
## select: dropped 60 variables (student_id, course_id, total_
points_possible, total_points_earned, percentage_earned, …)
```

Notice how because we loaded the {tidylog} package, details about how 60 variables were dropped (because they weren't selected) was printed when the above code was run.

Analysis

Use of {caret}

Here, we remove observations with missing data (per our note above about random forests requiring complete cases).

```r
# Checking how many rows are in our dataset
# We see that we have 606 rows
nrow(df)
## [1] 606
# calling the na.omit function to eliminate ANY rows that have ANY
missing data
df <- na.omit(df)
# checking whether our na.omit call worked as expected
# after running the code above, we see that we now have 464 rows
nrow(df)
## [1] 464
```

Machine learning methods often involve using a large number of variables. Some of these variables will not be suitable to use: they may be highly correlated with other variables or may have very little—or no—variability. For the dataset used in this study, one variable has the same (character string) value for all of the observations. We can detect this variable and any others using the following function:

```
# run the nearZeroVar function to determine
# if there are variables with NO variability
nearZeroVar(df, saveMetrics = TRUE)
##                     freqRatio percentUnique zeroVar    nzv
## int                  1.314815     9.0517241   FALSE  FALSE
## uv                   1.533333     6.4655172   FALSE  FALSE
## pc                   1.488372     3.8793103   FALSE  FALSE
## time_spent           1.000000   100.0000000   FALSE  FALSE
## final_grade          1.333333    93.1034483   FALSE  FALSE
## subject              1.648649     1.0775862   FALSE  FALSE
## enrollment_reason    3.154762     1.0775862   FALSE  FALSE
## semester             1.226601     0.6465517   FALSE  FALSE
## enrollment_status    0.000000     0.2155172    TRUE   TRUE
## cogproc              1.000000    96.9827586   FALSE  FALSE
## social               1.500000    96.1206897   FALSE  FALSE
## posemo               1.000000    96.7672414   FALSE  FALSE
## negemo              13.000000    90.7327586   FALSE  FALSE
## n                    1.333333    10.1293103   FALSE  FALSE
```

After conducting our zero variance check, we want to scan the `zeroVar` column to see if any of our variables failed this check. If we see any TRUE values for `zeroVar`, that means we should look more closely at that variable.

In the nearZeroVar() function we just ran, we see a result in the ZeroVar column of TRUE for the `enrollment_status` variable. If we look at `enrollment_status`, we will see that it is "Approved/Enrolled" for *all* of the students. Using variables with no variability in certain models may cause problems, and so we remove them first.

```
# taking the dataset and re-saving it as the same dataset,
# but without the enrollment status variable
df <-
    df %>%
    select(-enrollment_status)
## select: dropped one variable (enrollment_status)
```

As we have discussed elsewhere in the book, the data will often come to you in a format that is not ready for immediate analysis. You may wish to pre-process the variables, such as by centering or scaling them. For our current dataset, we can work on pre-processing with code below. We want to make sure our text data is in a format that we can then evaluate. To facilitate that, we change character string variables into factors. Factors store data as categorical variables, each with its own levels. Because categorical variables are used in statistical models differently than continuous variables, storing data as factors ensures that the modeling functions will treat them correctly.

```
# converting the text (character) variables in our dataset into factors
df <-
    df %>%
    mutate_if(is.character, as.factor)
## mutate_if: converted 'subject' from character to factor (0 new NA)
##             converted 'enrollment_reason' from character to factor
(0 new NA)
##             converted 'semester' from character to factor (0 new NA)
```

Now we will prepare the **train** and **test** datasets, using the {caret} function for creating data partitions. Here, the p argument specifies what proportion of the data we want to be in the **training** partition. Note that this function splits the data based upon the outcome, so that the training and test datasets will both have comparable values for the outcome. This means that since our outcome is final grade, we are making sure that we don't have either a training or testing dataset that has too many good grades *or* too many bad grades. Note the times = 1 argument. This parameter can be used to create *multiple* train and test sets, something we will describe in more detail later. Before we create our training and testing datasets, we want to "set the seed" (introduced in Chapter 11). Setting the seed ensures that if we run this same code again, we will get the same results in terms of the data partition. The seed can be any number that you like—some people choose their birthday or another meaningful number. The only constraint is that when you open the same code file again to run in the future, you do not change the number you selected for your seed. This enables your code to be reproducible. If anyone runs the same code file on any computer, anywhere, they will get the same result.

Now try running the code chunk below. Be sure to read the messages that R gives you to see what is happening with each step! One important note here: the numbers will differ slightly if you are running this on a Windows machine.

```
# First, we set a seed to ensure the reproducibility of our data
partition.
set.seed(2020)
# we create a new object called trainIndex that will take 80 percent
of the data
trainIndex <- createDataPartition(df$final_grade,
                                  p = .8,
                                  list = FALSE,
                                  times = 1)
# We add a new variable to our dataset, temporarily:
# this will let us select our rows according to their row number
# we populate the rows with the numbers 1:464, in order
df <-
    df %>%
    mutate(temp_id = 1:464)
## mutate: new variable 'temp_id' with 464 unique values and 0% NA
# we filter our dataset so that we get only the
# rows indicated by our "trainIndex" vector
```

```
df_train <-
    df %>%
    filter(temp_id %in% trainIndex)
## filter: removed 92 rows (20%), 372 rows remaining
# we filter our dataset in a different way so that we get only the
rows
# NOT in our "trainIndex" vector
# adding the ! before the temp_id variable achieves the opposite of
# what we did in the line of code above
df_test <-
    df %>%
    filter(!temp_id %in% trainIndex)
## filter: removed 372 rows (80%), 92 rows remaining
# We delete the temp_id variable from (1) the original data,
# (2) the portion of the original data we marked as training, and
# (3) the portion of the original data we marked as testing,
# as we no longer need that variable
df <-
    df %>%
    select(-temp_id)
## select: dropped one variable (temp_id)
df_train <-
    df_train %>%
    select(-temp_id)
## select: dropped one variable (temp_id)
df_test <-
    df_test %>%
    select(-temp_id)
## select: dropped one variable (temp_id)
```

Finally, we will estimate the models. We will use the train function, passing *all* of the variables in the data frame (except for the outcome, or dependent variable, final_grade) as predictors.

The predictor variables include three indicators of motivation: interest in the course (int), perceived utility value of the course (uv), and perceived competence for the subject matter (pc). There are a few predictor variables that help differentiate between the different courses in the dataset: subject matter of the course (subject), reason the student enrolled in the course (enrollment_reason), and semester in which the course took place (semester). We have a predictor variable that indicates the amount of time each student spent engaging with the online learning platform of the course (time_spent).

We also have a number of variables associated with the discussion board posts from the course. Specifically, the variables include the average level of cognitive processing in the discussion board posts (cogproc), the average level of social (rather than academic) content in the discussion board posts (social), the positive and negative emotions evident in the discussion board posts (posemo and negemo), and finally, the number of discussion board posts in total (n). We are using all those variables discussed in this paragraph to predict the outcome of the final grade in the course (`final_grade`).

Note that you can read more about the specific random forest implementation chosen in the {caret} bookdown page (http://topepo.github.io/caret/train-models-by-tag.html#random-forest). To specify that we want to predict the outcome using every variable except the outcome itself, we use the formulation `out-come ~ .`. R interprets this code as: predict the outcome using all the variables except outcome itself. The outcome always comes before the ~, and the . that we see after the ~ means that we want to use all the rest of the variables. An alternative specification of this model would be to write `outcome ~ predictor1, predictor2`. Anything that follows the ~ and precedes the comma is treated as predictors of the outcome.

We set the seed again to ensure that our analysis is reproducible. This step of setting the seed is especially important due to the "random" elements of random forest because it's likely that the findings would change (just slightly) if the seed were not set. As we get into random forest modeling, you might notice that the code takes a bit longer to run. This is normal—just think of the number of decision trees that are "growing"!

```
# setting a seed for reproducibility
set.seed(2020)
# we run the model here
rf_fit <- train(final_grade ~ .,
                data = df_train,
                method = "ranger")
# here, we get a summary of the model we just built
rf_fit
## Random Forest
##
## 372 samples
##  12 predictor
##
## No pre-processing
## Resampling: Bootstrapped (25 reps)
## Summary of sample sizes: 372, 372, 372, 372, 372, 372, ...
## Resampling results across tuning parameters:
##
##   mtry  splitrule   RMSE      Rsquared   MAE
##    2    variance    15.26965  0.5646105  11.182943
##    2    extratrees  16.99412  0.5228177  12.064817
##   10    variance    13.96625  0.5926815  10.144724
##   10    extratrees  13.87205  0.6205291  10.068379
##   19    variance    14.05020  0.5886314  10.023326
##   19    extratrees  13.41310  0.6319288   9.766645
##
## Tuning parameter 'min.node.size' was held constant at a value of 5
## RMSE was used to select the optimal model using the smallest value.
```

```
## The final values used for the model were mtry = 19, splitrule
= extratrees
##   and min.node.size = 5.
```

We have some results! First, we see that we have 372 samples, or 372 observations, the number in the train dataset. No pre-processing steps were specified
in the model fitting, but note that the output of `preProcess` can be passed to
`train()` to center, scale, and transform the data in many other ways. Next, we
used a resampling technique. This resampling is not for validating the model
but is rather for selecting the tuning parameters—the options that need to be
specified as a part of the modeling. These parameters can be manually provided,
or can be estimated via strategies such as the bootstrap resample or *k*-folds cross
validation.

As we interpret these findings, we are looking to minimize the Root Mean
Square Error (RMSE) and maximize the variance explained (Rsquared).

It appears that the model with the value of the `mtry` tuning parameter equal
to 19 seemed to explain the data best, the `splitrule` being "extratrees", and `min.`
`node.size` held constant at a value of 5. We know this model fits best because the
RMSE is the lowest of the options (13.41) and the Rsquared is the highest of the
options (0.63).

The value of resampling here is that it allows for higher accuracy of the model
(James et al. 2013). Without resampling (bootstrapping or cross-validation), the
variance would be higher and the predictive accuracy of the model would be lower.

Let's see if we end up with slightly different values if we change the resampling
technique to cross-validation, instead of bootstrap resampling. We set a seed again
here, for reproducibility.

```
set.seed(2020)
train_control <-
    trainControl(method = "repeatedcv",
                 number = 10,
                 repeats = 10)
rf_fit1 <-
    train(final_grade ~ .,
          data = df_train,
          method = "ranger",
          trControl = train_control)
rf_fit1
## Random Forest
##
## 372 samples
##   12 predictor
##
## No pre-processing
## Resampling: Cross-Validated (10 fold, repeated 10 times)
## Summary of sample sizes: 335, 334, 334, 336, 334, 334, ...
## Resampling results across tuning parameters:
```

```
##
##    mtry    splitrule    RMSE        Rsquared     MAE
##     2      variance     14.64664    0.5896743    10.965898
##     2      extratrees   16.24513    0.5854833    11.787050
##     10     variance     13.29633    0.6181503    9.829458
##     10     extratrees   13.00986    0.6599769    9.655362
##     19     variance     13.25465    0.6167849    9.683722
##     19     extratrees   12.59520    0.6635394    9.363926
##
## Tuning parameter 'min.node.size' was held constant at a value of 5
## RMSE was used to select the optimal model using the smallest value.
## The final values used for the model were mtry = 19, splitrule
= extratrees
##   and min.node.size = 5.
```

Tuning the random forest model

When we look at this output, we are looking to see which values of the various tuning parameters were selected. We see at the bottom of the output above that the value of `mtry` was 19, the split rule was "extratrees", and the minimum node size is 5. We let this model explore which value of `mtry` was best and to explore whether extra trees or variance was a better split rule, but we forced all iterations of the model to a minimum node size of five (so that minimum node size value in the output shouldn't be a surprise to us). When we look at the bottom row of the output, it shows the final values selected for the model. We see also that this row has the lowest RMSE and highest Rsquared value, which means it has the lowest error and highest predictive power.

We won't dive into the specifics of the statistics behind these decisions right now, but next we will try adjusting a few different parts of the model to see whether our performance improves. For a detailed statistical explanation of random forest modeling, including more about `mtry` and tuning a model, please see Chapter 8 in the book "An Introduction to Statistical Learning with Applications in R" (James et al. 2013).

What would happen if we do not fix `min.node.size` to five? We're going to let `min.node.size` change and let `mtry` change as well.

Let's create our own grid of values to test for `mtry` and `min.node.size`. We'll stick with the default bootstrap resampling method to choose the best model. We will randomly choose some values to use for `mtry`, including the three that were used previously (2, 10, and 19). Let's try 2, 3, 7, 10, and 19.

```
# setting a seed for reproducibility
set.seed(2020)
# Create a grid of different values of mtry, different splitrules,
and different minimum node sizes to test
tune_grid <-
    expand.grid(
        mtry = c(2, 3, 7, 10, 19),
```

```
        splitrule = c("variance", "extratrees"),
        min.node.size = c(1, 5, 10, 15, 20)
    )
# Fit a new model, using the tuning grid we created above
rf_fit2 <-
    train(final_grade ~ .,
          data = df_train,
          method = "ranger",
          tuneGrid = tune_grid)
rf_fit2
## Random Forest
##
## 372 samples
##  12 predictor
##
## No pre-processing
## Resampling: Bootstrapped (25 reps)
## Summary of sample sizes: 372, 372, 372, 372, 372, 372, ...
## Resampling results across tuning parameters:
##
```

##	mtry	splitrule	min.node.size	RMSE	Rsquared	MAE
##	2	variance	1	15.21257	0.5640999	11.115597
##	2	variance	5	15.26810	0.5638393	11.181907
##	2	variance	10	15.45130	0.5541338	11.348051
##	2	variance	15	15.56036	0.5497028	11.445290
##	2	variance	20	15.72194	0.5426742	11.573521
##	2	extratrees	1	16.92739	0.5217704	11.959970
##	2	extratrees	5	17.02815	0.5177077	12.076823
##	2	extratrees	10	17.28776	0.5060890	12.265775
##	2	extratrees	15	17.44764	0.5016608	12.390719
##	2	extratrees	20	17.67751	0.4891901	12.556140
##	3	variance	1	14.65669	0.5738730	10.730009
##	3	variance	5	14.71055	0.5718560	10.796714
##	3	variance	10	14.84534	0.5667383	10.938649
##	3	variance	15	15.01766	0.5573860	11.077530
##	3	variance	20	15.17448	0.5497694	11.222043
##	3	extratrees	1	15.73859	0.5602534	11.197195
##	3	extratrees	5	15.87463	0.5561978	11.312669
##	3	extratrees	10	16.18226	0.5450388	11.578177
##	3	extratrees	15	16.41014	0.5386357	11.749329
##	3	extratrees	20	16.64769	0.5297996	11.902915
##	7	variance	1	14.06354	0.5891298	10.265146
##	7	variance	5	14.05089	0.5901984	10.256999
##	7	variance	10	14.17334	0.5839552	10.372204
##	7	variance	15	14.24620	0.5806848	10.456265
##	7	variance	20	14.36375	0.5755600	10.560296
##	7	extratrees	1	14.27671	0.6067836	10.306448

```
##     7    extratrees    5         14.37512   0.6034048   10.371551
##     7    extratrees   10         14.54903   0.6000708   10.539154
##     7    extratrees   15         14.73613   0.5956554   10.679249
##     7    extratrees   20         14.99862   0.5858391   10.874959
##    10    variance      1         13.94020   0.5933172   10.118910
##    10    variance      5         13.95884   0.5925954   10.130894
##    10    variance     10         13.99612   0.5912951   10.177994
##    10    variance     15         14.06937   0.5871199   10.264013
##    10    variance     20         14.12505   0.5849011   10.326244
##    10    extratrees    1         13.81434   0.6225194   10.002114
##    10    extratrees    5         13.87943   0.6192667   10.082908
##    10    extratrees   10         14.07823   0.6131080   10.220691
##    10    extratrees   15         14.29597   0.6060346   10.383784
##    10    extratrees   20         14.42182   0.6028746   10.489607
##    19    variance      1         14.01330   0.5904613    9.988716
##    19    variance      5         14.04655   0.5882967   10.010647
##    19    variance     10         14.05683   0.5881496   10.029118
##    19    variance     15         14.07198   0.5876164   10.069665
##    19    variance     20         14.09864   0.5865583   10.079718
##    19    extratrees    1         13.35989   0.6335635    9.729254
##    19    extratrees    5         13.39873   0.6325685    9.746579
##    19    extratrees   10         13.51532   0.6285967    9.834457
##    19    extratrees   15         13.59740   0.6260692    9.903994
##    19    extratrees   20         13.74330   0.6213098   10.014353
##
## RMSE was used to select the optimal model using the smallest
value.
## The final values used for the model were mtry = 19, splitrule
= extratrees
##   and min.node.size = 1.
```

The model with the same values as identified before for mtry (19) and splitrule (extratrees), but with min.node.size equal to 1 (not 5, as before) seems to fit best. We know this model fits best because the RMSE is lowest (13.36) and the variance explained is highest (0.63) for this model, though the improvement seems to be fairly small relative to the difference the other tuning parameters seem to make.

While the output above gives us a good summary of the model, we might want to look more closely at what we found with our rf_fit2 model. The code below is a way for us to zoom in and look specifically at the *final* random forest model generated by our rf_fit2.

In the code chunk below, you'll notice we are selecting the finalModel output using a $ operator rather than the familiar select(). We cannot use {dplyr} and the tidyverse here because of the structure of the rf_fit2 object—we have stored a random forest model as a model, so it's not a normal data frame. Therefore, we extract with a $. We want to select only the final model used and not worry about the prior iterations of the model.

```
#Here, we select the "finalModel" output from the rf_fit2 model
rf_fit2$finalModel
## Ranger result
##
## Call:
##   ranger::ranger(dependent.variable.name = ".outcome", data = x,
mtry = min(param$mtry, ncol(x)), min.node.size = param$min.node.
size,   splitrule = as.character(param$splitrule), write.forest =
TRUE,   probability = classProbs, ...)
##
## Type:                              Regression
## Number of trees:                   500
## Sample size:                       372
## Number of independent variables:   19
## Mtry:                              19
## Target node size:                  1
## Variable importance mode:          none
## Splitrule:                         extratrees
## Number of random splits:           1
## OOB prediction error (MSE):        159.8603
## R squared (OOB):                   0.6599865
```

In looking at this output, we see the same parameters we noted above: *Mtry* is 19, the *node size* is 1, and the split rule is extra trees. We can also note the *OOB prediction error (MSE)*, of 159.86, and the proportion of the variance explained, or R squared, of 0.66. As before, we want the error to be low and the variance explained to be high.

Now that we understand how to develop a basic machine learning model and how to use different tuning parameters (such as node size and the splitting rule), we can explore some other related themes. We might wonder about how we could examine the predictive accuracy of the random forest model we just developed.

Examining predictive accuracy on the test dataset

What if we use the test dataset: data not used to train the model? Below, we'll create a new object that uses the rf_fit2 model we developed above. We will put our testing data through the model, and assign the predicted values to a column called pred. At the same, time, we'll make a column called obs that includes the real final grades that students earned. Later, we'll compare these predicted and observed values to see how well our model did.

```
# setting a seed for reproducibility
set.seed(2020)

# Create a new object for the testing data including predicted values
df_test_augmented <-
```

```
    df_test %>%
    mutate(pred = predict(rf_fit2, df_test),
           obs = final_grade)
## mutate: new variable 'pred' with 92 unique values and 0% NA
##         new variable 'obs' with 90 unique values and 0% NA
# Transform this new object into a data frame
defaultSummary(as.data.frame(df_test_augmented))
##      RMSE     Rsquared         MAE
## 12.9821088   0.5517269    9.9735400
```

We can compare this to the values above to see how our model performs when given data that was not used to train the model. Comparing the RMSE values, we see that the RMSE is about the same when we use the model on the test data as it was on the training data. We get a value of 12.98 on the test data here, and it was 13.36 on the training data. The Rsquared value is 0.55 here, as compared to the 0.63 we got when we passed the training data through `rf_fit2` earlier.

While we might have expected that the model performance would be worse for the testing data as compared to the training data, we actually are seeing marginal improvements here: the model does better with the test data than with the training data. These results suggest to us that the model is able to handle new data, as we get comparable—in fact, improved—results when running the model on data it has never "seen" before (the testing data). This is good news!

Results

Variable importance

One helpful characteristic of random forest models is that we can learn about which variables contributed most strongly to the predictions in our model, across all the trees in our forest.

We can examine two different variable importance measures using the **ranger** method in {caret}.

Note that importance values are not calculated automatically, but that "impurity" or "permutation" can be passed to the `importance` argument in `train()`. See more on this website (https://alexisperrier.com/datascience/2015/08/27/feature-importance-random-forests-gini-accuracy.html).

We'll re-run the `rf_fit2` model with the same specifications as before, but this time we will add an argument to call the variable importance metric.

```
# setting a seed for reproducibility
set.seed(2020)
# Specify the same model as earlier in the chapter (rf_fit2) with
the addition of the variable importance metric
rf_fit2_imp <-
    train(
        final_grade ~ .,
```

```
        data = df_train,
        method = "ranger",
        tuneGrid = tune_grid,
        importance = "permutation"
    )
# Extract the variable importance from this new model
varImp(rf_fit2_imp)
## ranger variable importance
##
##                                                          Overall
## n                                                        100.0000
## subjectFrScA                                              20.8268
## time_spent                                                13.6802
## subjectPhysA                                               5.2882
## semesterS216                                               4.0628
## negemo                                                     3.1369
## pc                                                         2.5582
## social                                                     2.3604
## posemo                                                     1.7236
## int                                                        0.9332
## cogproc                                                    0.7290
## enrollment_reasonScheduling Conflict                       0.5157
## enrollment_reasonLearning Preference of the Student        0.4661
## enrollment_reasonOther                                     0.4123
## uv                                                         0.3871
## enrollment_reasonCredit Recovery                           0.2332
## semesterT116                                               0.2124
## subjectOcnA                                                0.1797
## subjectBioA                                                0.0000
```

Our results here give us a ranked order list of the variables in the order of their importance. Variables that appear at the top of the list are more important, and variables that appear at the bottom of the list are less important in the specification of our final random forest model. Remember that we are predicting final grade in the course, so this list will tell us which factors were most important in predicting final grade in online science courses. It can be a bit hard to visually scan a variable importance list, so we might be interested in doing a data visualization.

We can visualize this variable importance list with {ggplot2}.

```
varImp(rf_fit2_imp) %>%
    pluck(1) %>%
    rownames_to_column("var") %>%
    ggplot(aes(x = reorder(var, Overall), y = Overall)) +
    geom_col(fill = dataedu_colors("darkblue")) +
    coord_flip() +
    theme_dataedu()
```

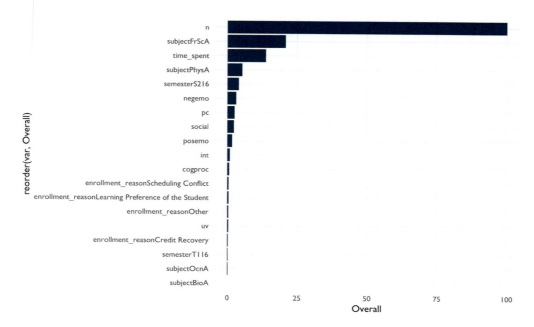

Figure 14.1: Variable Importance

Cool! We can now visualize which variables are most important in predicting final grade.

The first thing we notice is that the variable *n* is the most important. This variable indicates how much students write in their discussion posts. The second most important variable is `subjectFrScA`. The third most important variable is the amount of time students spend in their course. This is the course subject: forensic science. Being enrolled in the forensic science course has a large impact on final grade. That would indicate to us that the forensic science course—more than the other science subjects in this dataset—is strongly correlated with students' final course grades. We can keep scanning down the list to see the other variables that were indicated as less and less important for the model's predictions. Variable importance can help us to better understand the inner workings of a random forest model.

Overall, there are some subject level differences in terms of how predictive subject is. Biology (`subjectBioA`) shows up pretty far down the list, whereas Physiology is in the middle (`subjPhysA`), and forensic science is towards the top (`subjectFrScA`). What this tells us is that the course students are in seems to have a different effect on final grade, depending on the course. Perhaps grades should be normalized within subject: would this still be an important predictor if we did that? We won't dive into that question here, but you can see how the line of research inquiry might progress as you start to explore your data with a machine learning model.

A quick statistical note: above, we selected our variable importance method to be "permutation" for our demonstrative example. There are other options available in the {caret} package if you would like to explore those in your analyses.

Comparing random forest to regression

You may be curious about comparing the predictive accuracy of the model to a linear model (a regression). Below, we'll specify a linear model and check out how the linear model performs in terms of predicting the real outcomes. We'll compare this with the random forest model's performance (rf_fit2). Note that we are not actually re-running our random forest model here, but instead we are just making a dataset that includes the values that the rf_fit2 model predicted as well as the actual rf_fit2 values.

```r
# Make sure all variables stored as characters are converted to
factors
df_train_lm <-
    df_train %>%
    mutate_if(is.character, as.factor)
## mutate_if: no changes
# Create a linear regression model,
# using the same formula approach as in the random forest: ~ .
lm_fit <-
    train(final_grade ~ .,
          data = df_train_lm,
          method = "lm")
# Append the predicted values to the training dataset for the lin-
ear model,
# so we can see both the predicted and the actual values
df_train_lm <-
    df_train %>%
    mutate(obs = final_grade,
           pred = predict(lm_fit, df_train_lm))
## mutate: new variable 'obs' with 354 unique values and 0% NA
##         new variable 'pred' with 372 unique values and 0% NA
# Append the predicted values to the training dataset for the ran-
dom forest
df_train_randomfor <-
    df_train %>%
    mutate(pred = predict(rf_fit2, df_train),
           obs = final_grade)
## mutate: new variable 'pred' with 372 unique values and 0% NA
##         new variable 'obs' with 354 unique values and 0% NA
# Summarize, as data frames, the training data with the predicted
# and the actual values for both the linear model
defaultSummary(as.data.frame(df_train_lm))
##        RMSE    Rsquared         MAE
## 14.4343171   0.5556582  10.8476760
# and the random forest
defaultSummary(as.data.frame(df_train_randomfor))
##        RMSE    Rsquared         MAE
## 4.6020505  0.9678801  3.3933523
```

Our output will come in the order we wrote the code, so the linear model output is displayed above the random forest output.

We can see that the random forest technique seems to perform better than regression. Specifically, the RMSE is lower for the random forest (13.36 as compared to 14.43 for the linear model). Second, the variance explained (`Rsquared`) is higher in the random forest (0.63 as compared to 0.56 for the linear model).

It may be interesting to compare the results from the random forest to a more sophisticated model as well, like one using deep learning. As you expand your skills, you can explore and find out.

Conclusion

In this chapter, we introduced both general machine learning ideas, like training and test datasets and evaluating the importance of specific variables, and specific ideas, like how a random forest works and how to tune specific parameters so that the model is as effective as possible at predicting an outcome. Like many of the topics in this book—but, perhaps *particularly* so for machine learning—there is much more to discover on the topic, and we encourage you to consult the books and resources in the *Learning More chapter* to learn about further applications of machine learning methods.

Chapter 15

Introducing data science tools to your education job

Chapter overview

The purpose of this section is to explore what it is like to take newfound data science skills into your work place with the challenge of finding practical ways to use your skills, encouraging your coworkers to be better users of data, and developing analytic routines that are individualized to the needs of your organization. Whether you are a consultant helping an educational institution, an administrator leading teachers at a school, or a university department chair implementing a new program, there are things you can do to transform what you've learned in the abstract into more concrete learning objectives in the context of your education work place. We'll discuss this topic using two areas of focus: bringing your organization the gift of speed and scale, and the importance of connecting well with others. We'll close this chapter by discussing some of the ways that K–12 teachers in particular might engage a work culture that is bringing on data science as a problem-solving tool.

The gift of speed and scale

The power of doing data analysis with a programming language like R comes from two improvements over tools like Excel and Google Sheets: (1) a massive boost in the speed of your work and (2) a massive boost in the size of the datasets you can analyze. Here are some approaches to introducing data science to your education workplace that focus on making the most of these increases in speed and scale.

Working with data faster

Data analysts who have an efficient analytical process understand their clients' questions and participate by rapidly cycling through analysis and discussion. They quickly accumulate skill and experience because their routines facilitate many cycles of data analysis. Roger Peng and Elizabeth Matsui discuss epicycles of analysis in their book *The Art of Data Science*. In their book *R for Data Science*, Garrett Grolemund and Hadley Wickham demonstrate a routine for data exploration. When the problem space is not clearly defined, as is often the case with education data analysis questions, the path to get from the initial question to analysis itself is full of detours and distractions. Having a routine that points you to the next immediate analytic step gets the analyst started quickly, and having many quick starts results in a lot of data analyzed.

But speed gives us more than just an accelerated flow of experience or the thrill of rapidly getting to the bottom of a teacher's data inquiry. It fuels the creativity required to understand problems in education and the imaginative solutions required to address them. Quickly analyzing data keeps the analytic momentum going at the speed needed to indulge organic exploration of the problem. Imagine an education consultant working with a school district to help them measure the effect of a new intervention on how well their students are learning math. During this process the superintendent presents the idea of comparing quiz scores at the schools in the district. The speed at which the consultant offers answers is important for the purposes of keeping the analytic conversation going.

When a consultant quickly answers a teacher's analytic question about their students' latest batch of quiz scores, the collaborative analytic process feels more like a fast-paced inspiring conversation with a teammate instead of sluggish correspondence between two people on opposite ends of the country. We've all experienced situations where a question like "Is this batch of quiz scores meaningfully different from the ones my students had six months ago?" took so long to answer that the question itself is unimportant by the time the answer arrives!

Users of data science techniques in education have wonderful opportunities to contribute in situations like this because speedy answers can be the very thing that sparks more important analytic questions. In our example of the education consultant presented with a superintendent's curiosity about quiz score results, it is not too hard to imagine many other great questions resulting from the initial answers:

- How big was the effect of the new intervention, if any?

- Do we see similar effects across student subgroups, especially the subgroups we are trying to help the most?

- Do we see similar effects across grade levels?

The trick here is to use statistics, programming, and knowledge about education to raise and answer the right questions quickly so the process feels like a conversation. When there's too much time between analytic questions and their answers, educators lose the momentum required to follow the logical and exploratory path towards understanding the needs of their students.

Example: Preparing Quiz Data to Compute Average Scores

Let's take our example of the education consultant tasked with computing the average quiz scores. Imagine the school district uses an online quiz system and each teacher's quiz export looks like this:

```
library(tidyverse)
set.seed(2020)

quizzes_1 <- tibble(
    teacher_id = 1,
```

```
    student_id = c(1:3),
    quiz_1 = sample(c(0:100), 3, replace = TRUE),
    quiz_2 = sample(c(0:100), 3, replace = TRUE),
    quiz_3 = sample(c(0:100), 3, replace = TRUE)
)
quizzes_1
## # A tibble: 3 x 5
##    teacher_id student_id quiz_1 quiz_2 quiz_3
##         <dbl>      <int>  <int>  <int>  <int>
## 1           1          1      1     27     87     35
## 2           1          2     86     64     41
## 3           1          3     21     16     69
```

Tools like Excel and Google Sheets can help you compute statistics like mean scores for each quiz or mean scores for each student fairly quickly, but what if you'd like to do that for five teachers using the exact same method? First, let's tidy the data. This will prepare our data nicely to compute any number of summary statistics or plot results. Using `pivot_longer()` to separate the quiz number and its score for each student will get us a long way:

```
quizzes_1 %>%
    pivot_longer(cols = quiz_1:quiz_3, names_to = "quiz_number",
values_to = "score")
## # A tibble: 9 x 4
##    teacher_id student_id quiz_number score
##         <dbl>      <int> <chr>       <int>
## 1           1          1 1 quiz_1       27
## 2           1          1 1 quiz_2       87
## 3           1          1 1 quiz_3       35
## 4           1          1 2 quiz_1       86
## 5           1          1 2 quiz_2       64
## 6           1          1 2 quiz_3       41
## 7           1          1 3 quiz_1       21
## 8           1          1 3 quiz_2       16
## 9           1          1 3 quiz_3       69
```

Note now that in the first version of this dataset, each individual row represented a unique combination of teacher and student. After using `pivot_longer()`, each row is now a unique combination of teacher, student, and quiz number. This is often talked about as changing a dataset from "wide" to "narrow" because of the change in the width of the dataset. The benefit to this change is that we can compute summary statistics by grouping values in any of the new columns. For example, here is how we would compute the mean quiz score for each student:

```
quizzes_1 %>%
    pivot_longer(cols = quiz_1:quiz_3, names_to = "quiz_number",
values_to = "score") %>%
    group_by(student_id) %>%
    summarize(quiz_mean = mean(score))
```

```
## # A tibble: 3 x 2
##    student_id quiz_mean
##         <int>     <dbl>
## 1           1      49.7
## 2           2      63.7
## 3           3      35.3
```

Again, for one dataset this computation is fairly straightforward and can be done with a number of software tools. But what if the education consultant in our example wants to do this repeatedly for 25 teacher quiz exports? Let's look at one way we can do this fairly quickly using R. We'll start by creating two additional datasets as an example. To make things feel authentic, we'll also add a column to show if the students participated in a new intervention.

```
# Add intervention column to first dataset
quizzes_1 <- quizzes_1 %>%
    mutate(intervention = sample(c(0, 1), 3, replace = TRUE))

# Second imaginary dataset
quizzes_2 <- tibble(
    teacher_id = 2,
    student_id = c(4:6),
    quiz_1 = sample(c(0:100), 3, replace = TRUE),
    quiz_2 = sample(c(0:100), 3, replace = TRUE),
    quiz_3 = sample(c(0:100), 3, replace = TRUE),
    intervention = sample(c(0, 1), 3, replace = TRUE)
)

# Third imaginary dataset
quizzes_3 <- tibble(
    teacher_id = 3,
    student_id = c(7:9),
    quiz_1 = sample(c(0:100), 3, replace = TRUE),
    quiz_2 = sample(c(0:100), 3, replace = TRUE),
    quiz_3 = sample(c(0:100), 3, replace = TRUE),
    intervention = sample(c(0, 1), 3, replace = TRUE)
)
```

The method we'll use to compute the mean quiz score for each student is to:

1. Combine all the datasets into one big dataset: Use `bind_rows()` to combine all three quiz exports into one dataset. Remember, this can be done because each teacher's export uses the same imaginary online quiz system and export feature and thus use the same number of columns and variable names

2. Reuse the code from the first dataset on the new bigger dataset: Paste the code we used in the first example into the script so it cleans and computes the mean quiz score for each student

```
# Use `bind_rows` to combine the three quiz exports into one big
dataset
all_quizzes <- bind_rows(quizzes_1, quizzes_2, quizzes_3)
```

Note there are now nine rows, one for each student in our dataset of three teacher quiz exports:

```
all_quizzes
## # A tibble: 9 x 6
##    teacher_id student_id quiz_1 quiz_2 quiz_3 intervention
##         <dbl>      <int>  <int>  <int>  <int>        <dbl>
## 1           1          1     27     87     35            0
## 2           1          2     86     64     41            0
## 3           1          3     21     16     69            1
## 4           2          4     55     79      2            1
## 5           2          5     71     28     65            1
## 6           2          6     41     97     92            1
## 7           3          7     77     47      6            1
## 8           3          8     77     46     83            0
## 9           3          9     75     77     17            1
```

We'll combine the cleaning and computation of the mean steps neatly into one this chunk of code:

```
# Reuse the code from the first dataset on the new bigger dataset
all_quizzes %>%
    # Clean with pivot_longer
    pivot_longer(cols = quiz_1:quiz_3, names_to = "quiz_number",
values_to = "score") %>%
    # Compute the mean of each student
    group_by(student_id, intervention ) %>%
    summarize(quiz_mean = mean(score))
## # A tibble: 9 x 3
## # Groups:    student_id [9]
##    student_id intervention quiz_mean
##         <int>        <dbl>     <dbl>
## 1           1            0      49.7
## 2           2            0      63.7
## 3           3            1      35.3
## 4           4            1      45.3
## 5           5            1      54.7
## 6           6            1      76.7
## 7           7            1      43.3
## 8           8            0      68.7
## 9           9            1      56.3
```

Note here that our imaginary education consultant from the example is thinking ahead by including the intervention column. By doing so, she's opened the

possibility of collaboratively exploring any possible differences in the scores between the students who had the intervention and the students who did not when
she reviews and discusses these results with the school staff. Adding these types of
details ahead of time is one way to build conversation starters into your collabora-
tions. It is also a way to get faster at responding to curiosities by anticipating useful
questions from your clients.

The difference in time it takes to do this on three quiz exports using R versus
non-programming tools is perhaps not significant. But the speed of computing
means across larger volumes of data—say, 30 quiz exports—is truly useful to an
education consultant looking to help many educators.

Summary

While getting fast at answering analytic questions is not a silver bullet (but really,
what is?), it does have a chain effect that often leads to creative solutions. It works
something like this:

1. Answering analytic questions faster helps more people

2. Helping more people creates opportunities for more data science practice

3. Helping more people also helps educate those same people about the solutions data science tools can offer

4. Lots of practice combined with a common understanding of the value of data
   science tools in the education workplace nurtures confidence

5. Confidence leads to the courage required to experiment with interesting solutions for designing the best solutions for students

Here are more ways to get faster at answering analytic questions:

- Recognize when you are using similar chunks of code to do repetitive operations. Store that code in an accessible place and reuse it

- Keep a notebook of the questions teachers and administrators ask to help you
  develop an instinct for common patterns of questions. Write your code to
  anticipate these questions

- Learn to use functions and packages like {purrr} to work on many datasets at
  once

- Instill a prototyping habit by getting comfortable with quickly producing
  rough first drafts of your analysis. Your audience can give valuable feedback
  early and feel like you are quickly on the path to developing useful answers
  to their questions

Working with more data

Improving outcomes in education is about learning, obviously for the students, but
just as importantly for the people teaching the students. The more data is available

to examine, the more school staff learn about what is working for their students. Using R to prepare and analyze data so it is repeatable and easy to share increases the amount of data you can work with by an order of magnitude compared to tools like Google Sheets.

When cleaning and analyzing data is laborious, people tend to generate less data. This can be a problem because less data means less context for the data you do have. Without context, it is difficult to conduct one of the primary cognitive tasks of data analysis: making comparisons. For example, imagine a teacher whose students have an average quiz score of 75%. This information is helpful to the teacher because it shows her how close she is to some pre-determined average quiz score goal, say 95%. But that data alone doesn't tell the teacher how unusual that class average is. For that, you need context. Say that line of code used to compute this teacher's class average quiz score was applied to every classroom and she learned that the school average for the same quiz was 77%. From this information, the teacher learns that her class average is not very different from everyone else's. This is more information than just the knowledge that her class's average was less than her pre-determined goal of 95%.

This is where using R for data analysis enters the conversation. Without programming, working with data past a certain size, say 10,000 rows, is difficult because you have to interact with each row through the graphical user interface. Instead, you can work with larger datasets by using programming languages like R to issue complex instructions for acting on the data rather than using a mouse and keyboard to act on what you can see on the screen.

Example: replacing many student names with numerical IDs

Say, for example, an elementary school administrator wants to replace each student name in a classroom dataset with a unique numerical ID. Doing this in a spreadsheet using good old-fashioned data entry is fairly straightforward. Doing this for a whole school's worth of classrooms, though, demands a different approach. Rather than hand-enter a unique ID into a spreadsheet, the administrator can write an R script that executes the following steps:

1. Use `read_csv()` to store every classroom's student list into the computer's memory

2. Use `bind_rows()` to combine the separate lists into one long list

3. Use `mutate()` to replace student names with a randomized and unique numerical ID

4. Use `split()` to separate the data into classrooms again

5. Use {purrr} and `write_csv()` to create and rename individual spreadsheets to send back to teachers

With some initial investment into thoughtful coding on the front end of this problem, the administrator now has a script she can use repeatedly in the future when she needs to do this task again.

Other ways to reimagine the scale of your work

Reflect on your current scale, then push to the next level

When you've been using the same data analysis tools and routines for a long time, it's easy to forget to reflect on how you work. The analytic questions we ask, the datasets we use, and the scale of the analytic questions become automatic because they've delivered results. When you introduce data science techniques and R into your education analysis workflow, you also introduce an opportunity to ask yourself: How can I put this analytic question in context by analyzing on a larger scale?

When an education client or coworker asks for help answering an analytic question, consider the following:

1. At what level is this question about: student, classroom, school, district, regional, state, or federal?

2. What can we learn by answering the analytic question at the current level, but also at the next level of scale up?

If a teacher asks you to analyze the attendance pattern of one student, see what you learn by comparing to the attendance pattern of the whole classroom or the whole school. If a superintendent of a school district asks you to analyze the behavior referrals of a school, analyze the behavior referrals of every school in the district. One of the many benefits of using programming languages like R to analyze data is that once you write code for one dataset, it can be used with many datasets with a relatively small amount of additional work.

Look for lots of similarly structured data

Train your eyes to be alert to repositories that contain many datasets that have the exact same structure, then design ways to act on all those datasets at once. Data systems in education generate standardized data tables all the time. It's one of the side effects of automation. Software developers design data systems to automatically generate many datasets for many people. The result is many datasets that contain different data, but all have the same number of columns and the same column names. This uniformity creates the perfect condition for R scripts to automatically act on these datasets in a way that is predictable and repeatable. Imagine a student information system that exports a list of students, their teacher, their grade level, and the number of school days attended to date. School administrators that have a weekly routine of exporting this data and storing it in a folder on their laptop will generate many uniformly structured datasets. When you train your eyes to see this as an opportunity to act on a lot of data at once, you will find an abundance of chances to transform data on a large scale so school staff can freely explore and ask questions aimed at improving the student experience.

Cleaning data

Folks who work in education want to look at data about their students with tools like Excel, but the data is frequently not ready for analysis. You can empower these people to explore data and ask more questions by being alert to opportunities to prepare lots of data for analysis. Offer to clean a dataset! Then do it again and do it quickly. When you get into this habit, you not only train your data cleaning skills, but you also train your education client's expectations for how quickly you can prepare data for them.

Solving problems together

Steven Spielberg said,

> When I was a kid, there was no collaboration; it's you with a camera bossing your friend around. But as an adult, filmmaking is all about appreciating the talents of the people you surround yourself with and knowing you could never have made any of these films by yourself.
>
> (Murphy 2011)

Data science techniques are a powerful addition to an educational organization's problem-solving capacity. But when you're the only person who codes or fits statistical models, it's easy to forget that the best solutions magically arrive when many perspectives come crashing together. Here are some things to think about as you challenge yourself to introduce data science to your education workplace in a lasting and meaningful way.

Data science in education and empathy

One definition of empathy is seeing things as others do, which points to a barrier to our mission of discovering ways to use our data science skills to improve the experience of learners—it is all too easy to assume that our coworkers will be as inspired by possibilities of data science as we are. In 1990, Elizabeth Newton, then a Stanford University graduate student, asked research subjects to "tap" out well-known songs with their fingers and estimate how many people would recognize the songs (Newton 1991, Heath and Heath 2006). She found that they overestimated every time! When we know a subject well, we tend to forget the experience of not knowing that subject. So how do we make use of this knowledge?

First, listen carefully to your coworkers as they work with data. As you listen, aim to understand the thinking process they use when making sense of reports, tables, and graphs. This will help you understand the problems and solutions they gravitate towards.

Second, ask them if you can "borrow the problem" for a bit. "Borrowing a problem" is not solving it for them; it's using a little data science magic to get them unstuck so they can continue solving the problem the way they want to. If they're struggling to make a scatter plot from their pivot table data, offer to help by cleaning and summarizing the dataset before they try again.

Third, if your first attempt at borrowing the problem didn't help, make an effort to learn more. Doing data science together is a conversation, so ask them how it went after you cleaned the dataset. Then listen, understand, and try again. After many rounds of this process, you may find your coworkers willing to try new methods for advancing their goals.

A workplace going from not using data science to using data science regularly is a process that takes longer than you think. Responses to new ideas might include excitement and inspiration, but they might just as likely include resistance and fear. Changing the way an organization works requires new skills which often take years to learn. But here we are talking about one part of this change that is easily missed: listening to people and the system and using empathy to determine the unique place in your education organization that your data science skills will help students the most. Introducing data science techniques to your system is as much about having good people skills and empathy as it is about learning how to code and fit models.

Data scientists and non-data scientists in education are similar in this regard—they both get excited about and inspired by solving meaningful problems for their students. Once we recognize that that is the unifying goal, the exploration of how we do that with a diversity of expertise and tools begins. When we use empathy to connect with our coworkers about the common problems we are solving, we open the door to all kinds of solutions. Data science in education becomes a tool for a student-centered common cause, not an end in and of itself.

Here are some reflection questions to use to inspire connection in your education workplace. Practice these questions both as personal reflections and also as questions you ask your coworkers:

1. What does data analysis in our organization look like today?

2. How do I wish data analysis will look in the future?

3. What is the hardest challenge I face in building my vision of student learning?

4. What is one story about a rewarding experience I had with a student?

Create a daily practice commitment that answers someone else's question

In his book *Feck Perfuction*, designer Victore (2019) writes,

> Success goes to those who keep moving, to those who can practice, make mistakes, fail, and still progress. It all adds up. Like exercise for muscles, the more you learn, the more you develop, and the stronger your skills become.
>
> (p. 31)

Doing data science is a skill, and like all skills, repetition and mistakes are their fuel for learning. But what happens if you are the first person to do data science in your education workplace? When you have no data science mentors, analytics routines, or examples of past practice, it can feel aimless to say the least. The antidote to that aimlessness is daily practice.

Commit to writing code every day. Even the simplest three line scripts have a way of adding to your growing programming instincts. Train your ears to be radars for data projects that are usually done in a spreadsheet, then take them on and do them in R. Need the average amount of time a student with disabilities spends in speech and language sessions? Try it in R. Need to rename the columns in a student quiz dataset? Try it in R. The principal is hand-assembling 12 classroom attendance sheets into one dataset? You get the picture.

Now, along the path of data science daily practice you may discover that your non-data science coworkers start kindly declining your offers for help. In our experience, there is nothing mean happening here, but rather this is a response to imagining what it's like to do what you are offering to do using the more commonly found spreadsheet applications. As your programming and statistics skills progress, some of the tasks you offer to help with will be the kind that, if done in a spreadsheet app, are overwhelmingly difficult and time intensive. So in environments where programming is not used for data analysis, declining your offers of help are more perceived acts of kindness to you and probably not statements about the usefulness of your work. As frustrating as these situations might be, they are necessary experiences as an organization learns just how available speed and scale of data analysis are when you use programming as a tool. In fact, these are opportunities you should seize because they serve both as daily practice and as demonstrations of the speed and scale programming for data analysis provides.

Build your network

It is widely accepted that participating in personal and professional networks is important for surviving, thriving, and innovating. The path to connecting to a data science in education network is apparent if your education workplace has an analytics department, but it will take a little more thought if you are the lone data scientist. When looking for allies that will inspire and teach you, the mind immediately searches for other programmers and statisticians and to be sure, these are relationships that will help you and the organization grow in its analytic approach.

What the authors argue here is that data science in education is not just about bringing programming and statistics, but in the broader view is about evolving the whole approach to analytics. When viewed that way, members of a network broaden beyond just programmers and statisticians. The network grows to include administrators and staff who are endlessly curious about the lives of students, graduate students fascinated with unique research methodologies, and designers who create interesting approaches to measurement.

Networks for growing data science in education are not limited to the workplace. There are plenty of online and real-life chances to participate in a network that are just as rewarding as the networks you participate in during regular work hours. Here are a few to check out:

- Communities on Twitter like #RLadies and #rstats

- Local coding communities

- Conferences like rstudio::conf and useR!

- Online forums like RStudio Community

For K–12 teachers

We've used almost all of this chapter to explore what to think about and what to do to help you bring your data science skills to your education workplace. So far the discussion has been from the data scientist's point of view, but what if you are one of the many who have an interest in analytics but very little interest in programming and statistics? Teachers in elementary and high schools are faced with a mind-boggling amount of student data. A study by Data Quality Campaign (2018) estimated that "95 percent of teachers use a combination of academic data (test scores, graduation rates, etc.) and nonacademic data (attendance, classroom, behavior, etc.) to understand their students' performance". Fifty-seven percent of the teachers in the study said a lack of time was a barrier to using the data they have. Data literacy is also increasingly important within teacher preparation programs (Mandinach and Gummer 2013).

Yet the majority of teachers aren't interested in learning a programming language and statistical methods as a way to get better at analytics, and both time and professional development with respect to working with data are necessary (Datnow and Hubbard 2015). After all, most teachers chose their profession because they love teaching, not because they enjoy cleaning datasets and evaluating statistical model output. But to leave them out feels like a glaring omission in a field where perhaps the most important shared value is the effective teaching of students.

If you do happen to be an elementary or high school teacher who wants to use programming and statistics to improve how you use data, you will find the approaches in this book useful. But if you are not that person, there is still much to explore that will lead to a rewarding experience as you grow your analytic skill. This book lacks the scope to explore this topic thoroughly, but there are many ways to improve how you use data without requiring a programming language or deep knowledge of statistics.

For example, you can explore what is perhaps the most important element of starting a data analysis: asking the correct question. Chapter three of *The Art of Data Science* (Peng and Matsui 2015) provides a useful process for getting better at asking data questions.

Given how often data is served to us through data visualizations, it is important to learn the best ways to create and consume these visualizations. Chapter one of book *Data Visualization: A Practical Introduction* (Healy 2019) explores this topic using excellent examples and writing.

For practical applications of a data-informed approach, *Learning to Improve: How America's Schools Can Get Better at Getting Better* (Bryk et al. 2015) offers a thorough explanation of the improvement science process. The book is filled with examples of how data is used to understand problems and trial solutions.

The final recommendation for elementary and secondary teachers wanting to get better at analysis is this: find, and partner with, someone who can help you answer the questions you have about how to serve your students better. You have the professional experience to come up with the right ideas and the curiosity to see what these ideas look like in the classroom. Inviting someone who can collaborate with you and help you measure the success of your ideas can be a rewarding partnership for you and your students.

Chapter 16

Teaching data science

Chapter overview

This book is focused on the application of data science to education. In other words, this book focuses on how to apply data science to questions of teaching, learning, and educational systems. The previous chapters have addressed this topic through narrative and walkthroughs for common questions (or problems) and the types of data encountered in education. In this way, much of the book has focused on applying data science methods. However, for a book on data science in education, it is important to not only discuss the application of data science methods, but also to consider what we know about how to teach data science. In recognition of these dual meanings of data science in education, we've referred to the application of data science methods as "data science *in* education" and the teaching and learning of data science as "data science *for* education" (Rosenberg et al. 2020).

Naturally, educators who do data science are positioned well to try to teach others how to do data science. In addition, we expect readers of this book—many of whom will also be involved in education—will be interested in teaching others about data science.

This chapter is organized around three topics:

1. The pedagogical principles we considered when planning this book

2. Strategies for teaching data science

3. General strategies related to teaching and learning

The pedagogical principles we considered when planning this book

As the authors of a book about data science in education—and readers of books that taught us about data science—we considered what would make it effective for our readers when we set out to write it. The result of this process was a pedagogical framework that consists of four principles: problem-based learning, differentiation, building mental models, and working in the open. We consider each of these in turn.

Problem-based learning

Problem-based learning (PBL) is a method of instruction that asks learners to apply their skills and knowledge to solve a real-world challenge. We applied this principle to the design of this book by including walkthroughs for common data science and education questions. This is especially important in data science because we do not have all of the right answers in this text. Moreover, there is not one right statistical model to fit, technique to write code, or software solution to use.

Thus, the text features walkthroughs that reflect the types of challenges that educational data scientists may encounter in the course of their work. All of the data (as well as the code) is available, and readers may choose to approach the analysis of the data used in each walkthrough differently. Moreover, the walkthroughs are structured in such a way that readers return to some of the analytic challenges, but with different aims, over the course of the book: Walkthrough 1 in Chapter 7, Walkthrough 7 in Chapter 13, and Walkthrough 8 in Chapter 14 all use the same dataset on online science learning, but Walkthrough 7 expands Walkthrough 1 by its focus on modeling the effects of courses, and Walkthrough 8 takes a *predictive*, rather than explanatory, goal, through the use of machine learning. Other challenges, such as processing and preparing data, are introduced in the first walkthrough and—reflective of their importance and ubiquity—returned to in each of the subsequent chapters.

Differentiation

Differentiation is a method for providing multiple pathways for learners to engage with, understand, and ultimately apply new content and new skills. To differentiate this text, we first created personas of the common groups of readers we expected to read this book (see Wilson (2009) for an example of this approach).

The objective was to write in a way that helped readers see themselves in the scenarios. The personas were a way to imagine our audience and guide who we interviewed to prepare for the writing. The interviews equipped us to go beyond what we imagined the needs of our readers were and to include their voices in the way we presented the content.

We then aimed to differentiate the book by recognizing and providing background knowledge (either explicitly or through references to other resources) and recommendations for where to begin based on prior expertise. We also provided screenshots—particularly in "Getting Started with R and RStudio" and "Foundational Skills" (Chapters 5 and 6)—that are annotated and reflective of the content in the text to help show readers how to use what they are reading about.

Lastly, we considered inclusivity and availability when differentiating this book. For inclusivity, we considered our audience and the unique assets that those in education bring. This broader view of who participates in data science informed the types of challenges, topics, and data that we included. For availability, we considered how a wide audience is able to access and engage with the book.

Working in the open

We started writing this book in the open, on GitHub. This allowed us to share the book as it developed. Writing the book in the open also allowed others from the wider educational data science and data science community to contribute. These contributions included writing sections of the book in which contributors had specific expertise, asking clarifying questions, and, even creating a logo for the book which informed our choice of a color palette. We decided to write this book in the open after witnessing the success of other books on data science (such as Wickham (2019a) *Advanced R* (https://adv-r.hadley.nz/) book.

Building mental models

In "Foundational Skills", we introduced the *foundational skills framework*. The purpose of this framework was to emphasize four core concepts (projects, functions, packages, and data) that are relevant to and used in nearly all data science projects. We chose to introduce this *general* framework before walkthroughs, which introduce *specific* techniques, in part to help readers to build a "mental model" of data science: an understanding of how data science tools and techniques at a level deeper than particular functions or individual lines of code (see Krist, Schwarz, and Reiser (2019)'s framework for the development of *mental models* and this type of deeper understanding). Understanding both how R works as a programming language (what R code is) and how R and RStudio work as software programs can make it easier to troubleshoot the (inevitable!) issues and identify possible solutions in the course of working on educational data science projects.

Universal design

In our original proposal for this book (see Estrellado et al. 2019), we noted that Universal Design (Wiggins, Wiggins, and McTighe 2005; McTighe and Willis 2019) was a part of our pedagogical framework. As we worked toward completing the book, we recognized that we did not fully meet the aims we had laid out. Here is what we wrote in the proposal:

> Universal Design is a series of principles which guide the creation of spaces that are inclusive and accessible to individuals from all walks of life regardless of age, size, ability, or disability. While traditionally applied to physical spaces, we have extended these principles to the creation of a data science text in such a way that the text and accompanying materials will be designed for individuals from all walks of life, regardless of educational level, background, ability, or disability. Many of the seven guiding principles of Universal Design are readily transferable to the creation of a text, such as equitable use, flexibility in use (aided in large part through differentiation), simple and intuitive use, perceptible information, and tolerance for error.

While we did not adequately address these in the book, they remain important to us, and we hope to address them in a future edition of the book.

Strategies for teaching data science

You may be interested in teaching others data science. You may be doing this informally (such as by teaching a colleague in your school district or organization), in a formal environment (such as a class on data science for educational data scientists or analysts), or in some setting in-between (such as a workshop). There is some research on teaching data science, as well as practical advice from experienced instructors, that can inform these efforts.

Provide a home base for learners to access resources

Learning strategies, along with other important factors (such as learners' motivations and having a supportive atmosphere), can make a difference for learners. Especially when it comes to learning to do data science, there are many tools and resources to keep track of, such as:

- How to download and install R

- How to download and install R Studio

- How to install packages

- How to access resources related to the workshop or course (or simply other resources you wish to share)

- How to contact the instructor

- How to get help and learn more

Having a "home base" where you can remind learners to look first for resources can help to lower some of learners' demands in terms of remembering how these tools and resources can be accessed. One way to do this is through a personal website. Another is through GitHub pages. For some organizations, a proprietary learning management system—such as Desire2Learn, Blackboard, Moodle, or Canvas—can be helpful (especially if your learners are accustomed to using them).

When it comes to writing code, think early and often

It is important to get learners to start writing code early and often. It can be tempting to teach classes or workshops that front-load content about data science and using R. While this information is important, it can mean that those you are teaching do not have the chance to do the things they want to do, including installing R (and R Studio) and beginning to run analyses. Because of this, we recommend starting with strategies that lower the barrier to writing code for learners. Ways to do this include:

- Using R Studio Cloud

- Providing an R Markdown document for learners to work through

- Providing a dataset and ideas for how to begin exploring it

While these strategies are especially helpful for courses or workshops, they can be translated to teaching and learning R in tutoring (or "one-on-one") opportunities for learners. In these cases, being able to work through and modify an existing analysis (perhaps in R Studio Cloud) is a way to quickly begin running analyses—and to use the analysis as a template for analyses associated with other projects. Also, having a dataset associated with a project or analysis—and a real need to analyze it using R—can be an outstanding way for an individual to learn to use R.

Don't touch that keyboard!

Resist helping learners to the point of hindering their learning. Wilson (2009) writes about the way in which those teaching others about R—or to program, in general—can find it easier to correct errors in learners' work. But, by fixing errors, you may cause learners to feel that they are not capable of carrying out all of the steps needed in an analysis on their own.

This strategy relates to a broader issue, as well: issues that have to do with writing code that runs correctly (e.g., with the correct capitalization and syntax) can be minor to those with experience programming but can be major barriers to using R independently for those new to it. For example, becoming comfortable with where arguments to functions belong and how to separate them, how to use brackets in functions or loops, and when it is necessary to use an assignment operator can be *completely new* to beginners. Doing these steps for learners may hinder their capability later when they may have fewer resources available to help them than when you are teaching them. Consider taking the additional time needed to help learners navigate minor issues and errors in their code: it can pay off in increased motivation on their part in the long-term.

Anticipate issues (and sacrifice accuracy for clarity)

Don't worry about being perfectly accurate early on, especially if doing so would lead to learners who are less interested in the topic you are teaching. Especially in cases for which additional details may not be helpful to beginning learners, it can be valuable to not only anticipate these questions, but to have responses or answers that provide more clarity, rather than confusion.

For example, there are complicated issues at the heart of why data that is built-in to packages or to R (such as the iris dataset) appear in the environment after they are first used in an R session (see the section on "promises" in Wickham 2019a). Similarly, there are complicated issues that pertain to how functions are evaluated that can explain why it is important to provide the name of packages installed via `install.packages()` (whereas the names of arguments to other functions, such as `dplyr::select()` do not need to be quoted).

Start lessons or activities with visualizing data

There are examples from data science books by Wickham and Grolemund (2018) and past research (e.g., Lehrer and Schauble 2015) that suggest that starting with visualizing data can be beneficial in terms of learners' ability to work with data. Wickham and Grolemund (2018) write that they begin their book, *Data Science Using R*, with a chapter on visualization, because doing so allows learners to create something they can share immediately, whereas tasks such as loading data can be rife with issues and do not immediately give learners a product they can share. Lehrer, Kim, and Schauble (2007) show how providing students with an opportunity to invent statistics by displaying the data in new ways led to productive critique among fifth- and sixth-grade students and their teacher.

Consider representation and inclusion in the data and examples you use

One way to think about data is that it is objective and free of decisions about what to value or prioritize. Another is to consider data as a process that is value-laden, from deciding what question to ask (and what data to collect) to interpreting findings with attention to how others will make sense of them (e.g., O'Neil (2016)'s *Weapons of Math Destruction*, and Lehrer, Kim, and Schauble (2007)'s description of data modeling). From this broader view, choosing representative data is a choice, like others, that teachers can make. For example, instructors can choose data that directs attention to issues—equity-related issues in education, for example—that she or he believes would be valuable for students to analyze.

It is important to consider and question what data is collected and why, even with variables that we consider to be objective. For example, some variables are constructed to be dichotomous (e.g., gender) or categorical (e.g., race), but the data that is collected is based on decisions by the observer and may not be inherently objective.

This broader consideration of data is also important when it comes to which data is used for teaching and learning. For example, if a dataset only includes names of individuals from a majority racial or ethnic group, some learners may perceive the content being taught to be designed for others. While we may think that such issues are better left up to those we are teaching to decide on themselves, setting the precedent in classes, courses, and other contexts in which data science is taught can be important for how learners collect and use data in the future.

Draw upon other resources

We touched on a few strategies for teaching data science. There are others that go more into depth on this topic from different perspectives, such as the following:

- GAISE Guidelines (https://www.amstat.org/asa/education/Guidelines-for-As sessment-and-Instruction-in-Statistics-Education-Reports.aspx): guidelines for teaching statistics

- Data Science for Undergraduates (https://www.nap.edu/catalog/25104/data-science-for-undergraduates-opportunities-and-options): a report on undergraduate data science education

- R Studio Education (https://education.rstudio.com/)

There are also a number of data science-related curricula (for the K–12 level) which may be helpful:

- Bootstrap Data Science (https://www.bootstrapworld.org/blog/index.shtml)

- Exploring CS, unit 5 (http://www.exploringcs.org/curriculum)

- Chromebook Data Science (http://jhudatascience.org/chromebookdatascience/)

- Oceans of Data Institute Curricula (http://oceansofdata.org/our-work/ocean-tracks-high-school-learning-modules)

Last, there are also books that emphasize the importance—for teachers—of understanding their students—every student. These books include Paris and Alim (2017) and Kozol (2012), and will likely be valuable for teachers of data science who wish to understand and honor the diversity of their students. Moore Jr, Michael, and Penick-Parks (2017) and Emdin (2016) may be helpful for data science educators who aim to be aware and intentional about teaching students from backgrounds other than their own.

General principles and core ideas related to teaching and learning

The National Academy of Science commissioned a report, *How People Learn* (Bransford et al. 2000), that aimed to summarize research on teaching and learning from educational psychology and the learning sciences. In 2018, the report was updated in *How People Learn II* (National Academies of Sciences, Medicine, and others 2018) with a new emphasis on the social and cultural aspects of teaching and learning. Both reports include general strategies that may be helpful to those teaching data science.

In addition to these reports, there are some books that are more practical, including Hattie (2012), Lemov (2015), and Bambrick-Santoyo (2010). These may provide some answers to questions of how to teach data science and how to mitigate some of the anxiety that teachers may feel.

Below, we highlight some general teaching and learning principles and core ideas with an emphasis on strategies applicable to teaching and learning data science. These general strategies are more conceptual than those described in the last section, and are likely more useful as starting points for further research or reflection, instead of as specific techniques that can be brought to the next workshop, class, or peer-to-peer teaching session.

Teaching and learning are complex

One principle from *How People Learn II* is that learning is not just about what learners know or think, but is also about the developmental, cultural, contextual, and historical factors each individual brings to the table. In short, learning is complex. This is an asset to teachers, because learners often bring resources that can serve as a starting point for their learning trajectory in data science. Individual distinctions also mean that educators need to consider factors beyond what learners know, such as their prior educational experiences and what resources and other individuals they have access to at work and at home.

Learners learn many different things (consciously and unconsciously)

The authors of *How People Learn II* point out that individuals learn in response to different challenges and circumstances, including those in formal learning environments, such as workshops or classes. This learning also happens at a different rate for each individual. This principle implies a strategy that involves supporting learners doing data science, however and whenever they learn it. This means that it is both okay—and even to be expected—that learners may learn more from a problem they try to solve on their own, than from a workshop or class (or even a degree!). This also suggests that learners may learn things that we do not anticipate.

Meta-cognition is important (even though it sounds more sophisticated than it is!)

Educators and educational researchers often talk about meta-cognition, or thinking (and ideas) about thinking, as if it is something only very sophisticated learners do. In reality, it is much more commonplace, as people (and learners) are thinking about what they are learning and doing regularly. Instructors can support meta-cognition by asking their students to consider what they learned and what they would like to learn more about. Exit tickets can be a great way to do this, but a brief period in-class would also work. Another strategy is to help learners recognize when it is important to ask for help. Often in data science, the right question to the right person (or community) can save hours of work.

Learning strategies matter

While teachers are responsible for designing learning opportunities, learners also play an important role in their own learning! According to the authors of *How People Learn II*, learning strategies matter, including those that help students retrieve, summarize, and explain what they have learned to themselves and others (see National Academies of Sciences, Medicine, and others (2018) for an elaboration on these).

Teaching strategies, such as how content is spaced and sequenced, also help learners. Dirksen (2015)'s *Design for How People Learn* presents these strategies, based largely on instructional design research, that may be helpful to those teaching data science.

What is most important for teachers of data science is less the specific strategies, and more the commitment to teaching their students how to learn.

Conclusion

Data science educators do not need to reinvent the wheel when it comes to teaching about data science. Insights from other, related educational domains (such as statistics education and computer science education) may prove helpful to those seeking to teach data science to others, whether in a one-on-one setting, a workshop, or through a formal class. In this chapter, we sought to describe both the pedagogical principles for this book and some strategies for teaching data science. As scholarship and practice where it comes to teaching and learning data science continues to develop, we hope that those teaching (and producing scholarship about teaching) data science not only draw upon the findings of those in other domains but carve out a domain of their own—one with findings that may have implications for how statistics, computer science, or even subject matters such as science and mathematics are learned.

Chapter 17

Learning more

Introduction

If you're reading this book cover to cover, you've been through quite a journey! So far, you've:

- Learned about the challenges of doing data science in education

- Practiced some basic coding and statistics techniques

- Worked through examples of analytic routines using education datasets

- Reflected on introducing data science to your education organization over time

- Learned about teaching data science to others

We hope this book sparked an interest in data science that you want to nurture. We've talked to many people in your shoes—folks who care about educating students and want to help by using their data skills. Indeed we've found the common thread in our audience is wanting to use data to improve the experience of learners. It's important to nurture this passion by keeping the learning going.

Surrounding yourself with continuous learning experiences can turn this spark into a specialization that makes a real contribution to the lives of students. There are three reasons we feel these ongoing learning experiences are essential to realizing your vision for data in education. First, developing technical skills is a continuous process. The learning mindset is the same whether you're taking your first steps toward using data science techniques or you're a seasoned data scientist trying to make a bigger impact in education: there is always something new to learn about programming and statistics. Setting regular time aside to evolve your craft is a commitment to this mindset.

Second, education and data science are like most industries—they are constantly evolving. That means today's tools and best practices might be tomorrow's outdated techniques. To keep up with changes, it is important to develop a learning routine that exposes you to the pulses of these two fields. Sometimes this means learning a new technique, sometimes it means deepening expertise in a technique you haven't mastered, and other times, it means revisiting a skill you mastered long ago.

And last, when you surround yourself with learning experiences, you inevitably surround yourself with others who are learning. Along your journey, you'll interact with folks who are struggling through the same concepts as you, folks who are struggling through more complex concepts, and folks who are struggling with concepts you've already mastered. Participating in a community of learners has magical properties—it's a place to learn, teach, inspire, and get inspired all at once. In *Creative Calling*, Jarvis (2019) touches on this very point:

> Whether online or in person, connecting with a community will support your learning efforts. It will also expose you to a diverse set of ideas that will dramatically enrich your perspective on what you're learning. If you weren't in love with your new skill before, this step can tip the balance. Passion is infectious.

You'll need to use your intuition to find the areas where you want to deepen your knowledge. When you feel it, go there and dive in. Remember that the learning experience includes all kinds of activities. It's a combination of reading, doing, discussing, walking away, and coming back. Here are some activities to include in your practice. We hope you take these and construct your own system of rewarding learning experiences.

Adopt a growth mindset

It's normal to feel overwhelmed while learning skills like R and data science. This is particularly true when these fields themselves are learning and growing. The R, data science, and education communities are constantly developing new techniques to move the field forward. It's part of the beauty of this work!

When you're feeling overwhelmed by everything you're trying to learn, consider adopting a growth mindset. Carol Dweck argues that we think of ourselves as *being* or *not being* a type of person. For example, we might think of ourselves as "math people" or "reading people". What matters is whether or not this state is changeable. When we believe we can change, we adopt a desire to learn, choose to be around people who help us learn, and make the effort to learn. When we move from a *fixed* mindset to a *growth* mindset, we create the possibility of mastering new techniques and realizing our vision for using data in education.

The nuances of the growth mindset (Dweck 2015) are beyond the scope of this book, but we do encourage the general belief that we can learn how to apply these techniques. We encourage you to adopt a growth mindset as a way to inspire learning and belief that you can introduce data science in your education job. In doing so, you'll be joining other data scientists who created a way to contribute to their fields.

Discover new information

The content you surround yourself with matters. You can learn a lot and stay inspired by high quality books, blog posts, journals, journalism, and talks. In his book *Steal Like An Artist*, Kleon (2012) encourages people to surround themselves with great content:

> There's an economic theory out there that if you take the incomes of your five closest friends and average them, the resulting number will be pretty close to your own income. I think the same thing is true of our idea incomes. You're only going to be as good as the stuff you surround yourself with.

In our "Resources" chapter, we share books and online resources that inspire us and help us learn. Use these as a starting point and build on them by seeking out authors, data scientists, and educators that inspire you to learn and master your craft. There are lots of ways to do this. Some folks follow data scientists on social media and take note of articles or talks that are getting attention. Others read data-informed publications like *FiveThirtyEight* (https://fivethirtyeight.com/), *The Economist* (https://www.economist.com/), or *The Upshot* (https://www.nytimes.com/section/upshot) in the New York Times. Whichever you choose, make sure to stick with something that you're drawn to and you just might find yourself with a new learning habit that is rewarding and fun.

Ask for help

So far, we've discussed learning activities you can do on your own. Data science is a team sport, so eventually your learning will lead you to others in the data science community. You can do this in many ways, both virtual and in real life. Here are a few examples you can try online. Try these and learn about what you're comfortable with. Then build on that to surround yourself with many ways to ask and answer questions.

Discussion forums

Visiting discussion forums is a common way to learn and participate in the R community. Websites like RStudio Community (https://community.rstudio.com/) and Stack Overflow (https://stackoverflow.com/) are very popular ways to do this. On these forums you'll find many years' worth of discussion about R and statistics. It's quite unusual to search these and not find a way to get unstuck. Many discussions include a reproducible example of code that you can copy and paste into your own R console. This is a fantastic way to learn!

Consider learning best practices for asking forum questions. Including a reproducible example, or "reprex", to communicate problems is a widely-accepted norm. Bryan (2019)'s video about making reproducible examples is a great place to learn more.

GitHub repositories

When you want to learn more about how a package works or engage a package's online community, consider visiting its GitHub repository. {dplyr}'s repository (https://github.com/tidyverse/dplyr) is a great example. You can start with the README then dive deeper in the vignettes, which contain demonstrations of the package's functions. You can even browse the code on GitHub to learn more about how the packages work. Don't worry, you won't break anything!

When you're ready to see how the community engages a package's authors, you can read through the "Issues" page. Each repository's Issues page contains questions, feature requests, and bugs submitted by the programming community. Visit this page when you want to see if someone's already submitted the coding challenge you're working through. If you find you're working on something that's *not* a known problem, you can contribute by adding an issue. And finally, you can contribute to the development of packages by submitting code to the repository—this process is called a "pull request". To learn more about contributing to packages, check out Woo (2018)'s talk.

Share what you've learned

If you keep asking questions and finding solutions, you will soon find yourself ready to help others who are just getting started. The adage of learning by teaching applies here—answering someone else's question also helps you deepen your learning and build empathy for new learners.

Adopting a regular sharing routine is a great way to start helping others. A sharing routine encourages participation in the community, invites feedback for improvement, and calls on you to build your craft in a way that others can understand it.

So what can you share? Really, what *can't* you share? If you've built a cool function or visualization that took your project to the next level, you just might help or inspire someone else by sharing it. Maybe you've found an R package that really helped you—chances are it will help others.

Sharing isn't always about the output of your work, it can also be about *how* you work. Consider sharing a workflow you've developed or your experience at a recent data science conference. Anything that you learned or found interesting will be relevant to others too!

What you share doesn't have to be perfect. You can decide when you're ready to share. Some data scientist's blogs are polished and others are ideas-in-progress or shorter posts. You never know when someone will find value in your work, regardless of whether your work is in a refined state or not.

Lastly, you can select your best work from all your sharing and use it as an online work portfolio.

Where to share

There are many ways to share your work online. For rapid fire conversational sharing—Twitter. Be sure to use the hashtag "#rstats" to reach more data scientists. For long-form sharing, consider posting to a data science blog. Robinson (2018)'s blog post *Advice to aspiring data scientists: start a blog* is wonderful inspiration for getting started.

If you decide to post to a blog, there are tools to help you post data science content regularly. As noted earlier, Xie, Thomas, and Hill (2019)'s {blogdown} is designed to help you create websites using R Markdown and a static website creator called "Hugo". Blogdown makes it easy to create, run, and publish code directly from R Studio. Hill (2017) has a great introduction on getting started with {blogdown}.

When you do share a blog post or a tweet, broadcast what you have to say! On Twitter, use hashtags or "at" other community members to include them in the Tweet. On your blog, use blog aggregators that help share your posts to a wider audience. Here are two aggregators to get you started:

- R Weekly newsletter (https://rweekly.org/)

- R Bloggers (https://www.r-bloggers.com)

Finally, share the love by engaging your fellow data scientists! Retweet others, leave comments, and interact with the vibrant data science and R communities online.

Welcome others

If you find yourself becoming an evangelist for R and data science in education—that's what happened to us!—welcome folks who are curious and ready to learn. The strength of any community comes from its inclusiveness, safe learning environment, and capacity to welcome new members. The data science community is no exception—many members work hard to create an environment with active participants, engaging conversations, and celebrations for little and big data science wins. Our call to action is this: continue growing this inclusive and positive environment by being the community member you'd want in your own network.

Data science in education is a wonderful Venn diagram of communities, with new members joining every day. Welcoming, helping, and teaching new members is a great way to contribute to a positive community and to continue your own learning. What better way to inspire new members than to share your work and how it has impacted the lives of students!

Chapter 18

Additional resources

Chapter overview

In this chapter, we provide links and references to additional resources relevant to data science in education.

Data science courses

Anderson, D. J. (2019). University of Oregon data science specialization for the college of education. https://github.com/uo-datasci-specialization

> A series of courses that emphasize the use of R on data science in education (graduate-level).

Landers, R. N. (2019). Data science for social scientists. http://datascience.tntlab.org/

> A data science course for social scientists.

RStudio. (2019). Data science in a box. https://datasciencebox.org/hello/

> A complete course, including a curriculum and teaching materials, for data science.

Workshop materials

Staudt Willet, B., Greenhalgh, S., & Rosenberg, J. M. (2019, October). Workshop on using R at the Association for Educational Communications and Technology. https://github.com/bretsw/aect19-workshop

> Slides and code for a workshop carried out at an educational research conference, focused on how R can be used to analyze Internet (and social media) data.

Anderson, D. J., & Rosenberg, J. M. (2019, April). Transparent and reproducible research with R. Workshop carried out at the Annual Meeting of the American Educational Research Association, Toronto, Canada. https://github.com/ResearchTransparency/rr_aera19

> Slides and code for another workshop carried out at an educational research conference, focused on reproducible research and R Markdown.

Data visualization

Tufte, E. (2006). *Beautiful evidence*. Graphics Press LLC. https://www.edwardtufte.com/tufte/books_be

> A classic text on data visualization.

Healy, K. (2018). *Data visualization: A practical introduction*. Princeton University Press. http://socviz.co/

> A programming- and R-based introduction to data visualization.

Chang, W. (2013). *R graphics cookbook*. O'Reilly. https://r-graphics.org/

> A great reference and how-to for executing many visualization techniques using {ggplot2}.

Wilke, C. (2019). *Fundamentals of data visualization*. O'Reilly. https://serialmentor.com/dataviz/

> A fantastic conceptual introduction to data visualization.

Books related to data science in education

Geller, W., Cratty, D., & Knowles, J. (2020). *Education data done right: Lessons from the trenches of applied data science*. Leanpub. https://leanpub.com/eddatadoneright

> An exploration of best practices in educational work with data and data science. It includes chapters on data governance, working with IT, and managing data requests. This book will help you apply your data science skills effectively in an education system.

Krumm, A., Means, B., & Bienkowski, M. (2018). *Learning analytics goes to school: A collaborative approach to improving education*. Routledge. https://www.routledge.com/Learning-Analytics-Goes-to-School-A-Collaborative-Approach-to-Improving/Krumm-Means-Bienkowski/p/book/9781315650722

> This book emphasizes data-driven improvement using new sources of data and learning analytics and data mining techniques.

Articles related to data science in education

Dutt, A., Ismail, M. A., & Herawan, T. (2017). A systematic review on educational data mining. *IEEE Access, 5*, 15991-16005. https://ieeexplore.ieee.org/abstract/document/7820050

> A comprehensive review of past research on educational data mining, with an emphasis on methods used in past research.

Lee, V. R., & Wilkerson, M. (2018). *Data use by middle and secondary students in the digital age: A status report and future prospects.* Commissioned Paper for the National Academies of Sciences, Engineering, and Medicine, Board on Science Education, Committee on Science Investigations and Engineering Design for Grades 6–12. Washington, DC. https://digitalcommons.usu.edu/itls_facpub/634/

> A comprehensive and incisive review of both recent and foundational research on what is known about how learners at the K–12 level analyze data.

Lehrer, R., & Schauble, L. (2015). *Developing scientific thinking.* In L. S. Liben & U. Müller (Eds.), *Cognitive processes. Handbook of child psychology and developmental science* (Vol. 2, 7th ed., pp. 671–174). Wiley. https://www.wiley.com/en-us/Handbook+of+Child+Psychology+and+Developmental+Science%2C+7th+Edition-p-9781118136850

> Describes the "data modeling" approach which has been used to support learners at the K–12 level to develop data analysis-related capabilities.

Rosenberg, J. M., Edwards, A., & Chen, B. (2020). Getting messy with data: Tools and strategies to help students analyze and interpret complex data sources. *The Science Teacher, 87*(5). https://search.proquest.com/openview/efbd11290f17b5dd9ff27c9c491ca25b/1?pq-origsite=gscholar&cbl=40590

> An overview of digital tools (including R) and strategies for teaching data analysis to K–12 students (particularly in science education settings).

Rosenberg, J. M., Lawson, M. A., Anderson, D. J., Jones, R. S., & Rutherford, T. (in-press). Making data science count in and for education. In E. Romero-Hall (Ed.), *Research methods in learning design & technology.* Routledge. https://edarxiv.org/hc2dw/

> Defines data science in education (as the use of data science methods) and data science for education (as a context for teaching and learning).

Schneider, B., Reilly, J., & Radu, I. (2020). Lowering barriers for accessing sensor data in education: Lessons learned from teaching multimodal learning analytics to educators. *Journal for STEM Education Research*, 1–34. https://link.springer.com/article/10.1007/s41979-020-00027-x

> A study of the effects of a course designed to teach students in educational graduate programs to analyze data using learning analytics techniques.

Wise, A. F. (2020). Educating data scientists and data literate citizens for a new generation of data. *Journal of the Learning Sciences, 29*(1), 165–181. https://doi.org/10.1080/10508406.2019.1705678

> A description of some of the opportunities and challenges of learning to analyze data in light of new data sources and data analysis (and data science) techniques.

Wilkerson, M. H., & Polman, J. L. (2020). Situating data science: Exploring how relationships to data shape learning. *Journal of the Learning Sciences, 29*(1), 1–10. https://doi.org/10.1080/10508406.2019.1705664

> An introduction to a special issue of the *Journal of the Learning Sciences* on data science education.

Equity resources

O'Neil, C. (2016). *Weapons of math destruction: How Big Data increases inequality and threatens democracy* (1st ed.). Crown.

> An exploration of how big data has played a role in societal inequality and ways data scientists can build ethical algorithms.

We All Count: https://weallcount.com/

> A project on equity and ethics in data science.

Data for Black Lives: http://d4bl.org/

> A resource for activists, organizers, and mathematicians working at the intersection of data and justice for Black lives.

Programming with R

Wickham, H., & Grolemund, G. (2017). *R for data science*. O'Reilly.

> An excellent introduction to using R for data science that is focused on the tidyverse suite of packages.

Teetor, P. (2011). *R cookbook*. O'Reilly.

> Provides over 200 practical solutions for analyzing data using R.

Bryan, J., & Hestor, J. *Happy git and github for the useR*. Retrieved from https://happygitwithr.com

> A fantastic and accessible introduction to using Git and GitHub.

Statistics

Introductory statistics

Open Intro. (2019). Textbooks. https://www.openintro.org/

> Three open-source textbooks for statistics, one for high school students.

Navarro, D. (2019). *Learning statistics with R*. https://learningstatisticswithr.com/

> An introductory textbook with a focus on applications to psychological research.

Field, A., Miles, J., & Field, Z. (2012). *Discovering statistics using R*. Sage publications.

> Emphasizes many of the most common statistical tests, especially those used in psychology and educational psychology. Covers the foundations thoroughly and in an entertaining way.

Ismay, C., & Kim, A. Y. (2019). *ModernDive: Statistical inference via data science*. CRC Press. https://moderndive.com/

> An introductory statistics textbook with an emphasis on developing an intuition for the processes underlying modeling data (and hypothesis testing).

James, G., Witten, D., Hastie, T., & Tibshirani, R. (2015). *An introduction to statistical learning with applications in R*. Springer.

> An introductory (and R-based) version of a classic book on machine learning by Hastie, Tibshirani, and Friedman (2009).

Peng, R. D. (2019). *R programming for data science*. Leanpub. https://leanpub.com/rprogramming

> Emphasizes R as a programming language and writing R functions and packages.

Peng, R. D., & Matsui, E. (2018). *The art of data science*. Leanpub. https://leanpub.com/artofdatascience

> A wonderful teaching tool and reference for R users. It describes underlying concepts of R as a programming language and provides practical guides for commonly used functions.

Advanced statistics

Gelman, A., & Hill, J. (2006). *Data analysis using regression and multilevel/hierarchical models*. Cambridge University Press.

A fantastic introduction not only to regression (and multi-level/hierarchical linear models and Bayesian methods) but also to statistical analysis in general.

Hastie, T., Tibshirani, R., & Friedman, J. (2009). *The elements of statistical learning: data mining, inference, and prediction*. Springer Science & Business Media.

A classic text on machine learning.

West, B. T., Welch, K. B., & Galecki, A. T. (2014). *Linear mixed models: a practical guide using statistical software*. Chapman and Hall/CRC.

A solid introduction to multi-level/hierarchical linear models, including code in R (with an emphasis on the lme4 R package).

McElreath, R. (2018). *Statistical rethinking: A Bayesian course with examples in R and Stan*. Chapman and Hall/CRC.

A new classic, accessible introduction to Bayesian methods. We note that this book has been "translated" into tidyverse code by Kurz (2019).

R packages and statistical software development

Peng, R. D. (2019). *Mastering software development in R*. Leanpub. https://leanpub.com/msdr

Developing packages in R, including a description of an example package for data visualization.

Wickham, H. (2015). *R packages: Organize, test, document, and share your code*. O'Reilly. http://r-pkgs.had.co.nz/

A comprehensive introduction to (and walkthrough for) creating your own R packages.

A career in data science

Robinson, E., & Nolis, J. (2020). *Building a career in data science*. Manning. https://www.manning.com/books/build-a-career-in-data-science?a_aid=buildcareer&a_bid=76784b6a

Advice on the technical and practical requirements to work in a data science role.

Cheat sheets

RStudio Cheat Sheets. https://rstudio.com/resources/cheatsheets/

See especially the {dplyr}, {tidyr}, {purrr}, {ggplot2}, and other cheat sheets.

Chapter 19

Conclusion

Where to next?

To start closing our journey together, let's recap what we've learned so far. When we started writing this book, we set out to create a learning experience that had recognizable education examples as its foundation. We used these examples to explore the role of data scientists in education. Building on that context, we introduced basic R tools. In the analysis walkthroughs, we learned to apply data science techniques to datasets and scenarios we've seen in our education jobs. Our goal was to help you learn data science using datasets, functions, language, and analytic approaches that you'll keep using in your own education job. Finally, we discussed using these technical skills to positively influence how your education organization uses data.

After all that, we hope that you feel more prepared to take on the data-related questions and problems that matter to your students. We want you to feel excited about choosing your next steps. But there's one more thing we'd like to share about data science in education: how we keep our efforts going in the long term.

As exciting as the promise of data science can be, over time there are inevitable bumps in the road that all educators encounter. As you master doing data science with education datasets, your learning challenges will evolve beyond the problems of coding syntax and into the realm of larger questions about education systems. For example, you may take an interest in new coding or statistics techniques but struggle to find the right application in your education job. Or you may find yourself working alone on a data project when you need a collaborator as a thought partner. Or maybe you're wondering how a project you're working on aligns with your values as an educator.

When these questions come up, it can be inspiring and reinvigorating to reflect on the bigger picture. Try thinking a little less about what you learn and a little more about how you learn, why you learn, and the ways your work can positively affect students and staff in your education system. Think of this as a strategic move to bring back the excitement and hope you feel when you solve problems that truly make the lives of your students better. In this final chapter, we'll discuss ways to think about your journey that ground you in your service to people learning in your education system. Let's kick off the next stage of your learning!

Learn in the context of education

The mental models and technical skills we learn are separate from the places and people we practice them with. If you intentionally learn new skills in the context of your daily work, you'll naturally gravitate towards the skills that are right for the problems that you are trying to solve. It makes sense for an auto mechanic to learn the science of diagnostics while working on automobiles. It makes sense for a surgeon to learn about anatomy while mastering surgical methods. It makes sense for a farmer to learn about the ecosystem while growing crops. Like all these examples, data scientists concern themselves with mastering skills in service of solving meaningful problems for people.

We've already started learning the basics of data science in education by introducing tools like R. Mastering R will help you analyze data at scale. It will also help you share your work while your organization's data practices grow. But as these skills develop and become muscle memory, your time and attention can focus more and more on what this data tells us about the students and staff that actually generated the numbers to begin with. This is why we believe so strongly in teaching data science using language, problems, and datasets commonly found in education. It helps you make the cognitive jump from simply working on datasets to working on datasets in service to students.

We hope that you're excited to take what you've learned and share it with others. Remember that what you share is not just a way to analyze data, but a way to contribute to someone's school experience.

And speaking of sharing, let's talk about one of the most powerful creative tools we have available to us: each other.

Learn to collaborate with others

In the last section we talked about data in the service of people. But working with data is as much about working *with* people as it is about working *for* people. To understand why collaboration in data science is so important, we first have to see data analysis as a fundamentally creative process. We don't mean this in the same sense that art is creative. First, data science is creative because practitioners create a process that extracts meaning from data. Then second, they create output like writing, visualizations, and conversations that convey this meeting to an audience.

In most creative endeavors, collaboration is the magical ingredient that evolves an individual idea into something truly unique and responsive to the needs of an audience. Daniel Kahneman and Amos Tversky brought the world new knowledge about cognitive biases (see Kahneman 2011). Ben Cohen and Jerry Greenfield collaborated to create Ben and Jerry's Ice Cream. Data journalism like the kind you find at *FiveThirtyEight* and *The Economist* uses collaborative work to produce many visualizations and analyses that consistently deliver high-quality information.

When we started writing this book together, we knew early on that the best product would come from a truly collaborative experience. When you work with others to write words, write code, and think analytically, you learn practices that create inspiration and excitement about the ideas you want to bring to life. Here are some lessons that we learned in our journey:

- Building trust with your collaborators will lead to productive experimentation with new ideas. Build trust slowly with your collaborators by actively listening to feedback and taking risks with new ideas from your teammates.

- Adopting an experimental mindset will maximize the opportunities to fail fast and find the solutions that are right for the problem. If you and your collaborators brainstorm an idea that feels promising but ambiguous, try it out and evaluate the results. Do this together often.

- Asking for feedback and giving feedback when asked will lead to a refined end product. Ask your collaborators regularly for their reaction to a visualization you've made or a report you've written. Does their feedback provide evidence that you've made what you intended to?

- Starting a draft of a project then releasing it to a collaborator is an exercise that builds trust. During our editing process, Josh reminded us of his collaborative spirit by saying, "I no longer consider anything I've written in this book mine. Change anything you want!"

- Collaboration is contagious. There's a really easy way to make a work environment more collaborative: approach someone and invite them to collaborate. You might be surprised at how being an active collaborator inspires similar behavior from others.

Learn every time you code

Whether you're working on a solo project or on a collaborative project, you'll often find that completing it requires learning something new. Learning requires you to get comfortable with not knowing how to do something because it liberates you from the pressure to know all the time. And when we don't feel pressure to be perfect, our minds are free to enjoy the challenges of learning.

When some of us first started learning to program in R, the amount of things we didn't know was glaring. We'd never typed a line of R code in our lives. The thought of writing code that worked, much less using it to do data analysis, felt like a distant goal. After lots of practice and patience, we find ourselves writing code and doing data analysis every day in our education jobs. Yet we still have a long list of things we want to learn so we can push for new ways to understand the lives of our students. Our vocabulary of R syntax has grown, but we still regularly enjoy the experience of learning a new function, discovering a new package, or learning about a analytic routine. The difference between our early learning experiences with R and more recent experiences is that we've embraced learning as a necessary part of enjoying this craft.

It's daunting to begin learning a new function, concept, or statistical technique. We know it will require sustained discomfort, trial and error, and some frustration before we experience the sweet thrill of a well-executed code chunk. Have you ever noticed how hard it is to get started? But simply beginning the learning process is like strengthening a muscle through exercise: it's really difficult at first but with repetition, patience, rest, and kindness towards yourself, it gets easier.

So we encourage you to just start. Set a small goal to open up that book about machine learning you've been avoiding and get through that first paragraph. Or fire up RStudio and copy and paste that first code chunk from the GitHub repository you've been trying to understand. Or run the first example from the documentation of the package you've been trying to learn. Trust us—you get used to it and, eventually, you'll start to enjoy all that comes with learning.

But even the most motivated of us can't sustain high effort and challenges indefinitely. When you've hit a wall trying to learn a new concept, or you've tried to fix your code one too many times, it may be time to take a strategic break.

Learn to take strategic breaks to help solve problems

Taking breaks is one of the most strategic moves you can make when you're trying to break through to the other side of a programming challenge. And it's not just true of R programming. Ryan talks about one of the first times he saw taking breaks in action:

> I grew up in the 1980s and 1990s, when completing Super Mario Brothers was a monk-like endeavor. I spent hours on helping Mario navigate across green-colored plumbing that unexplainably stuck out from the ground. I practiced combinations of jumps and runs to avoid Koopas to eventually reach the end of a two dimensional level.

> Looking back, there were moments when playing this game reached levels of frustration comparable to pressing an impossibly small Lego piece into a complex Lego structure that fell apart in my hands. When these frustrating Mario moments came, there was only one strategy: attempting the challenge over and over again until the inevitable throwing of the controller.

> After throwing the controller, I'd engage some other activity. I'd take a nap, go outside, hang out with my sister, or watch TV. Strangely, when I returned to the game console to play again, I'd often progress through the same frustrating challenge on the first or second try. Some moments I succeeded so quickly it was hard to believe the level was ever a challenge to begin with.

> I learned a valuable lesson from indulging this exercise repeatedly for many years: during moments of frustration, the mind and body need a break. Taking breaks is a functional activity. It gives you time to synthesize all the learning that happened during repeated attempts to solve a problem. During the breaks the mind and body work to replenish energy to take on problems again. Taking strategic breaks is not failure, it's the mark of a professional who understands the most efficient way to get to viable solutions.

So when you need it, take a break and live to code another day. We need as many data scientists working in different corners of education as possible, and we don't want to lose you to burnout!

Learn more meaningfully by knowing your why

Our last bit of advice for staying connected to the bigger picture: make time to regularly reflect on why you're doing this work to begin with. Doing data science in education without reflecting on the cause you're trying to positively affect can make you feel a little like you're just spinning your wheels. Fortunately, working in education has a common built-in purpose: to provide the highest quality learning experience for students with the resources you have available.

To be clear, getting familiar with the "why" of your work is an ongoing process. As we learn and grow, our motivations evolve. But still, better to have this evolution be an intentional and self-aware journey. Here are some reflection questions that are useful to prompt the kinds of thinking that activate your "why":

- Think of what your own learning experience was like. Were there things you wish were different? Were there positive experiences you hope more people will have?

- Is there a teacher or school leader that you've worked with or that positively influenced your life as a student? What was it about them that you'd like to see more of in schools?

- Is there an education-related topic, like diversity, special education, or curriculum and instruction, that you have a natural passion for?

Most people don't have immediate answers to questions like these. It's good enough to just ask them regularly and reflect on the thoughts and feelings that come up. Finding your "why" and being able to talk about it is more like an exploration and less like a singular "aha" moment. But we believe asking these questions is a way to intentionally design meaning into your data science work. When there is a clear purpose and personal connection to why you use data science in education, you'll be reminded that your work affects the lives of learners, sometimes in profoundly meaningful ways.

That brings our time together to a close, but only for a short while. We hope to see you in the "data science in education" community, offering value, learning from others, bonding over challenges, and inspiring each other to be the best we can for our students.

Appendices

This chapter includes four appendices:

- Appendix A: Importing Data (associated with Chapter 6)

- Appendix B: Accessing Twitter Data (associated with Chapters 11 and 12)

- Appendix C: Social Network Influence and Selection Models (associated with Chapter 12)

- Appendix D: Colophon

Appendix A: importing data

This Appendix is provided to serve as a non-exhaustive resource for importing data of different file types into R; it extends some of the techniques introduced in the foundational skills chapter, Chapter 6. We note that while the bulk of the data that we use in this book is available through the {dataedu} package, although there are cases where you will be importing a .csv file or scraping data from the web.

Using functions to import data

You might be thinking that an Excel file is the first type of data that we would load, but there happens to be a format which you can open and edit in Excel that is even easier to use between Excel and R. This format is also supported by SPSS and other statistical software (like MPlus) and even other programming languages, like Python. That format is .csv, or a comma-separated-values file.

The .csv file is useful because you can open it with Excel and save Excel files as .csv files. A .csv file contains rows of a spreadsheet with the columns separated by commas, so you can also view it in a text editor, like TextEdit for Macintosh. Not surprisingly, Google Sheets easily converts .csv files into a Sheet, and also easily saves Sheets as .csv files. However we would be remiss if we didn't point out that there is a package, {googlesheets4}, which can be used to read a Google Sheet directly into R.

For these reasons, we start with—and emphasize—reading .csv files. To get there, we will download a file from the internet.

Saving a file from the Internet

You'll need to copy this URL:

```
https://goo.gl/bUeMhV
```

Here's what it resolves to (it's a .csv file):

```
https://raw.githubusercontent.com/data-edu/data-science-in-educa
tion/master/data/pisaUSA15/stu-quest.csv
```

This next chunk of code downloads the file to your working directory. Run this to download it so in the next step you can read it into R. As a note: there are ways to read the file directory (from the web) into R. Also, you could do what the next (two) lines of code do manually: Feel free to open the file in your browser and to save it to your computer (you should be able to 'right' or 'control' click the page to save it as a text file with a .csv extension).

```r
student_responses_url <-
    "https://goo.gl/bUeMhV"
student_responses_file_name <-
    paste0(getwd(), "/data/student-responses-data.csv")
download.file(
    url = student_responses_url,
    destfile = student_responses_file_name)
```

It may take a few seconds to download as it's around 20 MB.

The process above involves many core data science ideas and ideas from programming/coding. We will walk through them step-by-step.

1. The *character string* `"https://goo.gl/wPmujv"` is being saved to an *object* called `student_responses_url`.

```r
student_responses_url <-
    "https://goo.gl/bUeMhV"
```

2. We concatenate your working directory file path to the desired file name for the .csv using a *function* called `paste0()`. This is stored in another *object* called `student_reponses_file_name`. This creates a file name with a *file path* in your working directory and it saves the file in the folder that you are working in.

```r
student_responses_file_name <-
    paste0(getwd(), "/data/student-responses-data.csv")
```

3. In short, the `download.file()` function needs to know:

   • where the file is coming from (which you tell it through the `url`) argument and

   • where the file will be saved (which you tell it through the `destfile` argument).

The `student_responses_url` *object* is passed to the `url` argument of the *function* called `download.file()`. The `student_responses_file_name` *object* is passed to the `destfile` argument.

```
download.file(
    url = student_responses_url,
    destfile = student_responses_file_name)
```

Understanding how R is working in these terms can be helpful for troubleshooting and reaching out for help. It also helps you to use functions that you have never used before.

Now, in RStudio, you should see the downloaded file in the Files tab. This should be the case if you created a project with RStudio; if not, it should be whatever your working directory is set to. If the file is there, great. If things are *not* working, consider downloading the file in the manual way and then move it into the directory that the R Project you created it.

Loading a .csv file

Okay, we're ready to go. The easiest way to read a .csv file is with the function `read_csv()` from the package {readr}, which is contained within the tidyverse.

Let's load the {tidyverse} library:

```
library(tidyverse) # so tidyverse packages can be used for analysis
```

You may have noticed the hash symbol after the code that says `library(ti-dyverse)`. It reads `# so tidyverse packages can be used for analysis`. That is a comment, and the code after it (but not before it) is not run. The code before it runs normally.

After loading the tidyverse packages, we can now load a file. We are going to call the data `student_responses`:

```
student_responses <-
    read_csv("./data/student-responses-data.csv")
```

Since we loaded the data, we now want to look at it. We can type its name in the function `glimpse()` to print some information on the dataset (this code is not run here).

```
glimpse(student_responses)
```

If you ran that code, you would see that `students_responses` is a *very* big data frame (with a lot of variables with confusing names, to boot)!

Great job loading a file and printing it! We are now well on our way to carrying out analysis of our data.

Saving files

We just practiced loading a file *into* R from an external data source. Just as often, you might need to save a file *out of* R into an external software.

Using our data frame `student_responses`, we can save it as a `.csv` with the following function. The first argument, `student_reponses`, is the name of the object that you want to save. The second argument, `student-responses.csv`, what you want to call the saved dataset.

```
write_csv(student_responses, "student-responses.csv")
```

That will save a `.csv` file entitled `student-responses.csv` in the working directory. If you want to save it to another directory, simply add the file path to the file, i.e., `path/to/student-responses.csv`. To save a file for SPSS, load the haven package and use `write_sav()`. There is not a function to save an Excel file in the tidyverse package {readr} or in the tidyverse, but you can save as a `.csv` and directly load it in Excel.

Loading Excel files

If you want to load data from an Excel workbook, you might be thinking that you can open the file in Excel and then save it as a `.csv`. This is generally a good idea. At the same time, sometimes you may need to directly read a file from Excel. Note that, when possible, we recommend the use of `.csv` files. They work well across platforms and software (i.e., even if you need to load the file with some other software, such as Python).

The package for loading Excel files, {readxl}, is not a part of the tidyverse, so we will have to install it first using `install.packages()` (remember, we only need to do this once), and then load it using `library(readxl)`. The command to install {readxl} is commented out below so that the computer will not automatically run that line. It is here just as a reminder that the package needs to be installed on your computer before you use it for the first time.

Once we have installed readxl, we have to load it (just like {tidyverse}):

```
library(readxl)
```

We can then use the function `read_excel()` in the same way as `read_csv()`, where "path/to/file.xlsx" is where an Excel file you want to load is located:

```
my_data <-
    read_excel("path/to/file.xlsx")
```

Of course, if you were to run this, you can replace `my_data` with a name you like. Generally, it's best to use short and easy-to-type names for data as you will be typing and using it a lot.

Note that one easy way to find the path to a file is to use the "Import Dataset" menu. It is in the Environment window of RStudio. Click on that menu bar option, select the option corresponding to the type of file you are trying to load (e.g., "From Excel"), and then click the "Browse" button beside the File/URL field. Search for your desired file. Once you click on the file, RStudio will automatically generate the file path—and the code to read the file too—for you. You can copy this code or click Import to load the data.

Loading SAV files

The same considerations that apply to reading Excel files apply to reading SAV files (from SPSS).

You can also read .csv files directly into SPSS. Because of this and because of the benefits of using CSVs (they are simple files that work across platforms and software), we recommend using CSVs when possible.

To load an SPSS file, first, install the package {haven}.

```
install.packages("haven")
```

Then, load the data by using the function read_sav():

```
library(haven)
my_data <-
    read_sav("path/to/file.xlsx")
```

Google sheets

Finally, it can sometimes be useful to load a file directly from Google Sheets, and this can be done using the Google Sheets package.

```
install.packages("googlesheets4")
library(googlesheets4)
```

When you run the command below, a link to authenticate with your Google account will open in your browser.

```
my_sheets <- gs_ls()
```

You can then use the gs_title() function in conjunction with the gs_read() function to work with your data frame. We provide a brief example below; the package's documentation provides more details.

```
df <- gs_title('title')
df <- gs_read(df)
```

Appendix B: accessing Twitter data

The chapter on text analysis, Chapter 11, explores the content of tweets containing the #tidytuesday hashtag, while Chapter 12 explores the relationships between individuals evidenced through their interactions through the #tidytuesday hashtag.

As you may now be wondering about how you can collect and analyze tweets that contain *other* hashtags or terms, we have included some ideas (and considerations) for collecting your own Twitter data.

Accessing Twitter data from the last seven days

As we describe in Chapter 12, the {rtweet} package can be used to access Twitter data, with a key limitation: Only tweets from (approximately) the past seven days are able to be accessed. As a reminder, here is code to access data from a hashtag (in this case, #statschat, used by statistics educators), much like we did in Chapter 12, but for the #tidytuesday hashtag:

```
library(rtweet)
rstats_tweets <-
  search_tweets("#statschat")
```

Accessing historical Twitter data when you have access to already-collected status URLs

Because the creator of the interactive web application for exploring #tidytuesday content, #tidytuesday.rocks, searched for (and archived) #tidytuesday tweets on a regular basis, a large dataset from more than one year of weekly #tidytuesday challenges is available through the GitHub repository (https://github.com/nsgrantham/tidytuesdayrocks) for the Shiny application. These Tweets (saved in the data directory as a .tsv (tab-separated-values) file) can be read with the following function:

```
raw_tidytuesday_tweets <-
  read_delim(
"https://raw.githubusercontent.com/nsgrantham/tidytuesdayrocks/
master/data/tweets.tsv",
    "\t",
    escape_double = FALSE,
    trim_ws = TRUE
  )
```

Then the URL for the tweet (the status_url column) can be passed to a different rtweet function than the one we used, lookup_statuses(). Before we do this, there is one additional step to take. Because most of the Tweets are from more than seven days ago, Twitter requires an additional authentication step. In short, you need to use keys and tokens for the Twitter API, or application programming interface. The rtweet vignette on accessing keys and tokens (https://rtweet.info/articles/auth.html) explains the process. The end result will be that you will create a token using rtweet that you will use along with your rtweet function (in this case, lookup_statuses()):

```
token <-
  create_token(
    consumer_key = < add - your - key - here > ,
    consumer_secret = < add - your - secret - here >
  )
# here, we pass the status_url variable from raw_tidytuesday_tweets
# as the statuses to lookup in the lookup_statuses() function, as
# well as our token
```

```
tidytuesday_tweets <-
  lookup_statuses(raw_tidytuesday_tweets$status_url,
                  token = token)
```

The end result will be a tibble, like that above for #rstats, for #tidytuesday tweets.

Accessing historical data when you do not have access to status URLs

In the above case, we had access to the URLs for tweets because they were saved for the #tidytuesday.rocks Shiny. But, in many cases, historical data will not be available. There are two strategies that may be helpful.

First is TAGS (https://tags.hawksey.info/). TAGS is based in, believe it or not, Google Sheets, and it works great for collecting Twitter data over time—even a long period of time. The only catch is that you need to set up and start to use a TAGS sheet *in advance of the period for which you want to collect data*. For example, you can start a TAGS archiver in August of one year, with the intention to collect data over the coming academic year, or you can start a TAGS archiver before an academic conference for which you want to collect Tweets.

A second option is the Premium API through Twitter. This is an expensive option, but is one that can be done through rtweet, and can also access historical data, even if you have not started a TAGS sheet and do not otherwise have access to the status URLs.

Appendix C: social network influence and selection models

Behind the social network visualizations explored in the chapter on social network analysis, Chapter 12, there are also statistical *models* that can be used to further understand relationships in a network.

One way to consider these models and methods is by considering selection and influence, two *processes* at play in our relationships. These two processes are commonly the focus of statistical analyses of networks. Selection and influence do not interact independently: they affect each other reciprocally (Xu, Frank, and Penuel 2018). Let's define these two processes:

- *Selection*: the process of choosing relationships

- *Influence*: the process of how our social relationships affect behavior

While these are processes are complex, it is possible to study them using data about people's relationships and behavior. Happily, the use of these methods has expanded along with R. In fact, long-standing R packages have become some of the best tools for studying social networks. Additionally, while there are many nuances to studying selection and influence, these are models that can be carried out with relatively simple modeling techniques like linear regression. We describe these in Appendix C, as they do not use the tidytuesday dataset and are likely to be of interest to readers after mastering the preparation and visualization of network data.

After getting familiar with using edgelists and visualizations in the chapter on social network analysis, Chapter 12, a good next step is learning about selection and influence. Let's look at some examples:

An example of influence

First, let's look at an example of influence. To do so, let's create three different data frames. These will include:

- An edgelist data frame that contains the *nominator* and *nominee* for a relationship. For example, if Stefanie says that José is her friend, then Stefanie is the nominator and José the nominee. Data frames like this can also contain an optional variable indicating the weight, or strength, of their relation

- Data frames indicating the values of some behavior—an outcome—at two different time points

In this example, we'll create example data we can use to explore questions about influence.

Let's take a look at our three datasets:

- `data1`: an edgelist that contains a nominator, nominee, and strength of the relation

- `data2`: a dataset that contains the nominee and the values of some behavior at the first time point

- `data3`: a dataset that contains a nominator and the value of some behavior at the second time point

Note that we will find each nominators' outcome at time 2 later on. Here's how we can make these example datasets:

```
data1 <-  .
  data.frame(
    nominator = c(2, 1, 3, 1, 2, 6, 3, 5, 6, 4, 3, 4),
    nominee = c(1, 2, 2, 3, 3, 3, 4, 4, 4, 5, 6, 6),
    relate = c(1, 1, 1, 1, 1, 1, 1, 1, 1, 1, 1, 1)
  )
data2 <-
  data.frame(nominee = c(1, 2, 3, 4, 5, 6),
             yvar1 = c(2.4, 2.6, 1.1, -0.5, -3, -1))
data3 <-
  data.frame(nominator = c(1, 2, 3, 4, 5, 6),
             yvar2 = c(2, 2, 1, -0.5, -2, -0.5))
```

Joining the data

Next, we'll join the data into one data frame. This step can be time-consuming for large network datasets, but it's important for the visualizations and analysis that follow. The more time you can invest into preparing the data properly, the more confidence you'll have that your resulting analysis is based on a deeper understanding of the data.

```r
data <-
  left_join(data1, data2, by = "nominee")
data <-
  data %>%
  # this makes merging later easier
  mutate(nominee = as.character(nominee))
# calculate indegree in tempdata and merge with data
tempdata <- data.frame(table(data$nominee))

tempdata <-
  tempdata %>%
  rename(
    # rename the column "Var1" to "nominee"
    "nominee" = "Var1",
    # rename the column "Freq" to "indegree"
    "indegree" = "Freq"
    ) %>%
  # makes nominee a character data type, instead of a factor, which
can cause problems
  mutate(nominee = as.character(nominee))

data <-
  left_join(data, tempdata, by = "nominee")
```

Calculating an exposure term

Next we'll create an exposure term. This is the key step that makes this linear regression model special. The idea is that the exposure term "captures" how your interactions with someone over the first and second time points impact an outcome. The model describes a *change* in this outcome because it takes the first and second time points into account.

```r
# Calculating exposure
data <-
  data %>%
  mutate(exposure = relate * yvar1)

# Calculating mean exposure
mean_exposure <-
  data %>%
  group_by(nominator) %>%
  summarize(exposure_mean = mean(exposure))
```

The data frame `mean_exposure` contains the mean of the outcome (in this case, `yvar1`) for all of the individuals the nominator had a relation with.

Let's process the data more so we can add the variables `exposure_mean`, `yvar1`, and `yvar2`.

```
data2 <-
  data2 %>%
  # rename nominee as nominator to merge these
  rename("nominator" = "nominee")

final_data <-
  left_join(mean_exposure, data2, by = "nominator")

final_data <-
  # data3 already has nominator, so no need to change
  left_join(final_data, data3, by = "nominator")
```

Regression (linear model)

Calculating the exposure term is the most distinctive and important step in carrying out influence models. Now, we can use a linear model to find out how much relations—as captured by the influence term—affect some outcome. While this code is not run here, you could run the code in this appendix to see the results (and how changes in how the exposure term is calculated, such as by finding the sum, instead of the mean, of each individual's exposures, impact the results).

```
model1 <-
  lm(yvar2 ~ yvar1 + exposure_mean, data = final_data)

summary(model1)
```

So, the influence model is used to study a key process for social network analysis. It's useful because it's one way you can quantify *the network effect*. This is a metric that is not always considered in education, but we hope to see more of it. It also helps that it can be done with a relatively straightforward regression model.

An example of selection

Let's look at selection models next. Information from selection models can be useful to a wide audience—administrators, teachers, and students—because it describes how members of a network choose who to interact with. Here, we briefly describe a few possible approaches for using a selection model to learn more about a social network.

In the last section we used a linear regression model. In this example we'll use a logistic regression model. Logistic regressions model outcomes that are either a 0 or a 1. Thus, the most straightforward way to use a selection model is to use a logistic regression where all of the relations (note the `relate` variable in `data1` above) are indicated with a 1.

But here is the important and challenging step: all of the *possible relations* between members of a network are indicated with a 0 in an edgelist. Recall that an edgelist is the preferred data structure for carrying out this analysis. This step requires that we prepare the data by lengthening and widening it.

Once all of the relations are given a value of either a 1 or a 0, then a logistic regression can be used. Imagine that we are interested in whether individuals from the *same* group are more or less likely to interact than those from different groups. To answer this question, one could create a new variable called `same` and then fit the model using code (which is not run, but is included as an example of the code for this kind of selection model) like this:

```
m_selection <-
  glm(relate ~ 1 + same, data = edgelist1)
```

While this is a straightforward way to carry out a selection model, there are some limitations. First, it doesn't account for the amount of nominations an individual sends. Not considering this may mean other effects, like the one associated with being from the *same* group, are not accurate. Some R packages aim to address this by considering other variables like relationship weights. Here are some examples:

- The {amen} (Hoff et al. 2017) package can be used for data that is not only 1s and 0s—like a logistic regression—but also data that is normally distributed

- The Exponential Random Graph Model, or {ergm} R package, makes it easy to use these kinds of selection models. {ergm} (Handcock, Hunter, Butts, Goodreau, Krivitsky, and Morris 2019) is itself a part of a powerful and often-used collection of packages for social network analysis, {statnet} (Handcock, Hunter, Butts, Goodreau, Krivitsky, Bender-deMoll, et al. 2019)

These packages are examples of the richness R packages can bring to using social network analysis models and methods. As developments in social network analysis methods continue, more cutting-edge techniques and R packages will be available.

Appendix D: colophon

This book was written using bookdown (Xie 2016) using RStudio (RStudio Team 2015). The website (https://datascienceineducation.com) is hosted with Netlify (https://www.netlify.com/).

This version of the book was built with:

```
sessionInfo()
## R version 3.6.3 (2020-02-29)
## Platform: x86_64-apple-darwin15.6.0 (64-bit)
## Running under: macOS Catalina 10.15.4
##
## Matrix products: default
## BLAS:   /Library/Frameworks/R.framework/Versions/3.6/Resources/
lib/libRblas.0.dylib
## LAPACK: /Library/Frameworks/R.framework/Versions/3.6/Resources/
lib/libRlapack.dylib
```

```
##
## locale:
## [1] en_US.UTF-8/en_US.UTF-8/en_US.UTF-8/C/en_US.UTF-8/en_US.UTF-8
##
## attached base packages:
## [1] stats      graphics  grDevices utils     datasets  methods   base
##
## other attached packages:
## [1] forcats_0.4.0    stringr_1.4.0    dplyr_0.8.5      purrr_0.3.3
## [5] readr_1.3.1      tidyr_1.0.2      tibble_3.0.0     ggplot2_3.3.0
## [9] tidyverse_1.3.0
##
## loaded via a namespace (and not attached):
##  [1] tidyselect_1.0.0 xfun_0.12       haven_2.2.0     lattice_0.20-38
##  [5] colorspace_1.4-1 vctrs_0.2.4     generics_0.0.2  htmltools_0.4.0
##  [9] yaml_2.2.1       rlang_0.4.5     pillar_1.4.3    withr_2.1.2
## [13] glue_1.3.2       DBI_1.1.0       dbplyr_1.4.2    modelr_0.1.5
## [17] readxl_1.3.1     lifecycle_0.2.0 munsell_0.5.0   gtable_0.3.0
## [21] cellranger_1.1.0 rvest_0.3.5     evaluate_0.14   knitr_1.28
## [25] fansi_0.4.1      broom_0.5.4     Rcpp_1.0.3      backports_1.1.5
## [29] scales_1.1.0     jsonlite_1.6.1  fs_1.3.2        hms_0.5.3
## [33] digest_0.6.25    stringi_1.4.6   bookdown_0.18   grid_3.6.3
## [37] cli_2.0.2        tools_3.6.3     magrittr_1.5    crayon_1.3.4
## [41] pkgconfig_2.0.3  ellipsis_0.3.0  xml2_1.2.5      reprex_0.3.0
## [45] lubridate_1.7.4 assertthat_0.2.1 rmarkdown_2.1   httr_1.4.1
## [49] rstudioapi_0.11 R6_2.4.1        nlme_3.1-144    compiler_3.6.3
```

References

Allen, I. E., & Seaman, J. (2008). *Staying the course: Online education in the United States, 2008*. ERIC.

Bambrick-Santoyo, P. (2010). *Driven by data: A practical guide to improve instruction*. John Wiley & Sons.

Baker, R., & Siemens, G. (2014). Educational data mining and learning analytics. In Sawyer, R. K. (Ed.), *The Cambridge Handbook of the Learning Sciences* (2nd ed., pp. 253–274). Cambridge University Press.

Bates, D., Maechler, M., Bolker, B., & Walker, S. (2019). *Lme4: Linear mixed-effects models using 'eigen' and s4*. https://CRAN.R-project.org/package=lme4

Betebenner, D. W. (2019). *RandomNames: Generate random given and surnames*. https://CRAN.R-project.org/package=randomNames

Bransford, J. D., Brown, A. L., & Cocking, R. R. (2000). *How people learn* (Vol. 11). National Academy Press.

Breiman, L. (2001). Random forests. *Machine Learning, 45*(1), 5–32.

Bryan, J. (2017). *Project-oriented workflow*. https://www.tidyverse.org/blog/2017/12/workflow-vs-script/

Bryan, J. (2019). *Reproducible examples and the 'reprex' package*. https://community.rstudio.com/t/video-reproducible-examples-and-the-reprex-package/14732

Bryan, J. (2020). *Happy git with R*. https://happygitwithr.com/

Bryk, A. S., Gomez, L. M., Grunow, A., & LeMahieu, P. G. (2015). *Learning to improve: How America's schools can get better at getting better*. Harvard Education Press.

Conway, D. (2010). The data science venn diagram. *Drew Conway, 10*. http://drew-conway.com/zia/2013/3/26/the-data-science-venn-diagram

Data Quality Campaign. (2018). *Teachers see the power of data – But don't have the time to use it*. https://dataqualitycampaign.org/wp-content/uploads/2018/09/DQC_DataEmpowers-Infographic.pdf

Datnow, A., & Hubbard, L. (2015). Teachers' use of assessment data to inform instruction: Lessons from the past and prospects for the future. *Teachers College Record, 117*(4), n4.

Dirksen, J. (2015). *Design for how people learn*. New Riders.

Dweck, C. (2015). Carol dweck revisits the growth mindset. *Education Week, 35*(5), 20–24.

Elbers, B. (2020). *Tidylog: Logging for 'dplyr' and 'tidyr' functions*. https://CRAN.R-project.org/package=tidylog

Emdin, C. (2016). *For white folks who teach in the hood... And the rest of y'all too: Reality pedagogy and urban education*. Beacon Press.

Estrellado, R. A., Freer, E. A., Motsipak, J., Rosenberg, J. M., & Velásquez, I. C. (2019). *Taylor and Francis book proposal for data science in education*. https://github.com/data-edu/DSIEUR_support_files/blob/master/planning/T%26F%20Book%20Proposal%20for%20Data%20Science%20in%20Education.docx

Estrellado, R., Freer, E., Mostipak, J., Rosenberg, J., & Velásquez, I. (2020). *Data-edu: Package for data science in education using R*. https://github.com/data-edu/dataedu

Field, A., Miles, J., & Field, Z. (2012). *Discovering statistics using R*. Sage Publications.

Firke, S. (2020). *Janitor: Simple tools for examining and cleaning dirty data*. https://CRAN.R-project.org/package=janitor

Frank, K. A., Xu, R., & Penuel, W. R. (2018). Implementation of evidence-based practice in human service organizations: Implications from agent-based models. *Journal of Policy Analysis and Management, 37*(4), 867–895.

Gelman, A., & Hill, J. (2006). *Data analysis using regression and multilevel/hierarchical models*. Cambridge University Press.

Glossary of Education Reform. (2015). *Student subgroup*. https://www.edglossary.org/student-subgroup

Great Schools (n.d.). Aggregate data. In *Ed Glossary*. https://www.edglossary.org/aggregate-data/

Grimm, K. J., Ram, N., & Estabrook, R. (2016). *Growth modeling: Structural equation and multilevel modeling approaches*. Guilford Publications.

Handcock, M. S., Hunter, D. R., Butts, C. T., Goodreau, S. M., Krivitsky, P. N., Bender-deMoll, S., & Morris, M. (2019). *Statnet: Software tools for the statistical analysis of network data*. https://CRAN.R-project.org/package=statnet

Handcock, M. S., Hunter, D. R., Butts, C. T., Goodreau, S. M., Krivitsky, P. N., & Morris, M. (2019). *Ergm: Fit, simulate and diagnose exponential-family models for networks*. https://CRAN.R-project.org/package=ergm

Hastie, T., Tibshirani, R., & Friedman, J. (2009). *The elements of statistical learning: Data mining, inference, and prediction*. Springer Science & Business Media.

Hattie, J. (2012). *Visible learning for teachers: Maximizing impact on learning*. Routledge.

Healy, K. (2019). *Data visualization: A practical introduction*. Princeton University Press.

Heath, C., & Heath, D. (2006). The curse of knowledge. *Harvard Business Review*, *84*(12), 20–23.

Hill, A. (2017). *Up and running with blogdown*. https://alison.rbind.io/post/2017-06-12-up-and-running-with-blogdown/

Hoff, P., Fosdick, B., Volfovsky, A., & He, Y. (2017). *Amen: Additive and multiplicative effects models for networks and relational data*. https://CRAN.R-project.org/package=amen

Ismay, C., & Kim, A. Y. (2019). *Statistical inference via data science*. CRC Press.

James, G., Witten, D., Hastie, T., & Tibshirani, R. (2013). *An introduction to statistical learning* (Vol. 112). Springer.

Jordan, R. (2015). *High-poverty schools undermine education for children of color*. https://www.urban.org/urban-wire/high-poverty-schools-undermine-education-children-color

Kahneman, D. (2011). *Thinking fast and slow*. Macmillan.

Kearney, M. W. (2016). Rtweet: Collecting twitter data. *Comprehensive R Archive Network*. https://Cran.R-Project.Org/Package=Rtweet.

Kearney, M. W. (2020). *Rtweet: Collecting twitter data*. https://CRAN.R-project.org/package=rtweet

Kleon, A. (2012). *Steal like an artist: 10 things nobody told you about being creative*. Workman Publishing.

Kozol, J. (2012). *Savage inequalities: Children in America's schools*. Broadway Books.

Krist, C., Schwarz, C. V., & Reiser, B. J. (2019). Identifying essential epistemic heuristics for guiding mechanistic reasoning in science learning. *Journal of the Learning Sciences*, *28*(2), 160–205.

Kuhn, M. (2020). *Caret: Classification and regression training*. https://CRAN.R-project.org/package=caret

Kuhn, M. (2008). Building predictive models in r using the caret package. *Journal of Statistical Software*, *28*(5), 1–26.

Kurz, S. (2019). *Statistical rethinking with brms, ggplot2, and the tidyverse*. https://bookdown.org/ajkurz/Statistical_Rethinking_recoded/

Lee, V. R., & Wilkerson, M. H. (2018). *Data use by middle and secondary students in the digital age: A status report and future prospects.* https://pdfs.semanticscholar.org/811d/3e7bbbea05a8954c09823629e81819554382.pdf?_ga=2.195337642.763980897.1582512794-1526781779.1582512794

Leeper, T. J. (2018). *Tabulizer: Bindings for 'tabula' pdf table extractor library.* https://CRAN.R-project.org/package=tabulizer

Lehrer, R., Kim, M.-j., & Schauble, L. (2007). Supporting the development of conceptions of statistics by engaging students in measuring and modeling variability. *International Journal of Computers for Mathematical Learning, 12*(3), 195–216.

Lehrer, R. & Schauble, L. (2015). Developing scientific thinking. In L. S. Liben & U. Müller (Eds.), *Cognitive processes. Handbook of child psychology and developmental science* (Vol. 2, 7th ed., pp. 671–174). Hoboken, NJ: Wiley.

Lemov, D. (2015). *Teach like a champion 2.0: 62 techniques that put students on the path to college.* John Wiley & Sons.

Loeb, S., Dynarski, S., McFarland, D., Morris, P., Reardon, S., & Reber, S. (2017). *Descriptive analysis in education: A guide for researchers.* https://ies.ed.gov/ncee/pubs/20174023/pdf/20174023.pdf

Lüdecke, D. (2020). *SjPlot: Data visualization for statistics in social science.* https://CRAN.R-project.org/package=sjPlot

Lüdecke, D., Makowski, D., Waggoner, P., & Patil, I. (2020). *Performance: Assessment of regression models performance.* https://CRAN.R-project.org/package=performance

Mandinach, E. B., & Gummer, E. S. (2013). A systemic view of implementing data literacy in educator preparation. *Educational Researcher, 42*(1), 30–37.

McTighe, J., & Willis, J. (2019). *Upgrade your teaching: Understanding by design meets neuroscience.* ASCD.

Mohammad, S. M., & Turney, P. D. (2013). Crowdsourcing a word-emotion association lexicon. *Computational Intelligence, 29*(3), 436–465.

Moore Jr, E., Michael, A., & Penick-Parks, M. W. (2017). *The guide for white women who teach black boys.* Corwin Press.

Murphy, M. (2011). *The adventures of spielberg: An interview.* https://carpetbagger.blogs.nytimes.com/2011/12/20/the-adventures-of-spielberg-an-interview/

National Academies of Sciences, Engineering, and Medicine. (2018). *How people learn ii: Learners, contexts, and cultures.* National Academies Press.

National Center for Education Statistics. (2018). *Public elementary/secondary school universe survey.* https://nces.ed.gov/programs/digest/d17/tables/dt17_204.10.asp?current=yes

National Center for Education Statistics. (2019). Concentration of public school students eligible for free or reduced-price lunch. *The Condition of Education 2019*. https://nces.ed.gov/fastfacts/display.asp?id=898

National Forum on Education Statistics. (2016). *Forum guide to collecting and using disaggregated data on racial/ethnic subgroups*. https://nces.ed.gov/pubs2017/NFES2017017.pdf

Navarro, D. (2020). *Learning statistics with R*. https://learningstatisticswithr.com/

Newton, E. L. (1991). *The rocky road from actions to intentions* [PhD thesis]. Stanford University.

O'Neil, C. (2016). *Weapons of math destruction: How big data increases inequality and threatens democracy*. Broadway Books.

Paris, D., & Alim, H. S. (2017). *Culturally sustaining pedagogies: Teaching and learning for justice in a changing world*. Teachers College Press.

Pedersen, T. L. (2019). *Tidygraph: A tidy API for graph manipulation*. https://CRAN.R-project.org/package=tidygraph

Pedersen, T. L. (2020). *Ggraph: An implementation of grammar of graphics for graphs and networks*. https://CRAN.R-project.org/package=ggraph

Peng, R. D., & Matsui, E. (2015). *The art of data science. A guide for anyone who works with data*. Skybrude Consulting, LLC.

Pennebaker, J. W., Boyd, R. L., Jordan, K., & Blackburn, K. (2015). *The development and psychometric properties of LIWC2015*. https://repositories.lib.utexas.edu/handle/2152/31333

Raudenbush, S. W., & Bryk, A. S. (2002). *Hierarchical linear models: Applications and data analysis methods* (Vol. 1). Sage Publications.

R Core Team. (2019). *R: A language and environment for statistical computing*. R Foundation for Statistical Computing. https://www.R-project.org/

Reachable: Data collection methods for sexual orientation and gender identity. (2016). https://williamsinstitute.law.ucla.edu/wp-content/uploads/Reachable-Data-collection-methods-for-sexual-orientation-gender-identity-March-2016.pdf

Robinson, D. (2018). *Advice to aspiring data scientists: Start a blog*. http://varianceexplained.org/r/start-blog/

Robinson, D., & Silge, J. (2020). *Tidytext: Text mining using 'dplyr', 'ggplot2', and other tidy tools*. https://CRAN.R-project.org/package=tidytext

Rosenberg, J. M., Greenhalgh, S. P., Koehler, M. J., Hamilton, E. R., & Akcaoglu, M. (2016). An investigation of state educational twitter hashtags (SETHs) as affinity spaces. *E-Learning and Digital Media*, *13*(1–2), 24–44.

Rosenberg, J. M., Lawson, M. A., Anderson, D. J., & Rutherford, T. (2020). Making data science count in and for education. In E. Romero-Hall (Ed.), *Research Methods in Learning Design & Technology*. Routledge.

RStudio Team. (2015). *RStudio: Integrated development environment for R*. RStudio, Inc. http://www.rstudio.com/

Siemens, G., & d Baker, R. S. (2012). Learning analytics and educational data mining: Towards communication and collaboration. *Proceedings of the 2nd International Conference on Learning Analytics and Knowledge*, 252–254.

Silge, J., & Robinson, D. (2017). *Text mining with R: A tidy approach*. O'Reilly Media, Inc.

Snyder, T., & Musu-Gillette, L. (2015). *Free or reduced price lunch: A proxy for poverty?* https://nces.ed.gov/blogs/nces/post/free-or-reduced-price-lunch-a-proxy-for-poverty

Spillane, J. P., Kim, C. M., & Frank, K. A. (2012). Instructional advice and information providing and receiving behavior in elementary schools: Exploring tie formation as a building block in social capital development. *American Educational Research Journal, 49*(6), 1112–1145.

Spinu, V., Grolemund, G., & Wickham, H. (2018). *Lubridate: Make dealing with dates a little easier*. https://CRAN.R-project.org/package=lubridate

Stanley, D. (2018). *ApaTables: Create American psychological association (APA) style tables*. https://CRAN.R-project.org/package=apaTables

Trust, T., Krutka, D. G., & Carpenter, J. P. (2016). "Together we are better": Professional learning networks for teachers. *Computers & Education, 102*, 15–34.

Urbanek, S. (2019). *RJava: Low-level R to java interface*. https://CRAN.R-project.org/package=rJava

U.S. Department of Education. (2020). *IDEA Section 618 data products: State level data files*. https://www2.ed.gov/programs/osepidea/618-data/state-level-data-files/index.html#bccee

Victore, J. (2019). *Feck perfuction: Dangerous ideas on the business of life*. Chronicle Books.

West, B. T., Welch, K. B., & Galecki, A. T. (2014). *Linear mixed models: A practical guide using statistical software*. CRC Press.

Wickham, H. (2014). Tidy data. *Journal of Statistical Software, 59*(10). https://www.jstatsoft.org/article/view/v059i10/v59i10.pdf](https://www.jstatsoft.org/article/view/v059i10/v59i10.pdf

Wickham, H. (2015). *R packages*. O'Reilly Media.

Wickham, H. (2019a). *Advanced R* (2nd ed.). https://adv-r.hadley.nz/

Wickham, H. (2019b). *Tidyverse: Easily install and load the 'tidyverse'*. https://CRAN.R-project.org/package=tidyverse

Wickham, H., Averick, M., Bryan, J., Chang, W., McGowan, L., François, R., . . . Yutani, H. (2019). Welcome to the tidyverse. *Journal of Open Source Software*, *4*(43), 1686.

Wickham, H., & Bryan, J. (2019). *Readxl: Read excel files.* https://CRAN.R-project.org/package=readxl

Wickham, H., François, R., Henry, L., & Müller, K. (2020). *Dplyr: A grammar of data manipulation.* https://CRAN.R-project.org/package=dplyr

Wickham, H., & Grolemund, G. (2018). *R for data science.* O'Reilly Media.

Wigfield, A., & Eccles, J. S. (2000). Expectancy-value theory of achievement motivation. *Contemporary Educational Psychology, 25*(1), 68–81. https://doi.org/https://doi.org/10.1006/ceps.1999.1015

Wiggins, G., Wiggins, G. P., & McTighe, J. (2005). *Understanding by design.* Ascd.

Wikipedia. (2020). *Reproducible research.* https://en.wikipedia.org/wiki/Reproducibility#Reproducible_research

Wilson, G. (2009). *Teaching tech together.* https://teachtogether.tech/

Woo, K. (2018). *Anyone can play Git/R: Tips for first-time contributions to R packages.* https://speakerdeck.com/karawoo/r-tips-for-first-time-contributions-to-r-packages

Xie, Y. (2016). *Bookdown: Authoring books and technical documents with R markdown.* CRC Press. https://github.com/rstudio/bookdown

Xie, Y. (2019). *Bookdown: Authoring books and technical documents with R markdown.* CRC Press. https://bookdown.org/yihui/bookdown/

Xie, Y., Thomas, A., & Hill, A. P. (2019). *Blogdown: Creating websites with R markdown.* CRC Press. https://bookdown.org/yihui/blogdown/

Index